Celebrating

300 YEARS OF

DETROIT COOKING

1701 to 2001

This Detroit family has gathered together for a picnic lunch on a sunny summer day at
Belle Isle about 1897. They are all dressed very nicely, so this may have been a Sunday afternoon outing.

Tricentennial Edition - 2001

Celebrating

300 YEARS OF

DETROIT COOKING

⸙1701 to 2001⸙

Marguerite J. Humes, Editor

with *Shirley Hartert and Rennie Hughes*

DETROIT HISTORICAL SOCIETY GUILD • DETROIT, MICHIGAN 48202

The front cover photo was taken of the students in the Detroit Cooking School about 1889. The students are:

Nettie Thayer

Mary L. Clark

Hattie Fonda

Florence Ingallo &
Marie Willcox

Minnie Hazard

Published by the Detroit Historical Society Guild to
Celebrate their 50th Anniversary - 2001

Copyright© 2001 by the Detroit Historical Society Guild
5401 Woodward Avenue, Detroit, MI 48202

Printed in the United States of America

Library of Congress Catalog Control Number:
2001126360
ISBN 0-9671242-2-0

Book designed by Mary Primeau

This cookbook is dedicated to members of the Detroit Historical Society Guild To recognize their 50 Years of Service to The Detroit Historical Society And the Detroit Historical Museums

Jessie Field &
Maggie Suglis

Francis Maying
Bagley

Fannie Brooke &
Lily Kimball

Marian F. Robb

Jewel Range, Jr.

Square Top.

With Reservoir and Shelf.

A Toy Range.　　　　　Body about 8 x 12 Inches.

Modeled after the full size Jewel Range.　Working parts complete.　Nickel Plated Doors, Panels and Edges. Nickel Plated Leg Frame, and Ornamental Shelf.

Packed one in a box, with kettle, spider and cake griddle.

Contents

Foreword *9*
Acknowledgments *10*
Meet the Cookbook Committee *11*

PART I
Campfires To Cranes
Historical Highlights from 1701 to 1800 *14*
American Indian Pre-European Recipes *16*
American Indian Recipes 1701 to 1800 *26*
French-Canadian-English Recipes 1701 to 1800 *32*

PART II
Hearthstones to Fancy Kitchens
Historical Highlights from 1801 to 1900 *64*
Detroit Recipes from 1801 to 1900 *66*

PART III
Cast-Iron Stoves to Microwave Ovens
Historical Highlights from 1901 to 2001 *140*
Detroit Recipes from 1901 to 2001 *142*

Appendices
Detroit Historical Society Guild *215*
The People Who Built Dertroit *218*
Measurements and Weights *219*
Glossary *222*
Bibliography *225*
Index *227*

Opposite page:
This is a page from an advertising catalog published in 1881 by the Detroit Stove Works. The 100 page catalog advertised a variety of cooking and heating stoves, using wood or coal.
The Jewell Range was one of the most popular stoves of its day. This page shows the toy stoves they made for childrn.

Mother and daughter tending the family store in Detroit's Hungarian community called "Delray."
Photo taken by student from Center for Creative Studies, December 1973.

Foreword

This is a cookbook for people who love cooking, love history, and would enjoy a peek into the everyday lives of those who lived in Detroit a long time ago. This is a historical cookbook. It will present information about Detroit's social setting and cooking history from 1701 to 2001. Original recipes were first handed down orally by American Indians then written down and passed on from generation to generation. The same can be said about the wonderful recipes passed along, over the years, by immigrants from Europe and elsewhere. Also included are a few interesting recipes that were developed by native Detroiters.

Using historical anecdotes, common for the century, and historical overviews, the editor presents the continuous social and political development of Detroit from a small village of 500 inhabitants to a major mid-western city. The historical pictures and drawings, from the archives of the Detroit Historical Museum, help to present an image of Detroit: a beautiful city growing larger than ever imagined, from its initial founding 300 years ago.

The recipes themselves reflect the kinds of foods enjoyed by Detroit inhabitants from the beginning. It describes the everyday foods the American Indians and settlers ate, that were found in the forests and waters.

The earliest Detroiters were the American Indians who had been living in the area for hundreds of years. They lived from the land. The abundance of wild game, vegetables and fruits, in the area provided them with food, clothing and shelter. They added corn, beans and squash. The recipes contained in Part I will give you insight into their life, culture, foods, and how those foods were prepared. Many of these foods are still enjoyed by Native Americans. You may wish to visit the American Indian exhibit at the Detroit Historical Museum, that opened in May 2001, to learn more.

As the early French settlers arrived, they brought with them the foods they enjoyed. Many of their recipes were handed down to their descendants, as were the preparation methods. They also had to supplement their diet by gathering food from the woods and the waters and trade with the Indians. But the French eventually brought seeds, trees, and plants from Canada, as well as animals, to make farming easier. By 1730 more people lived on farms outside the fort than inside. Those farms produced wheat, oats, corn, chickens, cattle and pigs.

In Part II, recipes from the nineteenth century reflect the foreign foods and recipes brought to the Detroit area by the immigrants who came to settle farms and work. At the time, etiquette advice was considered important, and helpful hints about everyday life were a common theme in 19th century cookbooks. The recipes are interesting because, for the most part they were quite simple and nutritious. Vegetables and meats made up a large portion of their diet. Recipes often called for large amounts of butter, cream and eggs. Desserts were not too common. The ingredients, more often than not, were written in a paragraph style and sometimes you had to figure out how to make it. Not until the late 1800's did the more familiar style of recipe writing appear. Cooking was still done on the fireplace and hearth, with the crane moving the cookpot in and out to regulate temperature. In the mid-1800's, cast-iron cookstoves became available. Cooking over the fireplace was abandoned, and was now safer and more convenient. A wide array of pots, pans and cooking utensils soon were invented for the housekeeper's convenience. If you visit the Housekeepers Palace in the Streets of Detroit at the Detroit Historical Museum you can see some of these unusual pieces of housekeeping equipment. You will, no doubt, wonder what some of these things were used for.

Part III, the twentieth century seems to be sort of a free-for-all-cooking era. A wide variety of goods was being delivered to Detroit regularly on trains and boats. Complicated recipes calling for imported ingredients were becoming more common. Grocery stores carried canned goods and fresh foods were delivered daily by street peddlers with carts. Cookstoves continued to be improved upon throughout the century, and other conveniences like refrigerators, freezers, vacuum cleaners, blenders and microwaves came on the scene. These made housekeeping easier and more convenient. Dishes, silverware, linens, and other home goods were now readily available at the S.S. Kresge store and other special stores. There is a replica of this store in Streets of Detroit also.

Now, in the Twenty-First century, 2001, cooking has matured to the 45-minute dinner with the instant help of the microwave oven, and you can find a cookbook for each part of any meal.

We hope you will enjoy this historical cookbook.

Marguerite Joyce Humes
Editor and Cookbook Committee Chair

Acknowledgments

This project came about, and was sponsored by, the Detroit Historical Society Guild who published this cookbook to celebrate their Fiftieth Anniversary of service to the Detroit Historical Society and Museums.

With a project of this nature, there are many people to thank who have given freely of their time, talent, advice, and specialized knowledge. To these people, the committee wishes to express our heartiest thanks. All of the photographs and drawings were made available for use by the Detroit Historical Museum archives and collections.

A special word of thanks goes to the following Detroit Historical Museum staff: Patience Nauta, the Museum Registrar, who was so accommodating and helpful in selecting pictures of early Detroit, as well as pictures of the museum's collections; Cynthia Young, Curator of Social History, for her intimate knowledge of the museum's exhibits, and suggestions for including photos of them; Michael Kucharski, Graphic Design, for his hours at the computer, his good humor and willingness to help with the electronic end of the project; James Conway, the Museum Exhibit Manager, who facilitated the project and had to work around the research going on; James Jordan, Audio/Visual Technician, who graciously helped by taking special photos of the exhibits in the Streets of Detroit; Dennis Zembala, the Museum Director, for his enthusiasm; and Richard Strowger, Executive Director of the Society, who had helpful suggestions at the beginning of the project.

A big thank you also to Ralph Naveaux, Assistant Director for the Monroe County Historical Museum, for his assistance and recommendations in the search for information about French Canadian cooking, population and culture and to Jan Langone and Brian Dunnigan at the Clements Library for their interest and assistance with research and photographs.

Special thanks also go to Alice Nigoghosian, from the Wayne State University Press, who acted as consultant for the production of this book. Her expertise is gratefully appreciated.

The committee also appreciates the help of friends and members of the Guild who contributed old family recipes, special ethnic recipes and personal anecdotes, memories and stories about Detroit, that added sparkle and character to the cookbook. A huge word of thanks must also go to the committee members; Shirley Hartert, who helped with the research of history and recipes, and Rennie Hughes, who helped with research and typing; and to William Schwedler, a retired history teacher, who researched and wrote the Historical Highlights for each of the centuries.

M. J. H.

Meet the Cookbook Committee

MARGUERITE HUMES
Cookbook Committee Chair and Editor

I was a little girl growing up on the east side of Detroit near the Chrysler Plant. When I was five years old I cooked something for the first time — a breakfast. It was for my two younger sisters when my mother had just had another baby. She guided me in the whole process, of pulling the kitchen chair over to the stove, setting the pan and pouring in the water and the oatmeal when the water boiled. I even lit the burner; and better yet my sisters ate the oatmeal! It was so exciting! Ever since then I have loved to cook.

As a child our family dinners often included as many friends as relatives. My father was a good cook and would even take over the cooking now and then. Both my parents were gardeners as well. Cooking has always been a large part of my life. I'm sure I take after my Hungarian grandmother whose favorite phrase was "Az ebed keszen van", "dinner is served".

I find it especially rewarding to cook for a large group of people. For a few years, I ran a small catering business with a friend, then became more involved with organizing community activities such as Harvest Dinners, Festival Dinners, and fund-raising dinners. This was a different, yet enjoyable, aspect of cooking. Currently I work at the Wayne State University Press in Detroit, still cook, and teach Etiquette Classes in my spare time.

SHIRLEY HARTERT
Cookbook Committee Member

My family used homegrown vegetables and fruits either from the garden or Eastern Market. As a family, we canned every fall using a pressure cooker.

In the 1980's I began cooking professionally aboard the charter sailing vessel "Maranatha." The cruises took us to the Caribbean in the winter and back to the Great Lakes each summer. I cooked gourmet lunch and dinner cruises on the Detroit River for private parties and corporate entertaining for almost 10 years. Some of my recipes have appeared in Caribbean Charter Yacht Cookbooks as well. I was featured in numerous sailing magazine articles as well as in the Detroit News and Free Press and on television stations.

My German family arrived during the 1830's and my great grandfather Charles Klein served as a City Alderman in the late 1800's and operated a tavern on Clark Street. My parents were active with the Detroit Historical Society and the Museum. My dad Erwin Stoetzer operated the print shop in the Streets of Old Detroit and my mother Lenora was a docent. I am currently employed by St. John Health System Home Care – Physical Therapy.

RENNIE HUGHES
Cookbook Committee Member

My mother was a fashion designer and my father designed water sprinkler systems for a suburban company and was vice-president. My Italian mother was a wonderful cook as was my Italian grandmother. Seldom was I allowed to help with the cooking to any extent. When my grandmother prepared a meal for the family, which was very often, she did all the cooking and we were at the dinner table for hours. Each meal had several courses, and we children would sit on telephone books at the table with the adults and participate in the dining and conversation as well.

Fortunately, I inherited my mother's and grandmother's recipes, and I have a few favorites of my own such as Spinach Pie, which I like to take to Potluck Dinners. Currently I am working for Electronic Data Systems (E.D.S.).

outaouaks.

Pipe

Jac apeelun

Ottawa warrior at the end of the eighteenth century
holding a pipe. Courtesy Clements Library,
University of Michigan.

Part 1

CAMPFIRES TO CRANES
1701 to 1800

HISTORICAL HIGHLIGHTS OF 1701 TO 1800

As the Voyageur canoes slid silently over the sun-gilded water, Antoine de la Mothe Cadillac waved the steersman in the stern to make for the north shore of the strait, where there was a high clay bank. It was Cadillac's experience that chose this spot as the site for his new post, to be called Fort Pontchartrain du Detroit. It was July 24, 1701. The eighteenth century began with both France and England expanding their holdings in this new world of North America. Located on the strait between Lakes St. Clair and Erie, this was the first French settlement in the lower lakes.

Accompanying Cadillac, was his nine-year-old son, Antoine, Alphonse de Tonty, his second-in-command, and two priests—a Jesuit, Francois Vaillant, and an unidentified Recollect. The party also included fifty soldiers, fifty coureurs deBois (fur trappers) and one hundred Indians.

They built a palisade fort with walls twelve feet high. It was two hundred feet square with bastions at the corners. Log buildings were constructed within, among the first of which was St. Anne's Church.

In the fall of 1701, Madame Cadillac and Madame Tonty arrived bringing along six-year-old Jacques Cadillac. This was done so that neighboring Indians would see Detroit, as it soon came to be called, as a "permanent" settlement. Indian tribes were invited to settle near the fort in order to encourage the lucrative fur trade. Huron, Miami, Ottawa, and Chippewa (Ojibway) came and established villages surrounding the fort.

Between 1707-1711 Cadillac distributed sixty-eight small lots inside the fort, and seventy-five farms nearby. These were called "ribbon" farms with frontage on the strait (already being called the Detroit River). These ribbons sometimes stretched one to three miles inland. Many north/south streets bear the names of these early "habitants" as the settlers were called. Beaubien, St. Aubin, Chene and Dequindre are examples.

Rents were paid in furs or cash. Cows were brought from Montreal. Pigs were also brought, and to keep them safe from marauding wolves, they were kept on "Isle Aux Cochons" (Hog Island), now Belle Isle.

Detroit grew very slowly, as the French seemed more interested in the riches of the fur trade than in settling down as farmers. Cadillac's enemies, merchants in Montreal, feared that Cadillac's wilderness town would take too much business from them. Their pressure exerted at the French court earned Cadillac a "promotion". He was appointed Governor of the French Territory of Louisiana. He never returned to Detroit and eventually lost all of his Detroit holdings, ruining him financially.

After Cadillac left, Indian troubles began. More than one thousand Fox Indians arrived from Wisconsin to settle near Detroit. The new commander of Detroit ordered them to leave. They refused. The commander plotted with other Indians to destroy the Foxes. After defending themselves for nineteen days, they began a retreat. They were overtaken by Huron, Ottawa, and Potawatomi at Windmill Pointe and fought until barely one hundred survived and managed to escape. Fox Creek is named for them.

In 1749, the French Governor offered farm tools, chicken's, a sow, gun powder and lead to those who would move to Detroit. Only forty-six people accepted the offer. The total population of the fort and surrounding farms was only about nine hundred, and apart from soldiers, there were probably no more than one hundred permanent residents. Detroit was basically run as a military post. Life was rigorous, so people had to provide their own entertainments. The populace was lighthearted, sociable and hospitable to a fault. There was no school in Detroit, therefore many children grew up illiterate. Those who could afford it sent their children to Montreal to be educated by priests and nuns. The "Habitants" were devoted to their church, St. Anne's, and celebrated the numerous church holidays together.

The French and Indian War (1754-1760) was fought in the east. Major Robert Rogers (of New England) was sent along with two hundred loyal rangers to take over French posts in the west. On November 29, 1760, Major Rogers and his troops occupied Detroit. The French left and the "habitants" took an oath of allegiance to King George II of England. The transfer from French to British sovereignty was made with no apparent difficulty.

The Indians, however, did not understand the white man's ways. Favoring the French, Ottawa Chief Pontiac encouraged several tribes to unite and drive the British out of the western forts. Pontiac and his men captured most of the formerly French-held forts with bloody results. Detroit

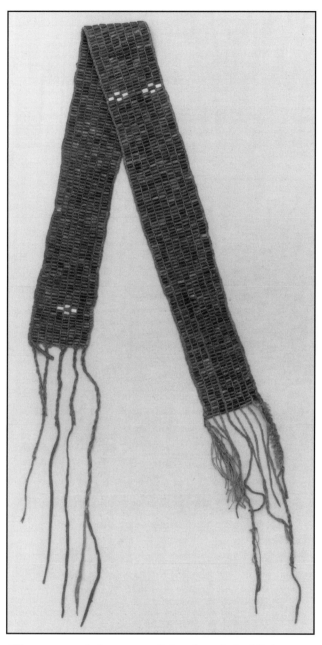

The wampum belt was a traditional symbol of diplomatic and ceremonial relationships among Indians in the northeast. The word stems from the Algonquinian, wampumpeag, meaning shell beads, made from the valuable shells of whelks and quahog clams. The beads were a trade item. Eventually, as the fur trade grew, wampum served more for money and less for ritual. ca. 1800. Photo courtesy of Cranbrook Institute of Science.

was the exception. Although besieged, Detroit was able to hold out and be re-supplied by ships sailing up the Detroit River and the British remained in firm control. In 1766, Pontiac and the other chiefs made peace with the British government.

Although the British flag flew over Detroit, most of the French "habitants" saw no reason to leave. The British allowed them to keep their farms, businesses, language, and church.

Though far removed from the American Revolution (1775-1781), the Treaty of Paris in 1783 made Detroit an official part of the United States of America. Since the fur trade was still lucrative, the British remained in Detroit. In 1794 U.S. Diplomat John Jay negotiated a treaty whereby the British agreed to evacuate the western forts by June 1, 1796. On July 11, 1796 the British hauled down the Union Jack and crossed the river into Canada.

The American Flag finally flew for the first time over Detroit. On July 13, 1796, Colonel John Francis Hamtramck arrived to take command of Detroit and secure the Fort, having been sent on ahead by General Anthony Wayne. In 1801, Detroit was still a small village of no more than 500 people, with about 2,000 more living on farms nearby. Dutch and German settlers had joined the French, English and American. At that time there was no post office, no school, no newspaper and no Protestant church.

Corn and Bread

There are two parts to this Indian recipe collection. The first part represents the traditional American Indian recipes from prior to 1701. The second part is from 1701 forward. Most of these recipes have been handed down verbally from past generations and were eventually written down. The ingredients and the directions are not complicated, and you will notice that there certainly is a wide variety of food represented. These recipes have been collected from several different Indian sources and are not intended to be a complete list, but only to give you an idea of the kinds of foods and preparation methods the Indians were using every day before European settlers arrived in the Detroit area.

Their food sources seemed to be everywhere. They hunted and trapped game animals, fished the waters, and collected wild onions, lettuce, garlic, carrots and other wild vegetables and fruits to round out their diet. Fruit trees were abundant, as well as berries of different varieties. They grew corn, beans and squash, which made up a large part of almost every meal. They cooked some hot foods in hollowed-out logs, birchbark baskets double-layered and sealed with tree resin, woven baskets (the liquid inside kept them from burning through), and earthenware pots, all of which were rather fragile. Many foods were also cooked on hot flat stones as well as on the hearth of their woodland fires.

Following the arrival of the European traders/settlers in 1701, the Indians could then trade furs, wild game and fish for other conveniences, such as iron cooking pots, spiders, kettles, gridirons, guns, and other implements that were useful to them. Cooking became much easier. The foods they ate were basically the same, but they now had the ability to cook a wider variety of foods safer and more conveniently. The second part of this recipe collection falls into this category. Some of the recipes may have additional ingredients not found in the first section because the French brought trade goods with them over a period of time.

Ash Cake – Chippewa

Cornmeal
Oak leaves (fresh)
Water

Make a stiff dough of cornmeal and warm water. Rake back the ashes of the fire, and spread oak leaves on the now clear floor of the firepit. Put the pone (dough) on the leaves and cover with more leaves. Pile red-hot ashes on the top layer of leaves.

Remove the pone when it is done. Eat in any manner that bread is eaten. Good topped with honey, maple syrup, or use to sop up soups or meat drippings.

Indian Nations

Indian villages occupied the site of Detroit as the first Europeans arrived in the area in 1701. At that time the Detroit River was an international boundary between two Indian civilizations: the Algonquin and the Iroquois. The Algonquin were chiefly hunters and fishermen; the Iroquois were predominantly farmers.

Indian Chestnut Bread – Traditional

Peel and scale one pound of chestnuts, then pound. Add enough corn meal to hold chestnuts together, mixing chestnuts and corn meal with boiling water. Wrap in green fodder or green corn shucks, tying each bun securely with bear grass. Place in a pot of boiling water and cook 2 hours.

The Indians taught the early settlers to make this bread.

Traditions

The recipes in this section are traditional recipes that may or may not be reproducible today. They are included here because of their authenticity and cultural value and should be respected for those reasons if no other. While they may not tempt your tastebuds, please remember that these recipes pre-date grocers and microwaves!

Corn Bread Baked on Bark

Corn meal
Pieces of bark from chestnut tree
    Mix enough water into corn meal to make a stiff dough. Put dough inside bark and stand it in front of the fire.

Indian Nations

The Iroquois were made up of Huron, or Wyandotte, Seneca and Erie Indians. The Algonquin tribe was made up of the Chippewa or Ojibway, Ottawa, Potawatomi and Fox.

Parched Corn – Ottawa

    Heat grease, add corn rubbed off dry cob. Shake around to heat corn evenly. Don't burn. Corn will almost pop. Use 1 layer of corn. Parches in about 5 minutes. Eat plain.

Boiled Parched Corn

2 cups dried sweet corn
Six cups spring water or the best you have
    Boil water, add dried sweet corn. Return to a boil. Continue to boil corn and add water as needed. Cook until tender. Add wild onions if you want to.

Wild Mustard

The seeds from the black mustard plant were used by the Indians to season their food. The plants are annuals and grow from four to six feet in height. The flowers are yellow and the seed pods are four-sided. The seeds are dried and pounded to a fine powder, then used as ordinary mustard.

Corn and Beans

    Skin flour corn with lye from hardwood ashes and cook it. Cook beans. Put together. Cook some more. Add pumpkin if you like. Can also add any nuts and cornmeal. Eat fresh. Will sour unless weather is cold.

Roasted Nuts

    Nuts were roasted by burying them in ashes and then covering the ashes with hot coals.
    They were stored in the upper chambers of the wigwam in handmade birch baskets.

Indian Artist

Quillwork, mostly done by the Woodland Indians in the Great Lakes region, is done with porcupine quills, bleached, dyed, trimmed and sewn in beautiful floral or woodland patterns by the Indian women. It takes a great deal of time and patience to decorate even one small item.

Corn Balls – Ottawa

    Grind corn kernels. Grind any berry. Mix 4 parts corn to 1 part berry together. Put grease in pot and brown mixture. Add more grease. Shape into balls. Dry in sun for later use in soup, etc. Can use blueberries, cranberries or other berries.

Drinks

Sage Tea – Ojibwa

6-10 fresh sage leaves or 2 teaspoons dried sage
1 pint water
    Steep 6 to 10 fresh leaves or 2 teaspoons dried sage in a pint of boiling water. Leaves are best if cut in early spring or early summer.

Relics

The archeological remains of Native American village sites were found mostly along the river from the foot of Woodward Avenue west to the River Rouge and larger village sites just north of Mt. Clemens along the shore of Lake St. Clair.

Field Mint Tea – Chippewa

10 large stalks fresh mint, washed
2 quarts water

Place mint and water in a large pan and bring slowly to a boil. Take from heat and let the 'tea' steep for 5 or more minutes (to desired strength). Strain and serve. Sweeten with honey if desired.

Indian Trails

The Sauk Fox Trail is now called Michigan Avenue. Other Indian Trails were Grand River, Fort Street, Jefferson, Woodward, Gratiot and Van Dyke. Very faint remains of the Saginaw Trail can still be seen in Royal Oak behind the Starr House on Crooks Road, south of 13 Mile. Paint Creek Trail is now Rochester Road.

Corn Soup Liquor

The liquor in which the corn bread was boiled was carefully drained off and kept in pots as a drink. It is said that the Indians were not fond of drinking water and preferred various beverages prepared from herbs or corn. One writer, James Adair, in "History of the American Indians" (London, 1775), p. 416, in discussing this subject, says: "Though in most of the Indian nations the water is good, because of their high situation, yet the traders very seldom drink any of it at home; for the women beat in mortars their flinty corn till all the husks are taken off, which having well sifted and fanned, they boil in large earthen pots; then straining off the thinnest part into a pot they mix it with cold water till it is sufficiently liquid for drinking; and when cold it is both pleasant and very nourishing; and is much liked even by genteel strangers."

Honey Drink

1 quart water
2/3 cup honey

Place water and honey in a large container with a tight fitting lid. Shake well to blend the two ingredients.

Moccasins

Indian moccasins or "skin shoes" from the Great Lakes make up an interesting portion of the American Indian collection of the Detroit Historical Museum.

Possum Grape Drink

Possum grapes, dried
Water
Corn meal

Shell off the grapes from the stems, wash, and stew them in water. When they are done, mash in the water they were cooked in. Let this sit until the seeds settle, then strain, reserving liquid.

Put the juices back on the fire and bring to a boil. Add a little cornmeal to thicken the juice. Continue cooking until the meal is done. Remove from the fire and drink hot or cold.

Lichen Tea – Traditional

A couple good handfuls of the greyish light green lichen that grows on the rocks.

Place the rinsed cleaned lichen in a boiling pot of water (no drying or curing the plant is necessary). Boil for 15 minutes or so, strain and let cool a bit. Then you have your own fine and nourishing wilderness brew!!

Always be sure of plant identification when gathering from the wild.

Polish Beavers

The beaver had been trapped out in Poland, which had been the main European source for pelts, and business men were seeking a new source. The region around Detroit was known as "the country of the beaver" and thus became a new source.

Fruit

Berries and Wild Rice – Ojibwa

Wild rice
Fresh cranberries
Water
Fresh blueberries
Fresh raspberries
Maple syrup

Cook rice and cranberries together in water until rice is done. Mix in the remaining berries, maple syrup.
Can be eaten warm or cold.

Bountiful Land - 1701

As the Europeans arrived to live in the area it was noted that Detroit was home to numerous animals and abundant plants growing in fertile soil at the beginning of the 18th century. The natural plants, trees, birds and animals of the Detroit area were eloquently described by Cadillac in a letter to one of the French officials in October 1701. "There are natural orchards with apples and plums which cover the floor of the forest. Vines hang heavy with grapes, and all the animals are fat and large. There are pheasants, quail, partridge, wild turkeys, woodcock and doves."

Other larger animals, not mentioned by him, included buffaloes, elk, moose, wolves, bears, rabbits, otters, lynxes, wildcats, beavers, black bears, deer and muskrats, all in the vicinity of Detroit.

Wild turkeys and quails were numerous, up to about 1850 and would often stray into the city. Innumerable flocks of ducks and geese, in their annual migrations could be heard easily as they flew overhead.

There were at least eighteen varieties of trees, including sugar maples, as well as coniferous trees of various kinds. The woods and forest rang with the sounds of numerous songbirds. Wild berries of all descriptions grew in the forests. Parts of the area were also somewhat swampy and wet.

This fertile environment meant that the American Indians were able to live well from the land, and the waters surrounding it.

Baked Apples

Apples (1 per serving)

Pick ripe apples. Cover the apples with hot ashes and live coals, cooking them until they are as soft as you want them.

Trade Item

Maple sugar was traded by the Indians for iron cooking pots, guns and beads, available from the French. It was called Indian Sugar by the settlers.

Maple Sugar and Fruit

Cranberries
Apples
Maple sugar
Water

Gather fruit. Add water and maple sugar. Cook until tender.

Apples and berries of all kinds were dried and stored for the winter. An Indian child might have some dried blueberries mixed with crushed corn and maple sugar on top for breakfast.

Fish and Soup

Fish and Mush – Algonquin

Barbequed fish
Cornmeal mush
Water

Cut barbequed fish into small chunks and boil in water to make a thick soup. Eat the fish soup with the mush. This dish was always used for sick people when fish was available. Barbequed means dried.

Coltsfoot Salt

Coltsfoot, a plant often found along streams and in swamps. The flowers are in bloom before the leaves appear. The undersides of the leaves are covered with a dense fuzz. The Indians formed the green leaves into balls and laid them out in the sun to dry, and then put them on a flat stone and burned them to ashes. The ashes are very salty and make a good substitute for salt.

Glossary of American Indian Words

Taken from the American Indian Exhibit at the Detroit Historical Museum – May 2001

English   Ottawa

ANIMALS
English	Ottawa
Animal	Ahwase
Badger	Missakakwidjish
Beaver	Ahmik
Bird	Penashe
Black Duck	Makateshib
Black Squirrel	Missinig
Cat	Kahshugans
Coyote	Pushquadashe
Deer	Wahsaushkashe
Dog	Ohnemooch
Duck	Shesheebaus
Eagle	Maezee
Elk	Ahtik
Fish	Keego
Fox	Wagoosh
Great Snapping Turtle	Mitchi-mikinaak
Hawk	Gebwaunushe
Horse	Papazegoonguhzhe

Wild Mint

The most common mints used by the Indians were Canada mint, spearmint and peppermint. All three varieties grow wild in the bush and forests. There are many ways the Indians used these plants for enhancing the taste of food. The Indians also used mint to make vinegar.

Traditional Fish Soup

Fish
Water
Coarse cornmeal
Wild onions
Wild greens

Boil fish of any kind in a pot with a quantity of water. If fish is not filleted, remove bones. Stir in coarse cornmeal to make a soup of suitable consistency. If wild onions and greens are available, toss them into the soup pot to add both color and flavor.

Fish Soup

Clean and bake a fish very brown. Put the fish into a pot of water and cook until done. Serve this soup with mush. Add anything you have.

Hot Soup Here

Soups were the mainstay of many American Indian diets. It was common to find a pot of soup simmering on the fire all day long. While there are definite recipes listed here, 'pot luck' was the bill of fare, and creativity was the key to a successful soup.

Crayfish – Traditional

Catch crayfish by baiting them with groundhog meat or squirrel meat. Pinch off tails and legs to use. Parboil, remove hulls and fry the little meat that is left. When crisp, it is ready to eat. Crayfish can also be used in a soup or stew after it is fried.

Boil the Sap

Maple syrup was made by the Indians by pouring the sap into a large hollowed out log and adding heated stones continuously until the sap was boiled down to the right consistency.

Fish Baked in Clay – Ojibwa

Pack any suitable fresh-caught fish (neither cleaned nor scaled) in a blanket of clay. Allow to dry for a few minutes by the fire, then bury this package in the hot coals, baking until the clay is hard (approximately 1 hour).

To serve, rake from the fire and hammer to break open the clay jacket. The cooked fish should split easily into 2 portions and the bones lift out. The intestines usually shrink into a tight ball and are easy to remove; the scales should be embedded in the clay. Sprinkle the steaming fish sections with your choice of herbs and nut oil.

Dumplings – Huron

Moisten a mass of corn meal with boiling water and quickly mold it into cakes in the closed hand moistened in cold water. Drop the dumplings one by one into boiling water and boil for half an hour. Dumplings were the favorite thing to cook with boiling meats, especially game birds.

To fish the dumplings from the pot everyone had a sharpened stick or bone. The dumplings were speared and held on the stick to cool and nibbled with the meat as it was eaten. The sticks after use were wiped off and stuck between the logs or bark of the wall for future use. Many of the sharpened splinters of bone now excavated from village and camp sites are probably nothing more than these primitive forks, or more properly food holders. Oho' sta' was one of the foods of which children were very fond, nor did grown people despise it as a bread with their meat.

Egg Soup

Beat eggs (bird) slightly and pour into boiling water. Season with grease. Add meat if you have it. Serve the soup with mush.

Beaver Fur

The supply of beaver in Europe was limited, but the supply of beaver was seemingly never-ending in the Great Lakes region. Traders established relationships with the Indians of the Iroquois and Algonquin tribes, trading beaver pelts for kettles, blankets, knives, and brandy.

Wild Vegetables

Fiddle Head Fern and Cattail Salad

Take large bunch fiddle head ferns. Pick in the spring when they are young and unopened. Wash them. Cut up wild onions and add. Pick cattails early in the spring also and peel first layer away to get to the tender shoots. The roots can be used as well. Wash and cut up. Add to rest. Add some wild lettuce, then add sunflower seeds if you have some and a little wild garlic. Mix together.

Most ingredients are found in the Spring and in marshy areas in the woods. Be sure to wash wild foods. You will get soaked on your search so wear boots.

Old Town

The original frontier settlement of Detroit spent 59 years as a New France village. The next 23 years were under British rule, and then 13 years as an American possession.

Young Milkweed Pods

Find small milkweed pods. Cook slow a short time. Eat hot or cold. Nice and crispy. Can add wild onions.

Mound Road

The Indian Mound Builders occupied a large part of the Midwest. The largest mounds are in Ohio and Indiana but some smaller ones were built within Detroit's city limits. One was near River Rouge, another is at Fort Wayne, and a third was in the northeast section of Detroit giving the name to Mound Road.

Steamed Cattails

10 fresh young cattail shoots
5-10 small tender garlic mustard leaves

Strip away the outer half on either side of a cattail. Cut the tender white base away from the green part of the leaves. (Dry and save the green part of the leaves for craftwork!) Gather, wash, and chop some garlic mustard leaves. Steam the white base of the cattail garnished with the garlic mustard.

Gather cattail shoots in the early spring when cattails are about 3 feet tall. Pull the outer two leaves of the cattail away from the stalk. Pull straight up on the cattail plant so the base pops out white and clean. This should not pull up the roots of the cattail and will not harm its growth next season. (Cattail roots are edible, too, but thatís another recipe.)

Ojawashkwawegad (Wild Green Salad) – Algonquin

Wild onions (substitute leeks), well chopped
Watercress
Sheep sorrel (substitute wood sorrel)
Dandelion leaves
Mix together.

Indian Vinegar

Indian vinegar is made from the sap of the sugar maple or birch tree. Also the buds and twigs and sap were allowed to ferment in the sun, then strained through a cloth. There is a fly which usually appears on the scene to tell you when the vinegar has fermented. It is called the vinegar fly; what else?

Young Milkweed Spears – Ojibwa

Young milkweed spears
Wood ashes
Garnish with nut butter or nut milk

Steam these young plant tops (do not boil) with the wood ashes in 1 cup water in a pot. Pour off this first bath, rinse thoroughly, and steam again in 1 cup fresh water without wood ashes for another 4 to 5 minutes. Rinse a second time and steam a third time in 1 cup water for yet another 4 to 5 minutes. Serve either hot or chilled with complements of nut butter or nut milk topping.

Maple Sugar Camps

In late February or early March, Indian families made sugaring camps in areas where maple trees were plentiful. Gashes were cut in the sugar maples, and sap was caught in hollowed out logs or birchbark containers, cut and folded at the corners so as to avoid breaking and leaking. The folds were also seamed with pine resin. The sap was often boiled and evaporated by lifting heated rocks with forked wooden sticks and placing the rocks in a large hollowed-out log container filled with sap. Clay pots, bark or basket containers were also used to boil sap until they became weak and started to leak.

The Indians made "grain sugar"–crystallized syrup; "cake sugar," before it crystallized it was poured into wooden molds to harden; and "wax sugar," poured on snow to make a chewy treat.

Maple sugar was stored in birchbark containers called mokuks. It was used throughout the year. Mixed with grain or berries, stirred into bear meat or used as a dip for roasted meat. It was also used as a trade item.

Greens

Dandelion, yellow dock, cowslips and milkweed plants can be cooked as greens. Select young, tender plants (cowslips before they blossom), sort out plants to remove bad ones or sticks and wash thoroughly. Cook in small amount of water for 10 minutes.

Milkweed plants can be cooked, the liquid drained off and the greens dried in the sun. When thoroughly dried, put into large birch baskets and store in the attic for the winter. Often these bags hung from the rafters of the wigwam.

Milkweed Buds

Gather milkweed buds and blossoms and wild garlic. Cook together with a little water. Add maple syrup if you like. Can also cook with other vegetables like wild carrot.

The Sacred World
Indian people honored all of nature. They believed each plant, animal and person had a reason for its life and needed the other.

Wild Rice

Wild rice
Cranberries
New cattail buds or roots, or crunchy somethings. Whatever is available
Meat broth
Boil up some wild rice in broth.

When it is almost done, add the crunchy somethings and a handful of cranberries. Add what herbs you like, a little sage perhaps, etc.

The thing to remember is to only add enough water to cover the rice and keep an eye on it so it doesn't dry up.

Wigwams
Most Indians in the Great Lakes region built wigwams, a conical shaped dwelling made of tree limbs and covered with either bark or rawhide. Inside there were platforms around the perimeter used for sleeping or sitting.

Baked Pumpkin with Wild Rice and Meat

1 pumpkin, seeds and 'pulp' removed
Broth or water
Wild rice

Add water (or broth) and wild rice inside and you get two dishes in one. Serve the pumpkin in shell and scoop out rice and pumpkin flesh at the table. A nice savory treat. Different, but a beautiful and healthy fall dish. Goes great with game dishes. Can add cooked squirrel meat with rice.

Taste
When it came to food, the basic Native American premise appeared to be we eat whatever the heck we can find.

Beans with Seeds, Nuts, Wild Rice and Meat

Mixed dried beans (any kind you like)
1 handful each – uncooked pumpkin seeds and uncooked sunflower seeds, wild rice
Nut meats if you like
Wild onions
Wild garlic
Venison, buffalo, bird
Water to cover all

Soak overnight. Wash once. Put more water in, twice as much as beans. Start cooking over fire. Add nuts. Cook till rice and beans are soft. Add onions and garlic. Cook some more.

Pine Needles for Stomach Cramps

Pine needles (yellow pine preferably)

Just yank a few pine needles off the nearest tree and chew them up. Swallow the juice. It will stop stomach cramps, spasms and hunger pains.

I have no idea how it works but it does and it also covers the smell of cigarettes and tobacco when hunting.

Everything Used

Woodland Indians made good use of every kind of food. They were gathered by the women and children after the first frost. Hickory nuts, chestnuts, and black walnuts were mixed with corn meal to make a heavy nourishing bread. They boiled chestnuts, hickories and corn to make a milk that was drunk hot or cold, and used in cooking.

Maple Sugar Candy

After you collect the sap . . . simmer, simmer, simmer . . . then, throw on the snow, or fill birchbark containers, slip a stick in the middle and wait until the 'lollipop' hardens. Unwrap, and enjoy. Not a difficult recipe, just takes time.

Wild Game

Baked Raccoon – Potawatomi

1 raccoon

Remove the skin and inner parts of raccoon, singe over fire and wash. Then parboil for 1 hour. Drain. Place in pot about 3 inches of hot water. Add 1 carrot, apple, and onion. Cook until tender.

Curfew at Ft. Pontchartrain

At 9 o'clock in the evening, the curfew bell would strike and the night watch would call out "9 o'clock and alls well. Curfew." Curfew is an adaptation of two French words: "couvre fue" meaning "cover the fire." At that, the residents would bank the fire for the night, so as to keep it going through morning.

Bird – Traditional

Clean the bird leaving it as whole as possible. Run a stick through it and roast before the fire. This is good served with cornmeal mush.

Winter Games

A popular Indian winter game was called "Snowsnake." In this sport they tried to see who was best at pushing a special wooden stick across the ice or snow.

Waboos – Rabbit – Traditional

Throw your waboos into a pot and cover with cold water. Keep over a hot fire. Throw in anything – potatoes, onions (wild onions are the best – throw a big huge handful in), beans, and cubed squash. The skin is good and soft once cooked. Take care not to let the waboos burn. Add sage. Throw in a handful of sunflower seeds, or what have you. Let it simmer till done – about another hour. You can thicken the soup with some maize-meal. Be careful of the bones.

Quail

Dress quail, put on a stick before the fire or over hot coals. Roast until very brown. Put browned quail in a pot of water and boil until well done. Thicken the soup with a little cornmeal.

Pheasants

Dress pheasant, cook before the fire until very brown, then stew or fry until done. Good with mush.

Trapping

Early American Indians often used the dead-fall beaver trap by baiting a line and attaching it to a heavy log. When the beaver or any other animal nibbled on the line the log fell and crushed the beaver.

Beaver Tail Stew – Huron

1 beaver tail
Wild onions
Wild tubers
Wild carrots

Skin over hot coals and cut beaver tail into 1-inch cubes. Boil for a couple of hours with the vegetables. Beavers eating birch taste better than beavers eating aspen.

Squirrel

Throw freshly killed squirrel into the fire to burn off the fur. Remove, scrape with a knife or sharp rock. Repeat this until the squirrel is rid of all fur. Wash the squirrel well with water and wood ashes until the skin is white. Remove the insides, cook on stick before the fire until brown.

Groundhog Stew

Catch groundhog, skin, parboil, and make a stew. Stew may be thickened with meal.

Weavers of Art

Corn husks, cattail leaves and other reeds and grasses were woven by the Indians into baskets, mats and bags.

Baked Beaver – Ojibwa

Skin and clean beaver. Cut up meat into small pieces. Parboil. Drain and wash pieces. Brown over fire in pot and cook until done adding a little water. Can add apples or other vegetables: wild onions, sage, carrots.

Family Life

The Iroquois traced descent on the mother's side. A matriarch ruled each long house and within it all the women were related; when a girl married, the husband moved, not the wife. The women named the children and reared them.

Opposum

Clean an opossum and parboil in plain water. Brown in bear fat until tender. Very greasy meat.

Farewell

After preparing food for the winter the Indians came together for a feast. Then they broke up into smaller groups to move to their seasonal hunting and fishing areas.

Dried Fish

Cut fish into strips or chunks. String on pieces of sharpened sticks and hang over or before a fire. Turn often and keep before fire until fish does not drip anymore. Save for later by stringing on thongs or bear grass. Use for making stew or soup.

Beans – Leather Britches

Snap the ends off the beans and string on heavy thread with needles. Hang in a sunny place to dry for two months.

To cook: Soak beans for 1 hour in two quarts of water. Bring to a boil. Reduce heat and simmer very slowly, stirring occasionally, for 3 hours. Add additional water if necessary. Serve hot with lots of broth as a vegetable. Corn pone is the perfect accompaniment and is good for sopping up the potlikker.

Winter Storage

The Indians prepared and stored a wide variety of food for use in the winter. Among these were berries that were dried in the sun, wild rice, parched corn and maple sugar. They were stored in woven baskets or birchbark containers. These containers were kept in the loft of the wigwam.

Dried Bear

Cut the meat in strips and dry before the fire. Hang these strips across the rafters of the wigwam on a basswood strip to keep dry all winter. It is best to cover the dried meat with a cloth if you have one. When you get ready to eat the bear meat, take it off the stick, beat it in the corn beater until it is like cornmeal. Put this in a pot of plain water and boil until the soup tastes good. Eat this with mush if you want it to taste the best.

Pemmican

Pemmican was a highly nutritious winter trail food made by the Indians. An Indian would find a handful sufficient for a day's rations. Settlers, President Theodore Roosevelt, explorers, and backpackers found it to be an ideal trail food.

Indian pemmican consisted of buffalo or venison, stripped of its fat, sun-dried, and pounded into powder with stones. Sometimes, it was left in jerky strips. Dried berries and melted fat were added. It was carried in a skin pouch.

Modern pemmican includes 1 pound of beef jerky, 2 tablespoons of sweetening, 2 ounces of dried berries (or raisins), and one pound of suet. Melt the suet and mix thoroughly with the meat mixture. It can be packed in plastic bags.

Corn and Bread

Hazelnutcakes – Chippewa

Unblanched hazelnuts, ground
Corn meal

Boil ground nut meats in water for 30 minutes, until the consistency of mush. Mix in corn meal; let stand about 20 minutes or until thick. Heat oil in iron skillet till drop of water sizzles. Drop nut mixture from tablespoon.

Brown well on one side, turn, and brown. Serve hot or cold as a bread.

Jack - Wax

Sugar maple trees are found only in the northeastern part of the United States. "Jack Wax" was made by taking thick syrup and pouring it on the snow. It then became a tasty chewy treat.

Bannock – Chippewa

Cornmeal
Water
Fat
Honey
Mix all this together, then fry in pan with grease. Chippewa and Ojibwa mean the same.

Ingami Pakwejiqan – Soft Bread – Ojibwa

Water
White corn flour
Butter
Sunflower seeds

Bring the water to a boil. Mix together the flour and salt. Pour the boiling water onto the dry ingredients while stirring. Continue to stir until the mixture becomes thick and uniform. Serve in a bowl topped with butter and the sunflower seeds. Can add blueberries or raisins.

Acorn Bread – Traditional – All Tribes

Acorn flour
Cornmeal
Whole wheat flour
2 eggs
Honey or fat
Milk

Combine flours, cornmeal. Add eggs, honey, fat and milk. Pour into greased pan and cook over fire until done.

Sewing With Sinew

Sinew was removed from the butchered animal and long strands were taken from the large muscles of the animal. Game animals as well as beef could be used. First it was washed and dried then rolled up into hanks and set to dry. When dry and ready to use for sewing, one strand was removed from the large hank. Holding each end of the sinew with the fingers, the person would run it from sides of the mouth back and forth until well dampened with saliva to make it pliable. Then one end of the sinew would be rolled on the knee to a rounded shape, as thread, working one end to a point to ease threading the needle. Sinew was used to sew clothing and moccasins as well as numerous other items.

Cornmeal Gravy

Put some water, milk (if you have it), salt, and red pepper in a pot where meat has been cooked (if you have meat), otherwise use a clean pot. Add cornmeal and cook until the meal is done. Eat this by itself, with bread for breakfast, or with vegetables if you have some.

Lacrosse

Lacrosse was a game that the Indians played. It was a fast, rough game. They called it baggataway.

Soup

Lichen Soup

Pick moss and wash well.
Use broth from boiled meat or fish.

Add moss and stir well. Add salt to taste and boil till soft. Put the meat or fish back in. Stir and serve hot. Enjoy.

The natives fed this soup to the British living at Fort St. Joseph in Ontario during the early 19th century to stave off starvation.

Corn Casserole

Take fresh green corn. Cut kernels down middle and scrape off pulp. Add corn flour. Mix up eggs with milk and add to corn. Bake in pot until firm.

Early Farmers

Indian women and children did the farming and gathering of wild vegetables from the woods to dry for winter use. One of the chores the children had, was to sit on top of a platform on poles in the middle of the garden, shaded by animal skins, and throw rocks at the birds and animals that came to eat the seeds or the vegetables.

Corn Soup – Ottawa

Take fresh corn – rub it on a grater to make the milk to run – scrape the whole works – kernel and milk into a pot – (it takes a bunch but be patient) – cook the soup – add scrap pork – fat back or hocks or what you have – and a bit of water – to thin for cooking – keep adding water while the pot boils to a creamy broth – add finely chopped green onions to taste – skim the soup when the meat is tender and falling apart – thin to a good consistency.

Planting

Early settlers planted seeds using the broadcast method, spreading seeds randomly over the tilled soil. The Indians showed them their method of planting seeds in rows. This method increased the yield of their crops. Often, fences made of sticks woven with smaller sticks or reeds were used around gardens to keep animals out.

Pumpkin Soup – Woodland Indians

1 small pumpkin
Bear grease or fat
Maple sugar or honey
Broth from venison or other meat
Thinly sliced green onion tops
Chopped hazelnuts
Roasted pumpkin and sunflower seeds for garnish

Place cooked pumpkin in pot. Add bear grease and maple sugar. Slowly stir in broth to consistency desired. Simmer over medium heat for about 5 minutes until hot. (If desired, serve in small pumpkin or squash shells.) Garnish with onions, nuts and hulled seeds.

Sunflower Seed Soup – Ottawa

Hulled sunflower seeds
Meat broth
Small green onions
Chopped fresh dill or other seasoning

Place sunflower seeds in a large pot. Add broth and green onions. Cook uncovered, over low heat for about 1 hour. Stir in dill.

Wild Vegetables

Large Mushrooms

Wash the mushroom, parboil, wash again, then fry in grease or animal fat.

Travelers

The Ojibwa people built beautiful birchbark canoes to use for hunting, fishing and traveling. They also built snowshoes and toboggans for traveling in the deep snow. Their clothing was made primarily with deerskin. Cradle boards were used to hold the babies.

Sweet Corn Mixture

Skin flour corn by putting it in lye from ashes. Cook the corn until it is done. Add beans and continue cooking until the beans are done. Add pumpkin and cook until it is done, then add walnut meal and a little corn meal. Add a little sugar or molasses if you'd like. Cook until the corn meal is done.

Watercress

Gather, wash, eat raw with salt or with hot grease poured over it.

Wild Peppermint Tea – Woodland Indians

Peppermint leaves
Honey

Boil water. Add the peppermint leaves. Let the tea steep. Add honey and pour into cups. The tea can be made from fresh leaves or dried leaves.

Sweetbay

There are several kinds of sweetbay trees growing in America. It is more frequently called the swamp magnolia or swamp laurel. The leaves are picked and sun-dried until they crumble easily. The dried leaves are used to flavor stuffings and soups.

Wild Cabbage

Wilt cabbage in a small amount of grease. Add some pieces of green peppers and cook until cabbage turns red. Serve this with cornbread.

Trading

The Indian tribes had been trading goods with one another, long before Europeans came. They exchanged things like corn, tobacco, woven mats, pottery, shells, and paints and dyes.

Yellow Dock

Some like yellow dock cooked with pieces of cooked salt pork for a special flavor. Butter or grease can be added to the milkweed greens. Dandelion greens can be flavored with salt, pepper and a bit of vinegar.

Wild Game

Venison and Wild Rice Stew

Place shoulder of venison in a large kettle uncovered with water and wild onions and cook slow for 3 hours until venison is tender. Add the wild rice, cover and simmer for 20 minutes. Stir, then simmer uncovered for an additional 20 minutes until rice is tender and liquid is absorbed.

Baked Raccoon – Ottawa

Clean raccoon, remove all fat, cut up. Put in large pot with water to cover raccoon; add salt. Bring to boil and simmer until tender. Remove meat from pot and put in baking pan. Add onion, carrots, cut up potatoes. Add water and cook until vegetables are done.

Glossary of American Indian Words

Taken from the American Indian Exhibit at the Detroit Historical Museum – May 2001

English	Ottawa
ANIMALS	
Moose	Moons
Muskrat	Wajashk
Otter	Neegig
Owl	Kookookuhoo
Panther	Keche Kahsuhgans
Porcupine	Kaug
Rabbit	Waboos
Raccoon	Asebun
OBJECTS	
Arrow	Mitigwanwi
Beads	Munedomen
Bow	Metegwahb
Canoe	Cheemahn
Gun	Paushkesegun
Knife	Mooko Mahn
Moccasin	Mahkesin

Muskrat Fiddle Head Stew

Clean the muskrat and be sure to remove the musk glands from the armpits. Put muskrat in a pot of water and parboil until scum forms. Drain off the water and the scum. Add more water and boil until tender. Then fry muskrat in a skillet with fat. Parboil fiddle heads and drain them, then add them to muskrat in the skillet along with a little water. Also add potatoes and any other vegetables you like. Cook until vegetables are tender.

Fiddle head ferns are a species of fern that grows by river banks. It is cut low to the ground when it first comes out of the ground and forms a coiled-up shape the like the far end of a fiddle. They are found only in the spring in marshy areas in the woods. The roots can also be used. Much of Detroit was an extremely wet and marshy area in the 1700's.

Chippewa Dill Jellied Eel

3 pounds eel
2 tablespoons coarse salt
2 1/2 cups water
1/4 cup white wine
2 wild onions, finely chopped
2 bunches fresh dill
10 whole peppercorns
2 teaspoons salt
2 bay leaves
1/4 cup fresh lemon juice
2 tablespoons fresh dill

Skin the eel by cutting around the neck behind the fins. Wrap the head in a piece of paper. Take hold of the skin and pull towards the tail. Then, split the eel open and take out the entrails. Cut the eel into 2-inch pieces and wash well in running water. Put in a single layer in a shallow pan. Sprinkle with coarse salt and pour in enough water to cover the pieces completely. Soak for 10 minutes, drain and rinse well in running cold water.

Place the eel in a kettle. Add the water, wine, onion, dill, peppercorn, salt and bay leaves. Bring to a boil over high heat. Reduce heat and simmer for 20 minutes. Remove from heat, stir in the vinegar and sprinkle the finely chopped dill on top. When thoroughly chilled, the liquid should form a soft jelly. Serve from the kettle.

Brush Cuts

The Ottawa men wore their hair in a sort of brush cut strip. They were the only Indians that wore this hairstyle.

Venison and Wild Rice Casserole – Chippewa

In a small roasting pan mix 1 cup of wild rice with water and mushrooms and other vegetables. On top place venison chops or steaks. Place 1 small onion (sliced) in pan and three strips of bacon if you have it over venison. Cook in pot until rice and venison are done. Eat and enjoy!

Ancient Method of Storing

Bones of buffalo, deer, moose and other animals were saved and chopped into pieces then placed in a large kettle which hung on a tripod set over an open fire, water was added and the whole was boiled and cooled to get the fat which rises to the top. The fat was stored in animal bladders which had been washed and scraped until thoroughly cleaned and dried. These bladders of grease were stored in the loft for use in cooking.

Beaver Tail Soup

Bones from a beaver
1 beaver tail
4 wild onions
4 quarts water
4 sweet bay leaves
1 tablespoon wild mustard

Separate the bones from the meat and break the bones into six pieces. Skin the tail by broiling the tail over the campfire. The scaly skin will come off in a blistered sheet to reveal the white, solid meat underneath. Put the bones and pieces of tail in a large kettle, add the water and salt. Bring to a boil, then cook slow for a while. Skim surface clean with a large spoon, then add the sliced onions, bay leaves, and wild mustard. Keep on simmering for a short time.

Remove the beaver tail pieces. Let drain on a plate and set aside to be added to the soup at a later time. Strain the soup into another large pot and boil down to about a quarter of its original volume.

Cut the meat from the tail into cubes about 1/2-inch square, add to the soup and serve hot. You can add to the taste with freshly cut mint, sprinkled over the individual servings.

Dyeing and Weaving

The Indian women were in charge of growing crops and gathering berries to dry. They were skilled weavers, and dyed cornhusks, cattail leaves, and other reeds which were woven into bags, mats and baskets for trade.

Dandelion and Fish

6 handfuls of dandelion greens
2 trout, salmon, or bass
Bacon grease (best) or fat
3 wild onions
White sage (few pinches)

Cut and clean fish. Cut into long strips. Chop onions. Wash and chop dandelion leaves. Grease fry pan slightly with bacon grease. Put on a semi-hot coal. Add onions and a few pinches of white sage. (Make sure sage is ground up a little.) Let cook about 3/4 of the way and then add the dandelion leaves. Cook until leaves are soft.

Indian Jerky

Jerky is dried meat, cut in long strips from large game or beef. To prepare sun-dried jerky, cut fresh meat into long thin strips about an inch wide and an inch thick. Rub the strips with salt and hang, spaced well apart on racks, in the sun to dry. When dry, store in sacks hung in a dry place.

Jerky can also be made by placing the strips in a corning solution for three or four days, then hung on racks over a slow burning, smoky fire for about two days. The strips should be placed well apart to keep them from touching each other. When dry, the strips should be wrapped in a protective covering such as cheesecloth to keep insects and dirt from settling on them.

Jerky will keep drying as long as it is exposed to the air and smoke. It is important not to leave it longer than a couple of days. Then take it down and store it in air-tight jars or other containers.

This recipe will make about 50 pounds of jerky meat.
Corning solution:
3 gallons water
2 pounds dark brown sugar
1 ounce saltpeter
1 ounce cayenne pepper
1 cup juniper berries, crushed
1 whole piece ginger

Bring water to a boil and add remaining ingredients. Boil for 5 minutes. Remove scum as it appears. Cool and store in a wooden barrel or earthenware crock.

Indian beaded bag. This beaded bag is part of the Chandler Indian collection at the Museum. The decorations are typical of those used by the Woodland Indians in the Great Lakes area. It is decorated with a combination of beads and porcupine quills in a floral pattern. Beads were among the items traded among the Indians. ca.1851

Special Recipe

Baked Corn

Fresh Tuscarora and/or sweet corn in which "milk" has "set"
Basswood leaves
For Traditional Preparation (preferred method):
Mortar and pestle
Iron kettle
Wood for fire
Tripod or "crane"

When the milk has set, Tuscarora and sweet corn is scraped from the cob and beaten to a paste in a mortar. This should be done just before the evening meal. After the housework is finished the housewife lines a large kettle with basswood leaves three deep. The corn paste is then dumped in, up to two-thirds the depth of the vessel and covered with a thick layer of leaves, then cold ashes to a finger's depth are now thrown over the leaves and smoothed down.

A small fire is built under the kettle which hangs suspended from a crane or tripod. Glowing charcoal is placed on the ashes at the top. The small fire is kept brisk and the coals at the top renewed three times. The cook may now retire for the night if her kettle hangs in a shielded place or in a fire pit. In the morning the ashes and top leaves are carefully removed and the baked corn dumped out. The odor of this steaming bread is most appetizing and it is eaten greedily with grease or butter. For winter's use the caked mass is sliced and dried in the sun all day, taken in at night to prevent dew from spoiling it and dogs or night prowlers from taking too much of it, and set out again in the morning to allow the sun to complete the drying. The bread is then ready to be stored away for the winter. When ready for use the winter's store of bread was taken from storage and a sufficient quantity for a meal thrown in cold water and put on the stove. Boiling for a little more than a half hour produces a delicious dish. Cornbread was one of the favorite foods of the Indians. One can hardly mention the name of it without showing that it brings memories of the pleasant repasts that it has afforded. In recent years the corn paste is prepared with a potato masher in a chopping bowl or by running the corn as cut from the cob through a food chopper. Baking is done in shallow pans in the oven. The food, so prepared, lacks a deliciousness that makes the older method still popular.

Glossary of American Indian Words

Taken from the American Indian Exhibit at the Detroit Historical Museum – May 2001

English   Ottawa

PEOPLE

English	Ottawa
American	Kitchimokoman
People of the 3 Fires	Anishinabe
Ancestor	Dodem
Bad Power Person	Mo-je Manido
Earth	A-Ki
Englishman	Shauguhnaush
	Jaganash
Frenchman	Wometegooshe
	Wemitigogo
Great Power Person	Ki-Je Manido
Moon (Grandmother)	Nokomis
Power Person	Manido
Sun (Grandfather)	Mishomis
Great Water	Mitchi-gan
Turtle Island	Mishiike-minis

DIRECTIONS

English	Ottawa
West	Red
South	Black
North	White
East	Yellow

FRENCH CANADIAN / ENGLISH 1701 TO 1800

Bread and Desserts

The French-Canadians brought with them a limited supply of their customary foods for their journey from Canada, but the everyday foods they had access to in Detroit were basically the same as those used by the Indians. Fish, wild game, corn, fruit and wild vegetables were the items the Indians traded at the fort for cooking kettles, beads, blankets and other goods. Within a few years the new settlers were growing wheat, as well as some other useful crops. In 1704 Cadillac brought three horses and 10 oxen to Detroit to plow the ground. Cows eventually made their appearance as did chickens. Many of the following French recipes use large amounts of cream, eggs and butter. Muskrat soon became one of their favorite dishes as well as pork. Roast suckling pig had been a long-time, special Christmas Day custom the French brought with them. These recipes are from a variety of sources including descendants of the original Frenchtown at River Raisin and include many that are historically based.

Although the British were quartered at Fort Pontchartrain, the major influence in the town for more than one hundred years was French. There are also some English recipes included in this section as they tried to make their presence felt as well.

French Bread

Beat together one pint of milk, four tablespoons of melted butter, or half butter and half lard, half a cupful of yeast, one teaspoonful of salt and two eggs. Stir into this two quarts of flour. When this dough is risen, make into two large rolls, and bake as any bread. Cut across the top diagonal gashes just before putting into the oven.

Dumplings

Two teacups of flour, some salt, two tablespoonfuls of melted butter, one teacupful of milk and four beaten eggs. Stir together. Drop by tablespoonfuls into boiling stew and cook until done.

Main Street Detroit - 1701
The newly built town of Detroit had one main street extending from end to end of the stockade east and west. It was named Ste. Anne Street. There were two narrow cross streets, St. Francois and St. Antoine. Ste. Anne Street was 20 feet wide and the other two were 15 feet or less.

Savory Herb Omelet

Mix six eggs together, add chopped onion, parsley and tarragon leaves. Pour into skillet and cook slowly over moderate fire until eggs are set. Then fold over in half and serve. Can add other fillings before folding in half. The French were very fond of tarragon.

Pastry for Meat Pies

Take one quart of flour and mix in one-half pint of butter or fat and one egg. Mix together and add water. Divide and lay paste into a deep dish and add meat, cover with paste and bake gently over fire.

French Crepes

One teacup milk
Three eggs, beaten
One teacup flour
Three teaspoons sugar

Whip together. Butter iron skillet and heat thoroughly. Pour a small amount of the batter onto the skillet. Rotate until it is evenly distributed and as thin as possible. Brown on one side, flip over and brown on other side. Stack in a covered dish in the oven to keep warm. Fill with fresh fruit, preserves, whipped cream, chicken, sausage, or creamed vegetables. Roll and serve in a row. Dessert crepes may be dusted with powdered sugar or syrup may be poured over the top.

Fried Bread – French

Mix sour milk with a little melted butter and enough flour to make a very soft dough. Cut dough into small pieces and drop into hot deep fat. Eat plain or with maple syrup.

Nice Clothes

Much of the clothing worn by Detroiters was imported and of a better quality than would be expected because the French government prohibited spinning and weaving in their colonies.

Cottage Cheese – English

Put a pan of sour or loppered milk where it is not too hot; let it scald until the whey rises to the top (be careful that it does not boil, or the curd will become hard and tough). Place a clean cloth or towel over a sieve, and pour this whey and curd into it, leaving it covered to drain two to three hours; then put it into a dish and chop it fine with a spoon, adding a teaspoonful of salt, a tablespoonful of butter and enough sweet cream to make the cheese the consistency of putty. With your hands make it into little balls flattened. Keep it in a cool place. Many like it made rather thin with cream, serving it in a deep dish.

Fern Soap

Early Indians used a variety of ferns, which when burned into ashes could be used as a skin cleaning soap. One of these was called soapwort.

French Toast

3 eggs, beaten
Milk or cream
Day old bread

Combine eggs and milk, mix well. Place in a large flat bowl. Dip slices of bread into the egg mixture and soak. Heat a griddle and coat it with lard. Fry the bread slices on both sides until lightly browned and the egg is cooked. Place on a plate and serve with butter and maple syrup.

Dried Fruits

Berries, peaches and other fruits were dried on plates to save for food preparation later.

Dried Pumpkin Seeds

Remove seeds from pumpkin. Wash and drain. Salt if desired. Spread on griddle over moderate fire to dry slowly. Stir often. Do not burn.

French Apple Tarts

Stew and strain the apples, add cinnamon, rosewater, wine and sugar to your taste. Lay in paste and squeeze orange juice, bake gently.

Cinnamon Custard

Put a stick of cinnamon to one quart of milk, boil well, add six eggs, two spoons of orange flower water, some mace; boil thick then stir in sweetening. Serve in small cups.

Brandy

Lemon and orange peels were saved to flavor brandy for cooking purposes.

English Custard

One quart of milk, some orange flavor, water, six eggs. Bake in deep dish.

Maple Pralines – French

Maple syrup
Walnuts

Cook maple syrup till thick. Pour into buttered pie tin. Sprinkle with broken nutmeats. Let harden.

Pound Cake

Take one pound of dried and sifted flour, the same of loaf sugar and butter; the well-beaten yolks of twelve and the whites of six eggs. Then with the hand beat the butter to a cream, add the sugar by degrees, then the eggs and the flour; beat it all well together for an hour, mixing half a glass of rose water, or twelve drops of the essence of lemon, and a nutmeg or a little cinnamon powdered. Bake it in a tin pan buttered in a Dutch oven.

Sage Tea
Wounds of any kind will heal more rapidly when washed with sage tea. It can also be used to relieve headaches.

Pumpkin Fritters – French

Eggs
Cooked pumpkin
Flour
Sugar
Spice
Melted fat

Mix well and drop onto hot griddle or fry in deep hot fat.

This rather elegant, handmade wooden doll belonged to Juliana Trumbull Woodbridge, as a child. She was the daughter of John Trumbull, and later married into the Woodbridge family. The jointed doll is wearing a dress made of a rough burlap material. ca. 1790-1795

Housekeeping
Most of the housewife's cooking utensils were iron. Some items may have been copper – a cauldron or pot, perhaps, or a bed warmer. Other items were of wood: some buckets and tubs, a few bowls, and possibly a butter churn. For cooking oil, melted bear fat was used.

Eau Sucre

Sweeten boiling water with sugar to your taste. This beverage is much used by French ladies. It is considered soporific, and good for fatigued or weak nerves.

Crunchy Treat
The Pralines of the North West Territory were made of dried corn, pounded fine and mixed with maple sugar.

Sour Dough Biscuits

One half pint starter
Salt
One pint flour
Butter, cut up

Mix together and drop by teaspoonful onto greased skillet. Bake over moderate fire.

Dried Pumpkin
Pumpkin was cut horizontally in thin slices and hung on a line in a warm room to dry.

White Tea

Put two teaspoonfuls of sugar into half a cup of good milk, and fill it with boiling water.

Sourdough Starter

Sourdough was produced by settlers using the wild yeast found in the air. Yeast, wild or tame, causes a fermenting action. Acetic bacteria, also always in the air, break down the alcohol produced by the yeast into vinegar, hence the sour taste.

For a starter, mix one cup of flour with one cup of water. Leave in a glass or crockery container covered with a light cloth. Set in a warm place for 2-5 days.

As soon as the starter ferments, it is ready for use. Starters vary in sourness. If too thin, the yeast works too fast and loses its bubbly quality. If too thick, it will work too slowly. If you would like to start a Frenchtown Starter, experiment a bit. The pleasant sour taste and fine texture will be your reward.

Woodland Food

Pumpkin was a great favorite along with cucumbers, watermelons, raspberries and pears and apples. Maple sugar was the principal sugar used by the French inhabitants. There was little salt used, most of it being imported from France.

Molasses Gingerbread

One tablespoon of cinnamon, allspice, four teaspoons pearl ash, dissolved in half pint water, four pounds of flour, one quart molasses, one-half pint butter. Knead well until stiff, the more the better. Bake fifteen minutes. Watch closely so it won't burn.

Nice Flavor

Peach kernels were saved to use later as a flavoring for foods. The whole inside kernel was powdered and used for flavoring custards and other foods.

Cider Syllabub

Sweeten a quart of cider with loaf sugar, grate nutmeg into it, then add milk into this. Then add sweet cream and mix.

Hot Cross Buns – English

Scald one-half pint of milk and add eight tablespoonfuls of melted butter, four tablespoonfuls of pulverized loaf sugar and one teaspoonful of salt. After it has cooled off, add one-half cupful of yeast, three eggs and one quart of flour. Mix in one-half pint of currants or raisins. When risen, make small buns. Cut a small cross on top. Bake in fast oven till brown. Mix one egg white with ten tablespoonfuls of powdered loaf sugar and make a cross on each bun.

Hot Cross Buns have been around since the Middle Ages and were originally made to honor the English Goddess of Spring. When the Christian faith came to the country, bakers added the tiny cross. Most likely, the town baker at the fort would bake all the breads and prepare these special Easter treats as well.

English Pancakes

One pint flour, two teaspoonfuls pounded loaf sugar, two egg yolks and three eggs and two tablespoonfuls of melted butter. Stir in one pint of milk and beat until frothy. Pour into hot skillet, turn over when brown. These cakes will be very thin. Sprinkle with some sugar.

Corn

Corn was the mainstay in the diet for settlers for the first 200 years. It was made into bread, soup, cakes, mush. Ashcakes were a mixture of water and corn and baked in the ashes of the hearth.

Pumpkin Pudding

Take a pint of pumpkin that has been stewed soft. Melt in half a pint of warm milk, a quarter of a pound of butter, and the same quantity of sugar, stirring them well together. If you can conveniently procure a pint of rich cream it will be better than the milk and butter. Beat eight eggs very light, and add them gradually to the other ingredients, alternately with the pumpkin. Then stir in a wine glass of rose water and a glass of wine mixed together; a large teaspoonful of powdered mace and cinnamon mixed, and a grated nutmeg. Having stirred the whole very hard, put it into a buttered dish and bake it three quarters of an hour. Eat it cold.

Campfire Corn Bread

Heat a Dutch oven and lid piping hot in the hot coals and ashes of the campfire.

Mix 1 quart of corn meal with 2 teaspoons salt. Moisten lightly by rapidly beating boiling water into the dough, until it is light. Place dough in Dutch oven, put on lid and bury in hot coals and ashes to bake.

Corncakes

The Journey Cake or "Johnny Cake" was sometimes cooked in a shovel over the open campfire.

English Crumpets

Beat together one-half pint of milk, one tablespoonful of melted butter, one-half teacup of yeast, a pinch of salt and one egg. Stir into this one cupful of flour. Pour two tablespoonfuls full of batter in skillet or griddle and cook over medium heat until brown. Turn over and brown other side. Serve hot with butter and jelly with hot tea.

Pancake Customs

English pancakes were traditionally served on Shrove Tuesday (the day before Ash Wednesday). Every household was supposed to use up all its eggs and milk before Lent began. This is similar to the French custom of crepes on Mardi Gras (Fat Tuesday).

French Sugar Pie

Milk
Brown sugar or molasses
3 tablespoons flour
Pinch of salt

Beat well and pour into a pie tin. Bake over fire until set.

Outdoor Bakery

In most French settlements there was a bakery where bread was made. In Detroit, the families within the stockade would get bread from the bakery. An engineer who came to Detroit in 1749 mentions the out door bakery with two large ovens.

Glacies – Drop Noodles for Chicken Soup

When the chicken is near the final stage of cooking, take one egg and beat it thoroughly. Pour in one-half cup of milk. Add several dashes of salt. Gradually stir in about one cup of flour – or, enough flour to make the batter just about the consistency of heavy cream. After the batter has been prepared, take the chicken out of the pan and bring the broth to a rolling boil. Tilt the mixing bowl of batter over the boiling broth and gently, but steadily, spoon out about two tablespoons of batter per stroke over the rim of the bowl into the broth. Allow the glacies to remain in the boiling broth for about five to seven minutes or until the batter has set firm. When done, spoon out and serve with the boiled stewing hen.

Laundress

Women washed the clothes in the sparkling waters of the Detroit River with a short wooden paddle called a battois.

Fruit

Maple Syrup Pie – French

Mix together three eggs with one cupful of maple syrup and one-half pint of brown sugar. Add two tablespoonfuls of melted butter, a pinch of salt, and two tablespoonfuls of flour. Bake in a pastry in moderate oven until set. Nuts can be added if you have some.

Cooking on a Hearth

Shortcake, biscuits, and cookies were sometimes baked in a spider – a long-handled pan with three legs.

The tin oven first appeared in 1832 which allowed the cook more freedom and variety in cooking her meals.

Drying of fruits and vegetables – they were either placed on the hearth or strung and suspended from the mantle to dry.

Stewed French Pears

Place alternate layers of washed, freshly picked grape leaves with peeled hard pears cut in half, in a kettle until full. Add 1 cup of sugar, some stick spices and 3 or 4 pieces of cracked ginger, (if you are lucky enough to have any). Fill the kettle with apple cider. Cover. Cook on a low fire until pears are tender, but not falling apart. Discard leaves before eating.

Pear Trees

The original pear trees were brought by the French to Detroit from Montreal. Some seedlings of these much-traveled, and much-loved, pear trees may still be found in Monroe, Michigan.

Corn Cob Syrup – American

Boil one dozen clean corn cobs (red ones are best) for one to two hours in enough water to have one pint of liquid when done. Strain and add 2 tablespoons brown sugar. Boil as long as you like – till it reaches the desired thickness.

Apple Tart – French

Cook cut-up apples with sugar in a deep kettle until done. Prepare a pastry dough and put over apples while hot. Bake in hot fire until top is brown. Can do the same with cherries.

King's Pasture

Under English rule, a 12-acre tract of land east of the Fort, but adjoining it, was set apart for use of the post. It was known as "the King's Garden." In 1773, this land was fenced off as private pasture. The people of the town protested, saying it reduced their pasturage. The fence was removed.

English Syllabub

2 cups fruit juice – 5 tablespoons grated lemon rind – 1/3 cup lemon juice – 1 1/2 cups sugar – 3 cups milk – 2 cups light cream – 4 egg whites – nutmeg.

Combine juice, lemon rind and lemon juice. Stir in 1 cup sugar and let stand until sugar dissolves. Combine milk and cream, add fruit juice mixture and beat with beater until frothy. Beat egg whites until stiff, add remaining 1/2 cup of sugar, a little at a time, beating constantly until whites stand in place. Pour fruit mixture into bowl, top with puffs of egg white and sprinkle with nutmeg.

Wild Grape Wine

Pick wild grapes when they are ripe. They are best after the first frost as they are sweeter. Crush in a large crock. Add about 1 pound of sugar per gallon of liquid. Let stand 5 or 6 days. Push grapes down once each day. After the 6th day, strain juice. Add sugar and water to make up 5 gallons. (The total amount of sugar would be 3 pounds per gallon.) Put in a jug or small barrel. Place air lock so that pressure can escape, and not let air back in. Let ferment until it ceases. Bottle and age at least 6 months.

Apple Beer

Peel apples and dry peelings in the sun or by the fireplace. Put in a crock and add boiling water to cover. Cover the crock and let sit for one or two days – till all the flavor comes out of the peelings. May add some sugar if desired.

Vegetables

Iron Skillet
Vegetables and Bacon – French

Boil 4 or 5 potatoes in their jackets. Heat a deep iron skillet and lightly brown 1/2 pound bacon, cut in 1 inch squares. Remove bacon, pouring off the grease, except 3 or 4 tablespoons. Cut a head of cabbage into slices. Add 1/2 cup water. Cover, cook lightly for about 20 minutes. Peel potatoes, dice and add to cabbage along with bacon. Salt to taste. Warm through only 10 minutes. Water may be needed, but allow mixture to brown the last few minutes to add to the taste.

Parched Corn

Take two ears of dried corn – dried right on the cob. Remove kernels from cob and place in very hot skillet. Cover and parch, stirring occasionally for 10 minutes. Serve cold or hot – and be sure teeth are in good working order. This is crunchy.

Pioneers often carried parched corn in their pockets to munch while traveling.

Wild Rice

Wild rice was often used as a stuffing for wild duck or eaten separately. Wash rice thoroughly. Put in boiling water, cook one hour. Stir so that it will fluff up.

"Three Sisters"

Squash, corn and beans were planted together by the American Indians. The corn stalks grew tall and the beans climbed on them. The beans produced nitrogen that was good for the soil. The squash kept the weeds down with their large leaves.

Gascony Style Eggs – French

Slice eggplant and dip in flour. Brown both sides in skillet. Place one egg on each slice of eggplant, cover and cook until egg is done. Top each egg with a slice of ham and pour fresh tomato sauce over the top.

Cadillac was from the Gascony region of France and this dish has long been a favorite of that area.

Onion Quiche – French

Slice onions and cook in butter. Mix eggs and milk together and add onions. Put pastry in bottom of Dutch oven; add filling and bake until set.

Mushrooms

Heat fat in skillet and add mushrooms, wild garlic, wild onion and parsley.

Daily Life - 1701

Daily life for the French settlers as well as the American Indians was devoted to providing shelter, clothing, and preserving enough fruit, vegetables and wild game to keep them through the cold winter months. This preparation began in the early spring with gathering maple syrup and cooking it down. Vegetable crops were planted, harvested and stored. The only white sugar available was shipped in the form of hard loaves and you needed a loaf cutter and a stone grinder to use it. Otherwise they used maple sugar, honey or molasses. Little salt was available.

Sauerkraut with Pork – Alsatian

Four pieces bacon, one cut-up onion, one-half quart sauerkraut, two tablespoons brown sugar or molasses, two cut-up potatoes, two sliced apples, four pork chops and chicken broth (if you have it). Can add a few peppercorns and bay leaf if you like.

Cook and stir bacon and onion in Dutch oven. Stir in sauerkraut and brown sugar. Add potatoes and apples. Add pork chops, pour in chicken or meat broth. Cook until meat is tender.

Mashed Potatoes with Turnips – French

Peel and cut up two turnips and four potatoes. Cook turnips a while then add the potatoes and onion. Cook until tender. Pour off water and mash vegetables with butter.

Green Beans—French Style

Cook onions in butter and add cooked green beans. Add butter, lemon juice and parsley.

Green Peas – French Style

Lay lettuce in deep dish. Place peas, onions and butter on top. Add a little water and butter. Cook until peas are tender. Cut up lettuce and serve.

Wild Game

Fried Quails

Pick and clean, cut in the middle of the back, fry in butter to a nice brown. Now put in an earthen or porcelain lined dish, one tablespoonful of nice butter and the same of flour; stir on a slow fire until butter is dissolved, then pour in slowly two-thirds glass of water and the same quantity of wine. Put in your birds that are nicely fried, simmer slowly one-quarter of an hour; toast some thin slices of bread (one toast to each bird); put in the dish you wish to serve, laying the birds on top; pour the gravy over all; serve very hot.

Creamed, Fried Partridges

Using 2 birds, cut into serving pieces and dredge with flour. Fry salt pork until crisp. Remove from pan and fry partridges in fat. When brown, add crisp pork. Pour 1 cup thick cream over all. Cover and simmer until done.

Celebration

On New Year's Day in French Town, barbecued pig, roast fowl, ragout made from pig hocks, with bowls of goutons, composed of a thick brown residue of rendered pork fat (for those whose stomachs could digest this delicacy) were served.

Blackbird Pie

Dress and clean well a dozen blackbirds as you do pigeons. Split each in half, put them in a stew pot with plenty of water and bring to a boil. Skim off rising scum, add salt and pepper to season, some minced parsley, a chopped onion, about 2 whole cloves, add about 1 cup of diced salt pork and boil until tender. Thicken broth with browned flour and boil up. Add 2 tablespoons of butter, mix and remove from fire. Cool. Dice 2 cups of potatoes. Grease baking dish, put in alternate layers of birds and potatoes. Moisten with rich broth, cover with pastry crust, cut slits in crust to let steam escape.

Roasting Over the Fire

Potatoes, corn, onions, nuts – by burying in warm ashes for insulation and then placing live coals on top of the ashes.

Meat – might be put on spit and turned often till done. Small boys had the job of turning the spit.

Turkey – hang it before fire by string attached to a beam above. Dripping pan was placed under and it was basted and turned till done.

Roast Muskrat – French

Marsh Squirrel

Soak muskrat for about 2 hours, in salt water to which 2 tablespoons of vinegar is added. Drain. Put onion, salt, pepper, celery, and muskrat in pan of cold water. Bring to a boil. When scum has formed, drain and rinse with cold water. Repeat process and scum will not form the second time – continue cooking until it has come to a good steady boil. Drain. Fry until meat is tender – or put in a roaster, cover with cream style corn plus a little water, top with crumbs, cook at least 1/2 hour in oven. Be sure to remove musk glands.

Roast Wild Duck

Canvass-back, Red-Head, and Mallard should be carefully picked, singed, drained, and trussed with neck twisted around to close opening in breast. For filling, use one cup wild celery, one-half cup chopped onions, one red pepper, and sweet h rb seasonings. Put filling in duck, sew the opening; butter well, bake one hour. Serve with currant jelly.

A Specialty

Sagammite was a dish of porridge made from cracked corn, eaten with cream and maple sugar. This dish was used in French Town for wedding feasts. The explorer Charlevoix mentioned Sagammite as early as 1722.

Woodcock

Tie the legs, skin the head and neck, turn the beak under the wing and tie it, tie a piece of bacon over it, and immerse in hot fat for two or three minutes. Serve on toast. Or split them through the back and broil, basting with butter and serving on toast. They may also be roasted whole before the fire for fifteen or twenty minutes.

Another Way of Cooking Fowl

Kill the fowl (no matter what kind it may be) by cutting off the head; hang up by the feet till free from blood; then carefully remove all the entrails and crop; use no water in the operation, save upon your hands before commencing; be careful not to remove or disturb the feathers; stuff the fowl with ordinary stuffing; then wrap the body up in wet brown paper and roast in the ashes of the fire as you would potatoes till done. The time consumed in roasting will depend on the age and kind of fowl. There is no danger of burning, if properly attended to and better be overdone than rare. When you think the fowl sufficiently done, take out of the embers and unroll carefully; remove the feathers and skin together; place upon a large dish and carry to the table. Sweeter fowl was never eaten.

Fried Muskrat – French

Before cooking muskrat, the musk glands located in the armpits must be properly removed. Failure to do so will result in a muskrat that tastes as if it had been soaking for several days in a sewer.

Immerse muskrat in a pan of water. Add two medium-sized chopped onions. Add a little salt and pepper. Parboil until a scum is no longer produced. Drain off the water and scum – leaving the onions with the muskrat.

Immerse the muskrat in water again. Add a little salt. Parboil until tender. Fry the muskrat in a skillet as you would a rabbit. Watch for bones.

Little Pigs

Wild pigs roamed the French Town area. The wild boars led the bands, followed by the sows and the sucklings. The 6-month-old pigs had distinctive "black" heads.

Barbecued Pig for New Year's Day – French

Take a suckling pig with a black head; smother it. With the help of a funnel pour into its snout a burning hot concoction of thyme, bayleaf, basil, sage, and rosemary which has been boiled in water for a half hour and strained through a clean cloth. Tie the snout, stretch the animal out on a plank and leave it there overnite. The next day, skin it like a hare, leaving the bristles around the tail and head. Clean out the insides; singe it over hot coals, lard it with bacon and soak for 1 day in vinegar with spices, slices of onions and carrots – turn several times. To roast it, cook on a spit until very brown.

Stewed Pigeons

Unless pigeons are known young, they are better braised or stewed in broth, than cooked in any other manner. Place slices of salt pork or bacon in bottom of stew pan. Lay pigeons side by side with breasts uppermost, add slice of carrot, an onion, a teaspoon of sugar and some parsley. Pour over enough stock to cover. If you have no stock, use boiling water. Now put thin slices of salt pork or bacon over tops of pigeons. Cover them as closely as possible adding boiling water or stock.

Clean Your Hearth

If you wish to have free-stone hearths dark, wash them with soap, and wipe them with a wet cloth; some people rub in lamp-oil, once in a while, and wash the hearth faithfully afterwards. This does very well in a large, dirty family; for the hearth looks very clean, and is not liable to show grease spots. But if you wish to preserve the beauty of a free-stone hearth, buy a quantity of free-stone powder of the stone-cutter, and rub on a portion of it wet, after you have washed your hearth in hot water. When it is dry, brush it off, and it will look like new stone.

Turtle Soup

Behead and bleed turtle, separate from the callopach and callopee, dismember, and clean well. Separate legs, neck, and other coarse parts. Dip in boiling water, and remove skin.

Remove fine, delicate inside meat, also cut into small pieces with the fat. Rinse in cold water and put all together in the kettle, adding 1 or 2 onions, and such sweet herbs as desired, salt and pepper; add about 2 quarts of cold water. Cook very slowly about 5 hours or more. Strain off the liquid, then pick out a quantity of the finer meat and bits of the fat and add to the soup. Add 2 or 3 hard-boiled eggs. Use turtle eggs if available, and chop fine. Add 1/2 cup of well-flavored wine. Thicken with browned flour. Reheat soup and serve.

Hearth Cooking

The gridiron was a specialized cast-iron pan shaped like a shallow frying pan but with an open lattice grid on the bottom. Iron pots were cleaned with sand.

Hunter's Partridge

Using four dressed and washed partridges, mix four cups shredded cabbage and four slices dried and crumbled bacon. Spoon mixture into each bird. Wrap each with four cabbage leaves and tie with string. Place in large skillet. Mix butter, chicken stock, carrots, thyme, tarragon and pepper. Pour over partridges. Bring to boil; cover and cook slow until done. Serve with pan sauce.

The Spit

A spit rested on the andirons in the fireplace. Often this was turned by hand, usually by a small boy. Meat was eaten in great abundance, except on fast days when dishes made with milk or eggs were popular.

Venison Steaks

Cut them from the neck, season with pepper and salt; heat the gridiron hot and grease the bars before laying the steak on; broil them well; turn once, taking care to save as much gravy as possible. Serve hot with currant jelly on each piece.

Warm Hats

When Louis XII appeared in his beaver fur hat it launched a desire for fashionable hats for men and women in Europe. A market for this new fashion led businessmen to the Detroit area to acquire beaver pelts to satisfy this new fad. There were at least eight different styles of the beaver hat made.

Soup

Soupe à la Baillarge – Traditional French

Beef shank
Cold water
2 onions, chopped
Peas or beans
Barley
Raw vegetables, diced (carrots, turnip, string beans, peas, shredded cabbage, fresh corn or hominy)
Whole potatoes, peeled
Corn on the cob
Carrots cut in large pieces
Turnips cut in large pieces

Wash meat and place in large pot with cold water. Bring to a boil and skim in order to obtain a clear broth. Add onions, beans and barley. Let simmer one hour. Add vegetables. Cook until tender.

The "Twelve Apostles"

Where Waterworks Park is now on East Jefferson, was the farm of Mr. Van Every. He had a row of 12 very large pear trees which were known up and down the river as the "twelve apostles." These French Pear trees grew to a height of 60 to 80 feet, and bore enormous crops of pears. There is a row of pear trees at the Detroit Historical Museum that are descendants of these ancient pear trees.

Pumpkin Soup

Cooked mashed pumpkin
Maple syrup
Meat broth

Mix and heat until warm – use broth to thin as necessary. Garnish with chives and toasted pumpkin seeds.

Peasant Fish Soup

Place three dressed fish in skillet. Add three-fourths pint of wine or water, one sliced onion, three wild garlics, mashed, and a bay leaf. Cook fish until done. Take fish out and set aside to keep warm. Mix in enough flour to thicken sauce. Place buttered bread in bowl and place fish on top. Pour sauce over fish.

Chowder

The French word for a hearty soup or stew is "chaudiere" Americanized to chowder.

Split Pea Soup

Wash split peas and soak overnight in cold water.

Boil with water and a marrow bone. After it has boiled somewhat, add 1 chopped onion, boil 3 hours, and return to kettle. Add 1 turnip and 1 carrot, season with salt and pepper, let it come to a rolling boil.

Habitant Pea Soup

Boil one quart of yellow split peas in Dutch oven. Add a good size piece of smoked pork, two chopped onions and a pinch of allspice. Cook slow one hour. Add carrots and cook slow until tender.

La Garbure – French Cabbage Soup

Cut up cabbage in quarters. Scald it; squeeze it between your hands to get all the water out. Tie each quarter and place in a kettle. Layer it with a knuckle, pickled pork, venison, or any other left-over meat.

Add onions, carrots, potatoes. Add a layer of bacon and cover with water. Simmer over low heat for at least two hours. When it is done, simmer some bread in the broth. Take out cabbage and serve with bread. The meat is served separately.

Log Houses

The newer log houses of early Detroit settlers were made with the logs standing upright with one end buried 4 feet in the ground, following the design of original French settlers.

Squash Soup

First cook garlic and onion in Dutch oven. Then add cooked squash, chicken broth or water and parsley and heat up over fire. Add another lump of butter and stir in some heavy cream. Serve hot.

Meat

Small Hot Patties – French

Make one recipe of pastry. Chop fine one cupful of leftover meat or fish. Add two tablespoonfuls of chopped mushrooms and two of chopped onion and some parsley, if you have it. Moisten with milk. Roll pastry out and cut into squares. Put meat onto squares and cover with a top. Brush some milk or egg on top. Cook in Dutch oven until brown, or in a skillet.

Beef and Kidney Pie

Cut up beef steak and beef kidney into small pieces. Roll them in flour and cook in fat until brown. Add one cup of water, two onions, mushrooms and thyme leaves. Make pastry for top and bake it on a flat iron. Pour meat into deep dish and put baked crust on top of meat mixture in dish.

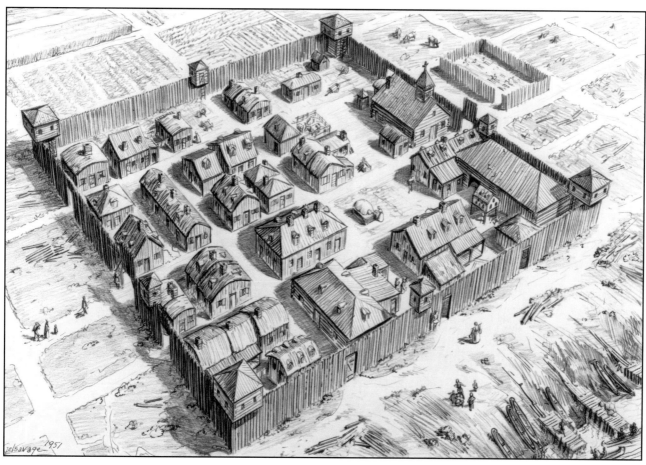

A drawing made by John Gelsavage, a contemporary artist, in 1951, taken from a map of Fort Pontchartrain drawn in 1760.

The Dutch Oven

The Dutch oven or bake kettle – had a flat bottom and stood on three legs about 2 inches long. It had an iron cover with a loop to lift it by. In it were baked bread, pork and beans, and meats of all kind. The food was put inside, and set over live coals on the hearth. The cover was heated and placed on top. Live coals were placed on the cover, and as they cooled, they were replaced with more live coals.

Meat Pie – English

Leftover meat
Onion, chopped
Carrots, diced
Potatoes, cut in cubes
Double pie crust

Place crust in the bottom of a pie plate. Fill with meat. Add top crust. Cut a vent opening to allow steam to escape. Place on a trivet in a Dutch oven. Bake until crust is browned. Serve warm.

Beef Ribs – English

Heat fat in Dutch oven. Cook beef until brown on all sides. Add two cut-up onions. Mix one tablespoon mustard, a teaspoon of curry powder, pinch of red pepper and water. Cover with lid and cook until tender.

Chicken Stew – French

Cut up one old stewing hen. Place the chicken in a pan and fill the pan with water until the chicken is almost covered with water. Add one heaping tablespoon of chopped onion and one heaping tablespoon of chopped celery and a pinch of salt. Bring to a steady boil. Boil until the chicken is tender and there is a rich film of fat on the surface of the water.

Cretons – French

Six pounds or more of pork shoulder. Cover with water – add 6 or more or less onions, salt, pepper, nutmeg, cinnamon, cloves or thyme, or whatever spice you prefer. Reduce all the water and liquid until you can almost make a path in it with your spoon. Stir as often as possible in such a way that meat becomes very thin. Use as a cracker spread.

Baking

Sometimes a beehive oven was built into the fireplace. It had a rounded top. A fire was built in it and, when ready, the hot coals, ashes, were removed. Temperature was tested by placing your arm into the oven. It was ready for use, if your arm did not burn before you counted to ten. Food was placed inside, and cover replaced. Foods that required hottest heat were baked first, as gingerbread, then in afternoon a pot of beans might be placed inside to cook all night.

Cornmeal Mush and Pork

To make a more filling meal out of the fried cornmeal mush and to vary the menu since it was served so often, the following recipe was used.

Simmer 1 pound pork with bones or any meat and bones left over until very tender. Remove meat and bones and boil broth down to 1 quart (or add water). Add 1 teaspoon salt and 1/2 teaspoon sage. Add 1 cup cornmeal dissolved in 1 cup of cold water. Add to broth and cook until it thickens, stirring frequently. Add shredded meat. Pour into greased bread loaf pans; chill; slice, dip in flour and fry in fat till brown and crispy. Serve hot with syrup or apple topping for breakfast.

Tourtiere

The "tourtè" was originally a pottery casserole dish. The famous French dish the "Tourtiere" was commonly cooked in it and the name was adapted to the meat pie. Pot pies were a favorite and were made mostly with chicken, game and vegetables.

Sausage

Empty intestines of hog, cut in lengths and lay for 2 days in salt and water. Turn inside out and soak one day longer. Scrape then rinse in soda water, wipe and blow into one end, having tied up the other with twine. If they are whole and clean, stuff with meat.

The meat for the sausage was ground by hand in a special grinder that seemed to take hours. Then the homegrown sage, salt and pepper were mixed with it. Before the casings were stuffed, a trial patty was cooked to see if the meat was seasoned right.For storage, the sausage was packed in crocks, and hot lard poured over each layer. This sealed out the air and kept it from spoiling.

Tourtè – French

Tourtè is the staple food of French Canada. Among the French of the Monroe County region, it is considered a treat reserved for holiday meals. This "folk" receipt has been modernized a bit, but it is still basically the same receipt that was used in the eighteenth century.

Any game cut up
Sausage
Chopped onion
Chopped raw potato

Let this steam in a skillet until it is soft. Place this into a pie shell. Make one vent hole in the center of the top crust. Bake the tourtè in moderate oven or fire until brown. Some of the French eat it cold with maple syrup on top.

Dinner

Game of many kinds helped vary the diet of early Detroiters. In the 1700's, pigeon, deer, bear, and wolves were often seen on the outskirts of town. Gamebirds, turkey, quail, ducks, and geese were to be had, as well as the squirrel.

Pork Pot Roast – French

In large Dutch oven brown pork roast in hot fat. Add four cups water and one cut-up onion. Cook slow until meat is tender then add cut-up carrots and turnips. Mix a little flour with water and pour into broth to thicken.

Wash Clean

Body washing in early days was considered a health hazard. Yet people did wash themselves and their clothing, however infrequently, and they made their own soap to do the job. More accurately it was usually the young ladies of the family who were given the monotonous task of soapmaking. Some soaps were made pleasant-smelling with fragrant herbs. Few homemakers depended on a written recipe. They knew by word of mouth that they could obtain enough lye from 5 or 6 bushels of wood ashes, to combine with 20 to 25 pounds of grease and fat, and they would end up with a barrel of soft usable soap.

Today we make soap with sodium hydroxide and this causes our soap to harden.

Oxtail Stew – English

Cook oxtails in Dutch oven, add water and seasonings. Cover and cook. Add carrots, turnips and onions and cook until tender. Mix flour and water and add to stew to thicken.

Fish

Fish were extremely important to the earliest settlers for religious reasons. Most of the new arrivals at Fort Pontchartrain were French Catholics, and they were bound by the 18th century church rules of fasting. Since the food supply was especially limited during the late winter, the ample supply of fish became the main source of protein for them during the Lenten season.

Fish Hash – French

Fresh fish, boned and skinned
Potatoes, boiled and cooled
Butter or margarine
Light cream

Cut up fish and set aside. Peel potatoes and cut up. Heat cream and butter in a soup kettle until butter melts. Add the fish and cook just until the fish turns flaky. Add potatoes and cook until potatoes are done.

Codfish Cakes – English

One pound of salt cod, placed in water overnight to remove the salt. Cook over a medium heat until tender, remove and drain. Chop to a medium-fine grade. Add to this 1/2 cup of cooked and mashed potatoes, 1 beaten egg, and a small chopped onion. Mix well and make into cakes. Fry on lightly greased pan until crusty. Cod was brought in.

Fishing in Detroit

Local Detroit fish included whitefish, sturgeon, pickerel, pike, perch, black bass, catfish, sunfish, and bullfish were plentiful – even being shipped later to Ohio and New York.

Boiled Whitefish

Clean the fish (gut and scale). Cut into chunks or strips about two inches wide. Fish may also be cut into fillets and skinned, if desired. Place in cold water; add seasonings such as salt, parsley, and onion, if desired. Bring to a boil and simmer on the side of the fireplace until the fish flakes easily. Serve warm.

Cooking - 1700's Style

Frying – Coals were raked out onto the hearth and the frying pan with legs (spider) was set directly upon them.

Boiling – Small amount of water – set kettle right up against fire, or on top of burning wood.

Larger amounts of water, or soups, stews, etc. – kettle was suspended over the flame. Temperature could be varied by swinging the crane into or out of the fire.

Fish with Peas – French

Any filleted fish can be used for this. Fresh water pan fish filleted are very nice for this dish.

Butter deep dish well. Arrange fish in it and cover lightly with cream. Cover with fine bread crumbs. Bake till flesh flakes and crust is brown and bubbly. Serve with cooked fresh peas arranged around dish.

Bouillabaisse (Fish Chowder) – French

Use any type of fish – carp, pickerel, perch. Cut into chunks, bones and all, but the heads. Cut up and add salt pork. Cover with water and stew until tender. Any type of vegetables may be added, such as potatoes, turnips, onions, celery, and carrots. Season as desired. Serve hot.

Dried Fish with Maple Sugar

When fish has been partly dried, the meat is removed from the bones. It was spread on a clean surface and worked by hand until it became a smooth, fine texture – like putty. Maple sugar was then worked into the mixture and it was stored in birchbark containers for winter use. This was originally an Indian recipe. Recipes were often traded.

Fish Balls

Fresh fish, boned
Water
Unpeeled, diced potatoes
Pepper
Oil
Maple Syrup
Herbs to taste (dill, parsley, fennel)

Boil fish and potatoes in a covered pot. Drain and mash. Add remaining ingredients and shape into balls. Fry in hot fat, turning until golden brown. Drain and serve, hot or cold

Fasting

French "habitants" also ate fish on fast days and, through a special dispensation, were permitted to eat beaver.

Pickled Fish – English

Fish
Cider Vinegar
Onions, thinly sliced
Dried juniper berries, crushed
Chopped, fresh dill
Peppercorns
Wood ashes (optional)

White fish and other fish can be pickled. Clean and cut into medium-sized pieces. Place in a crock on top of thin slices of onion. Simmer the cider vinegar with the juniper berries and seasonings. Stir in the wood ashes. Pour this mixture over the fish, adding more vinegar, if necessary, to cover. Cover the crock and let it stand from 2 days to 2 weeks. After 2 days the vinegar and spices should have softened and dissolved all internal bones. Serve cold.

Smoked Fish

Fish were often preserved by smoking them over a juniper or hickory fire. The smoke was contained in a smokehouse or barrel while the fish were drying.

Crayfish

Bring a kettle of water to rolling boil and add salt. Drop live crayfish into kettle and boil until its body turns deep red. Take it out and serve whole. Edible meat is in tail, legs, and claws. To get at this meat, bread off tail and dig out meat from underside. Pull legs and claws from body and crack open the hard shell.

Electric streetcars began running in 1893. At Woodward and Jefferson the *Queen Anne Soap* company sign was electric and could be seen up the street from the river.

Woodward Avenue covered with snow c. 1875-79. People and goods traveled around on horse drawn sleds.

This four-in-hand coach of 1897 circles Grand Circus Park with its stylish passengers. Note the man with the long horn to warn pedestrians.

Opposite page:
Detroit's first city hall was built in 1835 on the east side of Woodward at Cadillac Square. The first floor was occupied by market stalls for many years, and the public Central Market was behind it. Russell House Hotel can be seen in the background.

Opposite page below:
Proud owners of a grocery store near Cadillac Square in 1870.

This is a view of the Campus Martius on the west side of Woodward, showing the new cty hall built in 1872.

Detroit street scene Woodward Avenue from Clifford to Grand Circus on the West Side. Woodward Avenue was the
major retail street in Detroit through the 1950's.

Police Department from Elmwood Station 1884. Left to right: Capt. L. Guyman, Lieut. Michael Kenny, Sgt. Thomas G. Havens, Lieut. Frank L. Lucius and Lieut. Geo. W. Phillips who answered his last roll call May 6, 1908.

A more modern looking Deroit Police Dept. c 1912. Car is a Chalmers model 36.

This is Chief James Battle of Detroit's first Fire Department c. 1870. The horn at left was presented to the D.F.D. by Windsor F.D. to thank them for their help in fighting a fire in Windsor. The horn is in the collection of the Detroit Historical Museum.

Late 1800's electric street car on 14th avenue, with motorman and conductor.

Gratiot avenue near downtown new model street car. c. 1920. Ponchartrain Hotel in background.

The city bought Belle Isle in 1876 and worked to transform it into a beautiful park.
Belle Isle ferry dock is seen in background.

Belle Isle was extremely wet and swampy. Unemployed citizens were expected to come to the island and donate time to help with drainage, to funnel the water into a network of canals. The lighthouse in the background was designed by Albert Kahn, and is still there.

Scenic approach to the old Belle Isle Bridge before it was destroyed by fire in 1915 and replaced by the present bridge. In the foreground, is the future site of the Electric Park rollercoaster.

This dock was located east of the Belle Isle Bridge. Ferry boats would bring in workers from downtown Detroit. Mothers would bring their children and picnic dinners during the day and meet dad after work on the island. c. 1889.

You could sit in your canoe and enjoy the concert going on in the bandshell in the bridge over the canal. c. 1908

This is a picture of Belle Isle's Grand Avenue (Central Avenue) about 1905, showing the decorative floral planting. The Scripps flower conservatory and the aquarium opened up in 1904. The aquarium was the first one of its' kind in North America.

View of the Dossin Great Lakes Museum on Belle Isle Park from the Detroit River.

The three-paneled LaSalle Window which contains more than 700 pieces of stained glass and is part of the Gothic room at the Dossin Great Lakes Museum.

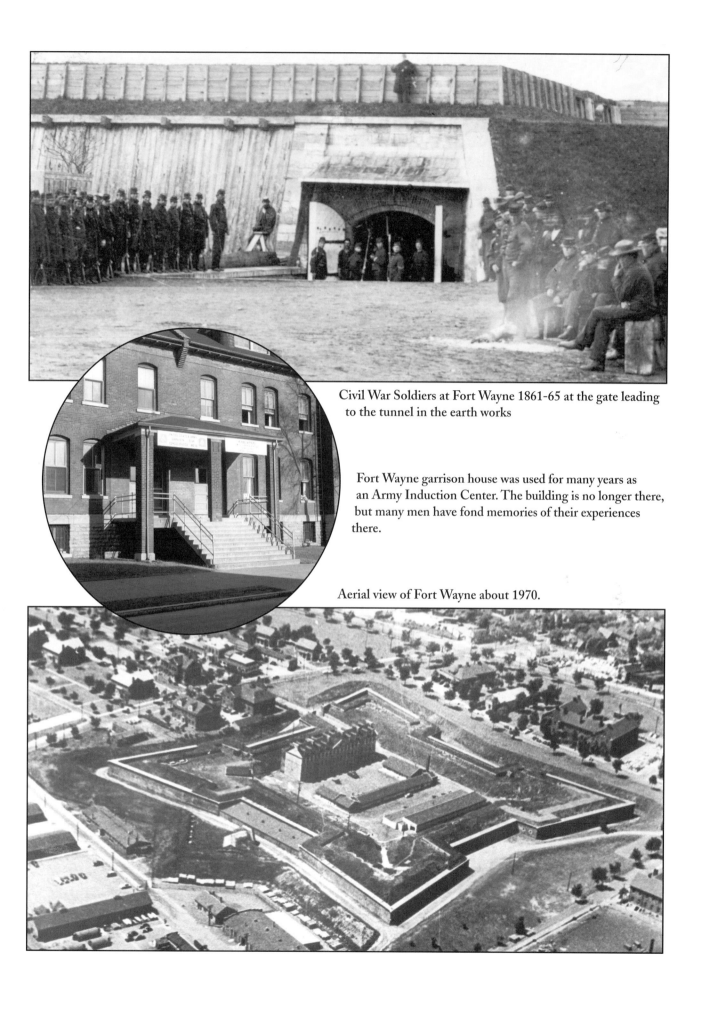

Civil War Soldiers at Fort Wayne 1861-65 at the gate leading to the tunnel in the earth works

Fort Wayne garrison house was used for many years as an Army Induction Center. The building is no longer there, but many men have fond memories of their experiences there.

Aerial view of Fort Wayne about 1970.

60

All of these toys are part of larger collections at the Detroit Historical Museum. Watch for periodic toy exhibits.

Henkel Milling began doing business in Detroit in 1855 and produced Henkel's Flour. In the early 1900's they began to produce *Velvet Cake Flour* and *Robinhood Flour*. In 1942 they acquired Commerical Milling, then International Milling in 1972 making it the largest U.S. company milling flour. In 1930 they published a recipe for pumpkin pie that appears in this cookbok. Peter Henkel's company was a Detroit business for 96 years.

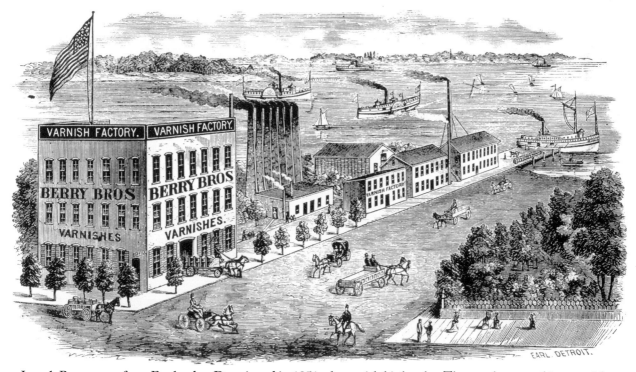

Joseph Berry came from England to Detroit and in 1851, along with his brother Thomas, began making varnish. Eventually, their company became one of the leading manufacturers of paint, varnish, glues and stains. Their company was in business for about 100 years until 1958. By the time Joseph Berry died his estate was worth $14,000,000. Some of the Berry descendants live in the Grosse Pointe area.

Thanksgiving Dinner, November 24, 1892 at Father Foote's. George H. Foote, *5th from the left*, was a wealthy Detroit waterfront landowner and in 1892 was instrumental in donating to the City of Detroit, one of the cannon used in the War of 1812. This photo was taken of the seventeen members of the Foote family by Alvond & Co., 55 Rowland St., a commercial photographer. The Foote home was located at 323 Lafayette Avenue.

Part 2

HEARTHSTONES TO FANCY KITCHENS
1801 to 1900

HISTORICAL HIGHLIGHTS OF 1801 TO 1900

Detroit was incorporated as a town in 1802. Three years later, in 1805, Detroit became the capitol of the newly-formed Michigan territory, which was to be run by a governor, a secretary, and three judges.

On June 11, 1805, Detroit was destroyed by fire which started in baker John Harvey's barn. A relief effort to help feed and shelter the villagers who were displaced by the fire was organized by Father Gabriel Richard. The territorial Judge Augustus Woodward's new plan for rebuilding the town called for a central hexagon with streets radiating from it. He determined that principal streets would be 200 feet wide, intermediate streets 120 feet wide, and the narrowest streets would be 60 feet wide. Judge Woodward believed that Detroit would grow to only about 50,000 residents and planned accordingly.

The First Methodist congregation was formed in 1810. At the start of the War of 1812, Governor Hull surrendered Detroit to the British without a shot being fired by raising a white flag on the flagpole. After Perry's victory at the Battle of Lake Erie, September 1813, the British retreated into Canada and Detroit once again flew the American flag.

On October 24, 1815, Detroit re-incorporated, negating all previous laws and adopting stringent fire regulations. Licenses were required for the sale of liquor. Gambling and games of chance were prohibited as was the keeping of more than one dog and working on the Sabbath.

Presbyterian minister John Monteith arrived in 1816, and the next year he was chosen by Judge Woodward to be the first president of the newly-formed University of Michigan. Monteith and Father Richard were the only professors appointed to be teachers and were expected to teach in eight different disciplines. In 1817, the idea for a Public Library was conceived, but this did not become a reality until 1831.

The Michigan Essay and Impartial Observer, Detroit's first newspaper printed only four issues. The Detroit Gazette, fared better, offering a four-page paper, the first three pages were printed in English and page four was in French.

Due to an influx of New Englanders to the area, Thanksgiving was celebrated for the first time in Detroit on November 25, 1824. The following year saw the opening of the Erie Canal combined with steam-powered ships operating on the Great Lakes. This opened Detroit and Michigan to more rapid settlement.

Jefferson Avenue was paved with cobblestones, while other streets were paved with cedar rounds embedded in tar, which was quieter but had the tendency to float away in rain storms.

Father Richard was elected as a territorial Representative to Congress, and Detroit replaced legislative trustees with a "Common Council."

The First Baptist Church opened. Systems were developed to deliver water to homes and businesses, and the Herald newspaper began publication, all during the 1820's. Beginning in 1830, African Methodists organized their first Detroit church. New towns that were growing in the area, such as Mt. Clemens, Utica, Rochester, Pontiac, Ann Arbor, Ypsilanti, and Port Huron meant more trade markets for Detroit.

In 1831 the Democratic Free Press and the Michigan Intelligencer (all one title) began publishing. The name was so long that it was soon shortened to the Free Press.

The Catholic Diocese of Detroit was created in 1833 and a second Catholic parish, Holy Trinity, opened mainly to serve the Irish, since St. Anne's was seen as a French church. Both Father Richard and Governor Porter died of cholera in the epidemic of 1832. One of every eight Detroiters died of cholera during the several epidemics.

On January 26, 1837, Michigan entered the Union as the twenty-sixth state, with Detroit as its capitol. The capitol was moved to Lansing in 1847.

Detroit's population in 1840 was 9,124. During this decade $50,000 was approved for construction of a fort on sixty-six acres along the river. This became Fort Wayne, from which never a shot was fired. But it secured Detroit during the Civil War. Detroit boasted fifteen churches and seventeen religious societies. Telegraph service began between Detroit and Ypsilanti. 1849 saw the incorporation of the Detroit Savings Bank, later Detroit Bank and Trust, renamed recently to Comerica Bank; German immigrants organized the Harmonie Society, a social and entertainment club; and the first Michigan State Agricultural Fair was held. H.R. Johnson used illuminating gas in his hotel at the foot of Third Street but was sure to turn it off at 10 p.m. because the residents would turn off the fire, and gas would leak out.

About 21,019 people called Detroit home in 1850. It was during this decade that Lewis Cass installed the first furnace in his home and Zachariah Chandler installed one in his large dry goods store on Jefferson near Woodward. All principal Detroit streets had coal-burning lamps mounted on tall posts. In Detroit, there were nineteen public schools and twenty-one teachers.

The second half of the nineteenth century saw a proliferation of industries which were to turn Detroit into a modern industrial city. John J. Bagley and Daniel Scotten became wealthy in the tobacco industry; when Scotten died in 1899, he left an estate valued at seven million dollars. Detroit was a leading manufacturer of cigars and chewing tobacco. Jeremiah Dwyer started a farm reaper and stove works; as more capital was acquired the company became Detroit Stove Works; joined later by Michigan Stove Company and the Peninsular Stove Company. They made cook stoves, ranges, parlor and heating stoves, gas ranges and heaters, plus furnaces for general heating.

With railroads and steamships for transportation, Eber Brock Ward was able to establish an iron industry with Detroit at its heart. Blast furnaces and rolling mills were built to further the steel industry.

In 1859, Walter Harper and his long-time housekeeper Ann Martin, donated their extensive properties to the city to be utilized for a hospital and a school for poor boys. Also during this time the YMCA opened and Temple Beth-El was incorporated.

With 45,619 people, Detroit, in 1860 was rapidly becoming a modern city. The fire department gave up hand-powered fire engines and bucket brigades for horse-drawn steam engines.

1861 saw the beginning of the Civil War; the First Michigan Infantry regiment left for duty on May 13th. All told, of Michigan's population of 500,000, 91,000 went to war; 14,500 Michigan men died. The Soldiers and Sailors Monument on Woodward at Campus Martius, unveiled in 1872, honors these valiant men. Money to commission the monument was donated by Bela Hubbard, a wealthy farm owner and active citizen.

After many futile attempts, a metropolitan police force was formed in 1865. It was run by the state since lawless elements had gained political power in Detroit. Patrol wagons were added in 1885, as were telegraph signal boxes.

1869 saw the opening of the Detroit Opera House, the opening of the Detroit Medical College, and for the first time children of African-American descent attended the public schools.

By 1870, 80,000 people lived in the city, arc lights brightened downtown streets. It was 1873 when James Edmund Scripps founded the Detroit News and began publication. The new city hall also opened that year. Proposals were made for a railway bridge or tunnel to Canada. William Davis of Detroit invented a freezing process and refrigerated railway cars.

In ten years Detroit's population had reached 116,000. The '80's witnessed a bridge built to Belle Isle. Frederick Law Olmsted, designer of New York City's Central Park, was hired to design this Detroit jewel. Hazen Pingree was elected mayor, inheriting a very corrupt city government. Seven members of the common council were indicted for accepting bribes from public contractors. Pingree rooted out corruption, and he promoted a public lighting plant to control Detroit's street lights. Telephones came into service in 1889.

During the '90's Detroit's salt industry began producing rock salt, soda ash, and caustic soda. With a population of 206,000, Detroit was becoming an industrial giant, not only in tobacco, stoves, and railway cars, but in seeds. Ferry Seed Company was the largest in the world. A burgeoning medical and pharmaceutical industry, led by Parke-Davis, began in the 90's. The Berry Brothers started a varnish and paint business. Detroit also boasted ship-building, dry-docks, lumber yards, machine shops, a brick industry, whole-sale dry goods, hardware, meat-packing, and engine and boiler manufacturing

The Spanish-American War of 1898 was brief, but bitter. Detroit General Russell A. Alger was Secretary of War in President McKinley's cabinet. As usual, Detroiters rushed to volunteer.

As Detroit prepared to celebrate its bi-centennial it had a population of 285,704 compared to only 2,000, one hundred years earlier.

HEARTHSTONES TO FANCY KITCHENS

Cooking in the 1800's was an adventure. The recipes in Part II are from that era. Into the 1800's and almost through the end, recipe books were written in a paragraph style, using measurements such as 1 gill of yeast, or 3 pints of flour and one teacup of milk. The ingredients list was usually rather short and the directions were sometimes not too clear. Many of the recipes in this section are easy to follow and will be delicious if you are willing to try them.

In 1800 cooking on a hearth with a gridiron, or swinging the Dutch oven over the fire on a crane made it difficult to get good results when it came to making something special like a cake. So one-pot meals with meat and vegetables were the usual fare, and wild game was on the menu often. Flour puddings with fruit and bread puddings seemed to be among the favorites for dessert since baking utensils like cake and pie pans were not widely available. Most of the recipes call for large amounts of cream, butter and eggs, which Detroit settlers had in abundance. Leavenings, like baking powder, were not generally available yet, so cooks made their own yeast for their breads and depended on a lot of eggs to make the cake rise or the pudding thicken. Occasionally, special ingredients, like lemons or oranges were available, so there are some recipes using these. As hearthstones gave way to iron stoves a whole new generation of cooks began to practice their craft. A wide variety of foods such as those presented here were cooked with good results and the cooks of days gone by are fondly remembered by their descendants.

In this era, we are also beginning to see the influence of immigrants to Detroit, especially from 1850 on. The Germans, Irish, Polish and others had a strong influence on Detroit culture as the immigrant population gew. Advice about housekeeping, cooking, child rearing and everyday manners began to appear in books and articles, as people from many cultures began to settle in.

Bread

About Bread

Among all civilized people bread has become an article of food of the first necessity; and properly so, for it constitutes of itself a complete life sustainer, the gluten, starch and sugar which it contains representing ozotized and hydro-carbonated nutrients, and combining the sustaining powers of the animal and vegetable kingdoms in one product. As there is no one article of food that enters so largely into our daily fare as bread, so no degree of skill in preparing other articles can compensate for lack of knowledge in the art of making good, palatable and nutritious bread. A little earnest attention to the subject will enable any one to comprehend the theory, and then ordinary care in practice will make one familiar with the process.

To Make Yeast

Boil one quart of Irish potatoes in three quarts of water. When done, take out the potatoes, one by one, on a fork, peel and mash them fine, in a tray, with a large iron spoon, leaving the boiling water on the stove during the process. Throw in this water a handful of hops, which must scald, not boil, as it turns the tea very dark to let the hops boil.

Add to the mashed potatoes a heaping teacupful of powdered white sugar and half a teacupful of salt; then slowly stir in the strained hop tea, so that there will be no lumps. When milk-warm add a teacupful of yeast and pour into glass fruit jars, or large, clear glass bottles, to ferment, being careful not to close them tightly. Set in a warm place in winter, a cool one in summer. In six hours it will be ready for use, and at the end of that time the jar or bottle must be securely closed. Keep in a cold room in the winter, and in the ice box in summer. This yeast will keep two weeks in winter and one week in summer. Bread made from it is always sweet.

Excellent Bread for Breakfast

1 quart of flour
Lard the size of a walnut
1 small Irish potato, boiled and mashed fine
1 heaping teaspoonful of salt
Half a teacup of good yeast, into which put a tablespoonful of white sugar

Make up a soft dough with cold water in summer and milk-warm water in winter. This must be kneaded for thirty minutes, and then set to rise, in a cool place in summer, and a warm one in winter; must never be kept more than milk warm.

Two hours before breakfast, make the dough into the desired shapes, handling it lightly, without kneading it, first rubbing lard over the hands, and taking especial care to grease the bread on top. Then set it to rise again.

Thirty minutes are sufficient for baking it, unless it be in the form of a loaf or rolls, in which case, it must be baked fifteen minutes longer. Excellent muffins may be made by the above receipt, adding two eggs well beaten, so that from the same batch of dough both plain bread and muffins may be made. Iron moulds are best for baking.

For those who prefer warm bread for dinner, it is a good plan to reserve a portion of the breakfast dough, setting it away in a cool place till two hours before dinner, then make into turnovers or twist, set it to rise and bake it for dinner, as for breakfast. Very nice on a cold day, and greatly preferable to warmed-over bread.

Corn Pone

Mix with cold water into a soft dough one quart of southern corn-meal, sifted, a teaspoonful of salt, a tablespoonful of butter or lard melted. Mold into oval cakes with the hands and bake in a very hot oven, in well-greased pans. To be eaten hot. The crust should be brown.

French Rolls

Three cups of sweet milk, one cup of butter and lard, mixed in equal proportions, one-half cup of good yeast, or half a cake of compressed yeast, and a teaspoonful of salt. Add flour enough to make a stiff dough. Let it rise over night; in the morning, add two well-beaten eggs; knead thoroughly, and let it rise again. With the hands, make it into balls as large as an egg; then roll between the hands to make long rolls, (about three inches). Place close together in even rows on well-buttered pans. Cover and let them rise again, then bake in a quick oven to a delicate brown.

Velvet Rolls

3 pints of flour
2 eggs
1 teacup of sweet milk
1 teacup of yeast
1 tablespoonful of lard, and the same of butter

Mix well and beat the dough till it blisters.

Let it rise, work in a small quantity of flour, beat as before and make into rolls. After the second rising, bake quickly.

Spider Corn-Cake

Beat two eggs and one-fourth cup sugar together. Then add one cup sweet milk, and one cup of sour milk in which you have dissolved one teaspoonful soda. Add a teaspoonful of salt. Then mix one and two-thirds cups of granulated corn-meal and one-third cup flour with this. Put a spider or skillet on the range, and when it is hot melt in two tablespoonfuls of butter. Turn the spider so that the butter can run up on the sides of the pan. Pour in the corn-cake mixture and add one more cup of sweet milk, but do not stir afterwards. Put this in the oven and bake from twenty to thirty-five minutes. When done, there should be a streak of custard through it.

Johnnie Cake

Sift one quart of Indian meal into a pan; make a hole in the middle and pour in a pint of warm water, adding one teaspoonful of salt; with a spoon mix the meal and water gradually into a soft dough; stir it very briskly for a quarter of an hour or more, till it becomes light and spongy; then spread the dough smooth and evenly on a straight, flat board (a piece of the head of flour-barrel will serve for this purpose); place the board nearly upright before an open fire, and put an iron against the back to support it; bake it well; when done, cut it in squares; send it hot to table, split and buttered.—Old Plantation Style

Egg Biscuit

Sift together a quart of dry flour and three heaping tea-spoonfuls of baking-powder. Rub into this thoroughly a piece of butter the size of an egg; add two well-beaten eggs, a tablespoonful of sugar, a teaspoonful of salt. Mix all together quickly into a soft dough, with one cup of milk, or more if needed. Roll out nearly half of an inch thick. Cut into biscuits, and bake immediately in a quick oven from fifteen to twenty minutes.

Boston Corn Bread

One cup of sweet milk, two of sour milk, two-thirds of a cup of molasses, one of wheat flour, four of corn-meal and one teaspoonful of soda; steam for three hours, and brown a few minutes in the oven. The same made of sweet milk and baking-powder is equally as good.

Light Bread

2 quarts of flour
1 teaspoonful of sugar
1 teaspoonful of salt
Half a teacup of yeast
1 egg, well beaten
1 pint of water

Sift the flour and divide it into three parts. Mix one third in the batter, one third in the jar to rise in, and pour the other third over the batter. Let it stand two hours and then work it well, adding a small piece of lard before baking.

Food for Infants Brought Up By Hand

Take two parts of good cow's milk to one part of water, and sweeten it a little with loaf sugar. Warm it so as to be of the temperature of milk just taken from the cow.

Sally-Lunn

1 quart of flour
1 teaspoonful of salt
1 tablespoonful of white sugar

Rub in a heaping tablespoonful of butter and lard in equal parts, then rub in an Irish potato, mashed fine.
Half a teacup of yeast
3 eggs well beaten

Make up the dough to the consistency of light bread dough with warm water in winter, and cold in summer. Knead half an hour. When it has risen light, handle lightly, put into a cake-mould and bake without a second kneading.

Parker House Rolls – Unfermented

These rolls are made with baking-powder, and are much sooner made. Stir into a quart of sifted flour three large tea-spoonfuls of baking-powder, a tablespoonful of cold butter, a teaspoonful of salt and one of sugar, and a well-beaten egg; rub all well into the flour, pour in a pint of cold milk, mix up quickly into a smooth dough, roll it out less than half an inch thick, cut with a large biscuit-cutter, spread soft butter over the top of each, fold one half over the other by doubling it, lay them a little apart on greased tins. Set them immediately in a pretty hot oven. Rub over the tops with sweet milk before putting in the oven, to give them a glaze.

Pocketbook Rolls

1 quart of flour
1 teaspoonful of salt
2 teaspoonfuls of sugar
2 tablespoonfuls of lard
3 tablespoonfuls of yeast
2 eggs

Mix up these ingredients with warm water, making up the dough at 10 A.M. in summer and 8 A.M. in winter. Put in half the lard when it is first worked up, and at the second working put in the rest of the lard and a little more flour.

Roll out the dough in strips as long and wide as your hand, spread with butter and roll up like a pocketbook. Put them in buttered tins, and, when they are light, bake them a light brown.

Nothings

Take one egg, two tablespoonfuls cream, butter the size of a walnut, flour to make the dough very stiff; work it well and roll it very thin. Cut the size of a saucer. Fry in lard and sprinkle with powdered sugar.

Nun's Puffs

Boil one pint of milk with half a pound of butter. Stir them into three-quarters of a pound of flour and let them cool. Then add nine eggs, yolks and whites to be beaten separately, and whites to be added last. Fill cups or tins half full and bake. When done, sprinkle with white sugar while hot. Very nice for tea.

Etiquette - 1852

The rule is, never to introduce one person to another without knowing that it is agreeable to both. Ladies are always to be consulted beforehand. Gentlemen are introduced to ladies, not ladies to gentlemen.

A common form is, "Mr. Jones, Mr. Smith–Mr. Smith, Mr. Jones." Messrs. Jones and Smith bow, shake hands, express their happiness at being made acquainted with each other.

When more ceremony is required, the introducer says, "Miss Smith, permit me to introduce Mr. Jones to your acquaintance," or, "allow me to present."

Coffee-house, steamboat, and stage-coach acquaintances last only for the time being. You are not obliged to know them afterwards, however familiar for the time.

Compliments of
The Wagner Baking Co.
Sole Manufacturers of
QUAKER BREAD.   OVER

Talk

Great caution should be used with regard to the habits of talking in a family. Talk of things rather than of persons, lest your children early imbibe a love of gossiping.

Baking Powder Recipe

1 pound, 2 ounces pure cream of tartar
1/2 pound cooking soda
1/4 pound cornstarch

Mix and sift thoroughly 4 times, and store in closely covered jars.

To Clean Combs

If it can be avoided, never wash combs, as the water often makes the teeth split, and the tortoiseshell or horn of which they are made, rough. Small brushes, manufactured purposely for cleaning combs, may be purchased at a trifling cost; with this, the comb should be well brushed, and afterwards wiped with a cloth or towel.

Twist

From the dough of loaf bread or French rolls, reserve enough to make two long strips or rolls, say, fifteen inches long and one inch in diameter. Rub lard well between the hands before handling and shaping these strips. Pinch the two ends so as to make them stick together. Twist them, pressing the other ends together to prevent unrolling.

Scones – English Origin

2 cups flour
1/2 teaspoonful salt
3 teaspoonfuls baking powder
2 tablespoonfuls butter
1/2 to 2/3 cup milk

Sift the flour, salt, and baking powder together, rub in the butter, and mix thoroughly with the milk. Roll to 1/2-inch thickness and cut into 8 triangular pieces. Bake in a fairly hot oven for 10 to 15 minutes. Serve with clotted cream and jam.

Mice Control

Mix corn meal and cement, half-and-half. Place in shallow containers where mice run.

Breakfast

Eggs

Properly cooked, eggs are a very wholesome and nutritious diet. Always be certain, however, that they are fresh, before attempting to make a dish of them. Some persons use Krepp's family egg-tester, to ascertain if an egg is sound. Full directions, as to the mode of using it, accompany the egg tester; so it is unnecessary to give them here. A simple mode of testing the soundness of an egg, is to put it in water; and if fresh it will sink to the bottom.

Eggs for Breakfast

Heat in the oven a common white dish, large enough to hold the number of eggs to be cooked, allowing plenty of room for each. Melt in it a small piece of butter, break the eggs, one at a time, carefully in a saucer, and slip them in the hot dish. Sprinkle over them pepper and salt, and let them cook four or five minutes. It is a great improvement to allow to every two eggs a tablespoonful of cream, adding it when the eggs are first put in.

Recipe for Making Hens Lay

Shell Indian corn, put it in a pot with some red pepper, (if you have no red the black will do) boil it till it is soft, feed the hens on it.

Ham and Egg Pudding – A Spring Dish

6 eggs beaten very light
A light pint of flour
A pint of milk
A small piece of butter
Salt and pepper to the taste

Sprinkle some slices of boiled ham (both fat and lean) with pepper, and lay them across a deep dish that has been greased. Then pour the pudding batter over the bacon and bake quickly.

Scalloped Eggs

Hard-boil twelve eggs; slice them thin in rings; in the bottom of a large well-buttered baking-dish place a layer of grated bread-crumbs, then one of eggs; cover with bits of butter, and sprinkle with pepper and salt. Continue thus to blend these ingredients until the dish is full; be sure, though, that the crumbs cover the eggs upon top. Over the whole pour a large teacupful of sweet cream or milk, and brown nicely in a moderately heated oven.

The Housekeeper's Palace was a four-story building located at 178 Grand River, that sold numerous, and unusual, cooking and housekeeping gadgets that had been invented for the housewife. Here you see a sampling of some of them from the permanent exhibit located in the Streets of Detroit at the Detroit Historical Museum. All of the housekeeping and cooking utensils shown in the picture are from the museum's collection. The façade of the building is modeled after the original.

Buttermilk Cakes

1 quart of flour
2 eggs, well beaten
1 1/2 pints of buttermilk
1 teaspoonful of salt

Beat very light, after mixing the ingredients. Just before baking, stir in a little soda, mixed in a little of the buttermilk.

Bake on a griddle, free from grease.

Sour Milk Cakes

1 pint sour milk
1 pint flour
Butter size of a small egg
1 tablespoonful of sugar
1 saltspoonful of salt
Half teaspoonful of soda

Bake in hot and well-greased iron clads.

Mixed Eggs and Bacon

Take a nice rasher of mild bacon; cut it into squares no larger than dice; fry it quickly until nicely browned, but on no account burn it. Break half a dozen eggs into a basin, strain and season them with pepper, add them to the bacon, stir the whole about, and, when sufficiently firm, turn it out into a dish. Decorate with hot pickles.

Liniment
One egg beaten light, half a pint spirits turpentine, half a pint good apple vinegar. Shake well before using. Good for sprains, cuts, or bruises.

Omelet of Herbs

Parsley, thyme, and sweet marjoram mixed gives the famous omelette aux fines herbes so popular at every wayside inn in the most remote corner of sunny France. An omelet "jardiniere" is two tablespoonfuls of mixed parsley, onion, chives, shalots and a few leaves each of sorrel and chervil, minced fine and stirred into the beaten eggs before cooking. It will take a little more butter to fry it than a plain one.

Eggs
Eggs can be kept for some time by smearing the shells with butter or lard; then packed in plenty of bran or sawdust, the eggs are not allowed to touch one another; or coat the eggs with melted paraffine.

Corn-Meal Griddle-Cakes

Scald two cups of sifted meal, mix with a cup of wheat flour, and a teaspoonful of salt. Add three well-beaten eggs; thin the whole with sour milk enough to make it the right consistency. Beat the whole till very light, and add a teaspoonful of baking-soda dissolved in a little water. If you use sweet milk, use two large teaspoonfuls of baking-powder instead of soda.

Asparagus Omelet

Boil with a little salt, and until about half cooked, eight or ten stalks of asparagus, and cut the eatable part into rather small pieces; beat the eggs, and mix the asparagus with them. Make the omelet as above directed.

Omelet with parsley is made by adding a little chopped parsley.

Apple Omelet

Apple omelet, to be served with broiled spare-rib or roast pork, is very delicate. Take nine large, tart apples, four eggs, one cup of sugar, one tablespoonful of butter; add cinnamon or other spices to suit your taste; stew the apples till they are very soft; mash them so that there will be no lumps; add the butter and sugar while they are still warm; but let them cool before putting in the beaten eggs; bake this till it is brown; you may put it all in a shallow pudding-dish or in two tin plates to bake. Very good.

Fresh Eggs
In shaking an egg, if it makes a sound, it is not a good egg, and should be rejected. The water test consists in putting them in water deep enough to cover; the "good eggs" will lie flat at the bottom, while the "bad eggs" will stand upright, like many other unsound things in the world. The "candling" process consists in looking through the egg at a light, or holding it between you and the sun. If it shows up clear and spotless, so that the yolk can be perceived, it is good; otherwise it is not.

Wheat Griddle-Cakes

Three cups of flour, one teaspoonful of salt, three teaspoonfuls of baking-powder, sifted together; beat three eggs and add to three cupfuls of sweet milk, also a tablespoonful of melted butter; mix all into a smooth batter, as thick as will run in a stream from the lips of a pitcher. Bake on a well-greased, hot griddle, a nice, light brown. Very good.

Flannel Cakes

1 quart of flour
1 pint of meal
1 teacup of milk
1 teacup of yeast
3 eggs
2 teaspoonfuls of salt

Beat well together and let it rise till usual time in a warm place. Excellent.

Breakfast Casserole

1 1/2 cups cheese, grated
6 slices white bread, cubed – crust included
1 1/2 pounds pork sausage, browned and drained
4 eggs
1 1/2 teaspoons dry mustard
1 teaspoonful salt
2 cups milk

In 3-quart casserole or 9 x 13 greased pan layer bread, cheese and sausage. Beat 4 eggs, mustard, salt and milk. Pour egg mixture over layered ingredients. Bake for 1 hour uncovered in moderate oven.

Egg Pie

Take six hard-boiled eggs, slice, season with salt, pepper, and butter, bake in a paste, top and bottom.

Gravy for Biscuits or Potatoes

Heat in fry pan:
1/4 cup fat
4 tablespoonfuls flour

Brown on slow heat until golden. Gradually stir in 2 cups cold milk or water and cook a few minutes more. Season to taste. Left over pork or pork sausage added for variation is excellent.

Fried hamburger, drained and added to the above gravy and served with any kind of potatoes, mashed, boiled or baked, makes a very good meal.

Fresh side pork probably made the best gravy using fat from the fried side pork. Large families relied on this meal for good tasty food.

Love

You cannot be loved by people unless you earn their esteem.

You cannot draw happiness from a world bank in which you have made no deposit.

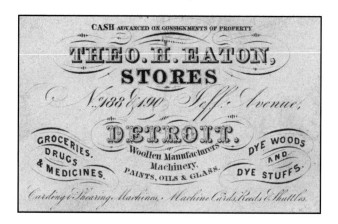

Oatmeal with Stewed Apples

Bring to boiling:
2 cups water
Stir in:
2 cups old-fashioned oats
Add:
1 apple, chopped or thinly sliced
1/4 teaspoonful cinnamon
1/4 teaspoonful salt

Cook covered 10 minutes. Serve up hot with honey and milk.

Orange Pancake Puff

1 cup water
1/2 cup butter
1/2 teaspon orange peel, grated

Boil ingredients in large saucepan. Add and stir into ball:
1 cup mix (1 scant cup flour)
1 1/2 teaspoons baking powder
1/2 teaspoon salt

Add, one at a time, and beat 4 eggs. Spread batter on bottom and sides of 2 greased 9-inch ie plates. Bake in hot ovenfor 15 minutes, then in modetate oven for 10 minutes or 'til golden. Cut into wedges and serve with choice of toppings. Serves 8.

Creamy Fruit Topping

Combine:
1 cup sour cream
1 tablespoonful honey
1 teaspoonful orange peel, grated
1/4 teaspoonful cinnamon

Fold in: 1 can fruit cocktail, drained

Household Hints

A sink should be scalded out every day, and occasionally with hot lye. On nails, over the sink should be hung 3 good dish-cloths, hemmed, and furnished with loops – one for dishes not greasy, one for greasy dishes, and one for washing pots and kettles. These should be put in the wash every week.

Flour should be kept in a barrel, with a flour-scoop to dip it, a sieve to sift it, and a pan to hold the sifted flour, either in the barrel or close at hand. The barrel should have a tight cover to keep out mice and vermin.

Rye should be bought in small quantities, say 40 or 50 pounds at a time, and be kept in a keg or half-barrel, with a cover.

Molasses, if bought by the barrel or half-barrel, should be kept in the cellar. No vessel should be corked or bunged, if filled with molasses, as it will swell and burst the vessel, or run over.

Scotch Eggs

8 hard-cooked eggs, peeled
1/4 cup all-purpose flour
1 pound bulk pork sausage
3/4 cup dry bread crumbs
1/2 teaspoonful ground sage
1/4 teaspoonful salt
2 eggs, beaten
Vegetable oil

Coat each hard-cooked egg with flour. Divide sausage into 8 equal parts. Pat one part sausage onto each egg. Mix bread crumbs, sage and salt. Dip sausage-coated eggs into beaten eggs; roll in bread crumb mixture.

Heat fat (1 1/2 to 2 inches) in 3-quart saucepan. Fry eggs, 4 at a time, turning occasionally, 5 to 6 minutes. Drain on paper towels. Serve hot or cold. 8 servings.

Buttery Peach Topping

1 can peaches (16 ounces)
2 tablespoonfuls butter
1 tablespoonful orange juice
1 teaspoon orange peel, grated
2 teaspoonfuls cornstarch
1/8 teaspoonful nutmeg

Combine in saucepan. Boil 2 minutes. Serve warm over Pancake Puff.

Ham Pie

8 ounces fresh mushrooms
1 pound thick ham slices, cooked and cut into bite-sized pieces
1 pound boneless chicken breasts
2 tablespoonfuls butter or margarine
Pepper to taste
2 cups water
2 tablespoonfuls flour
2 tablespoonfuls butter
1 onion, chopped
1 tablespoonful chicken or ham base
Pastry for a 2-crust pie or prepared pastry circles

Preheat oven to hot temperature and line 9-inch deep-dish pie pan with one pie crust/pastry circle.

In a large frying pan melt 2 tablespoonfuls butter and sautè the mushrooms. Remove mushrooms and set aside. In same pan, brown the chicken breasts over medium heat for approximately 15 minutes and then cut into bite-sized pieces.

Layer the ham and then the chicken in the pie pan, making a total of 4 layers. Top with the mushrooms.

Melt 2 tablespoonfuls butter and cook onions until tender. Stir in flour. Slowly add water and soup base, stirring constantly. Cook until liquid thickens and is bubbly.

Pour liquid over ham, chicken and mushrooms.

Cover pie with second pie crust, cutting small slips in top to allow steam to escape.

Bake in hot oven for approximately 25 minutes or until crust is golden brown.

Makes 6 hearty servings.

In the 1700s this pie could have been served as the main midday meal, or even for breakfast. Today, the addition of a green salad would make this a hearty and filling winter meal. The substitution of white turkey meat for the chicken would be a tasty way to use up left-over turkey today.

Cakes

1800's Recipes

In the early part of the 1800's, recipes were generally written in a prose or paragraph style. Cooks had fewer ingredients available to work with, so recipes were simple both in content and direction. Baking utensils such as cake pans, etc. were not widely available which made baking more difficult. As more ingredients and cookware became available recipes became more involved.

Following is an example of a simple recipe – followed by the same recipe retyped in a modern format which is easier to read. Note there is no milk listed in the original recipe. This cook must have added an unknown quantity, based on familiarity with recipe. I have added this ingredient to complete the recipe in the one that follows.

Sweet Strawberry Cake

Three eggs, one cupful of sugar, two of flour, one tablespoonful of butter, a teaspoonful, heaped, of baking-powder. Beat the butter and sugar together, and add the eggs well beaten. Stir in the flour and baking-powder well sifted together. Bake in deep tin plate. This quantity will fill four plates. With three pints of strawberries, mix a cupful of sugar and mash them a little. Spread the fruit between the layers of cake. The top layer of strawberries may be covered with a meringue made with the white of an egg and a tablespoonful of powdered sugar. Save out the largest berries, and arrange them around in circles on the top in the white frosting. Makes a very fancy dish, as well as a most delicious cake.

Sweet Strawberry Cake

3 eggs
1 cup of sugar
1 tablespoonful butter
2 cups flour
1 1/2 teaspoonfuls baking powder
3/4 cup milk

Cream butter and sugar together, and add beaten eggs. Add sifted dry ingredients alternately with milk. Pour into four greased and floured tin plates. Bake in moderate oven 25-30 minutes.

Mash three pints strawberries with one cup sugar. Spread between layers, saving a few nice berries for top. Whip one egg white with tablespoonful of sugar into a meringue for top of cake and arrange saved berries around the edge.

Leavening 1850s

Baking powder was invented in mid-19th century as a convenient substitute for yeast, which was homemade and generally unpredictable, especially in cold weather.

Yeast was often kept in the kitchen in the form of "starter," i.e., part of the last batch of bread dough in which yeast was already working. This practice continues for homemade sourdough bread and biscuits. At the end of the 18th century it was discovered that wood ashes could release carbon dioxide gas in dough, and the pearl ash industry boomed. In 1792 America decimated its forests to export 8,000 tons of pearl ash to Europe.

The next improvement was baking soda (bicarbonate of soda) which the cook could combine with buttermilk or sour milk to get the desired reaction. With sweet milk, a cook added some cream of tartar. Baking soda was also called "saleratus." This arrangement was soon superseded by commercial preparations. Preston & Merrill of Boston produced the first commercial baking powder.

Old Fashioned Bride's Cake

Cream together one scant cup of butter and three cups of sugar, add one cup of milk, then the beaten whites of twelve eggs; sift three teaspoonfuls of baking-powder into one cup of corn-starch mixed with three cups of sifted flour, and beat in gradually with the rest; flavor to taste. Beat all thoroughly, then put in buttered tins lined with letter-paper well-buttered; bake slowly in a moderate oven. A beautiful white cake. Ice the top. Double the recipe if more is required.

Stove Polish

Stove lustre, when mixed with turpentine and applied in the usual manner, is blacker, more glossy and more durable than when mixed with any other liquid. The turpentine prevents rust, and when put on an old rusty stove will make it look as well as new.

Cream Cake

Four eggs, whites and yolks beaten separately, two teacups of sugar, one cup of sweet cream, two heaping cupfuls of flour, one teaspoonful of soda; mix two teaspoonfuls of cream of tartar in the flour before sifting. Add the whites the last thing before the flour, and stir that in gently without beating. Bake in a moderate oven for one hour.

Marguerites, or Jelly Cakes

Rub together one pound sugar, one pound of butter, till perfectly light. Beat six eggs till very thick, leaving out the whites. Sift one and a half pound of flour into the eggs, butter, and sugar, one teaspoonful of mixed spices (cinnamon, mace, and nutmeg), and half a glass of rose water. Stir the whole well, and roll it on the paste-board about one-quarter inch thick. Then cut out the cakes and bake them a few minutes. When cold, spread the surface of each cake with peach jam or any marmalade. Beat the whites of four eggs very light, and add enough powdered sugar to make them as thick as icing. Flavor it with lemon or rose water and with a spoon put it on each cake, high in the centre. Put the cakes in the oven, and as soon as they are of a pale brown take them out.

Cake Without Eggs

Beat together one teacupful of butter, and three teacupfuls of sugar, and when quite light stir in one pint of sifted flour. Add to this, one pound of raisins, seeded and chopped, then mixed with a cup of sifted flour, one teaspoonful of nutmeg, one teaspoonful of powdered cinnamon, and lastly, one pint of thick sour cream or milk, in which a teaspoonful of soda is dissolved. Bake immediately in buttered tins one hour in a moderate oven.

Making Fruit Cakes

In making fruit cake, prepare the fruit the day before. In winter time, this may be easily and pleasantly done after tea. It requires a longer time to bake fruit cake, than plain. Every housekeeper should have a close cake-box in which to put cake after cooling it and wrapping it in a thick napkin.

White Fruit Cake

1 pound white sugar
1 pound flour
1/2 pound butter
Whites of 12 eggs
2 pounds citron, cut in thin, long strips
2 pounds almonds, blanched and cut in strips
1 large cocoanut, grated

Before the flour is sifted, add to it one teaspoonful of soda, two teaspoonfuls cream tartar. Cream the butter as you do for pound cake, add the sugar, and beat it awhile; then add the whites of eggs, and flour; and after beating the batter sufficiently, add about one-third of the fruit, reserving the rest to add in layers, as you put the batter in the cake-mould. Bake slowly and carefully, as you do other fruit cake.

Pound Cake

Cream:
1 pound butter
1 pound confectioners' sugar
    Add:
6 eggs, one at a time
1 teaspoonful vanilla
    Add:
3 cups sifted cake flour

Bake in greased and floured tube pan, in moderate oven for 1 hour.

Submitted by Mary Ellen Busch

French Chocolate Cake

The whites of seven eggs, two cups of sugar, two-thirds of a cup of butter, one cup of milk and three of flour, and three teaspoonfuls of baking-powder. The chocolate part of the cake is made just the same, only use the yolks of the eggs with a cup of grated chocolate stirred into it. Bake it in layers – the layers being light and dark; then spread a custard between them, which is made with two eggs, one pint of milk, one-half cup of sugar, one tablespoonful of flour or corn-starch; when cool, flavor with vanilla, two teaspoonfuls. Fine.

Orange Cake

8 eggs
1 1/2 pounds sugar
1 1/2 pounds flour
3/4 pound butter
1 pint milk
2 teaspoonfuls cream tartar
1 teaspoonful soda

Beat the eggs very light, and mix in the sugar and creamed butter. Pour in half the milk, and dissolve the cream tartar and soda in the other half. Add the sifted flour as quickly as possible after the foaming milk is poured in. Bake in jelly-cake pans.

Take six oranges, grate the peel and squeeze the juice with two pounds pulverized sugar. If you use sweet oranges, add the juice of two lemons. After stirring to a smooth paste, spread between the layers of the cake. Ice, or sprinkle over sugar the last layer on top of the cake.

English Pound Cake

1 pound of butter
1 1/4 pounds of flour
1 pound of pounded loaf sugar
1 pound of currants
9 eggs
2 ounces of candied peel
1/2 ounce of citron
1/2 ounce of sweet almonds
When liked, a little pounded mace

Work the butter to a cream; add the sugar, then the well-beaten yolks of eggs, next the flour, currants, candied peel, which should be cut into neat slices, and the almonds, which should be blanched and chopped, and mix all these well together; whisk the whites of eggs, and let them be thoroughly blended with the other ingredients. Beat the cake well for 20 minutes, and put it into a round tin, lined at the bottom and sides with strips of white buttered paper. Bake it from 2 hours to 2 1/2, and let the oven be well-heated when the cake is first put in, as, if this is not the case, the currants will all sink to the bottom of it. A glass of wine is usually added to the mixture, but this is scarcely necessary, as the cake will be found quite rich enough without it.

Most early settlers used heavy cast-iron kettles, Dutch ovens and gridirons. Tin ware was soon added to the early kitchens for baking pies and cakes. But they would rust easily. Granite iron ware was much easier to care for since it had a smooth finish.
This is an advertising tradecard, c. 1860

Old Fashioned Groom's Cake

2 1/4 pounds butter
3 pounds dark brown sugar
3 cups buttermilk
15 eggs, separated
6 pounds seedless raisins
6 pounds currants
4 pounds dates, cut fine
1 1/2 pounds citron
1 1/2 pounds candied pineapple
1 1/2 pounds candied cherries
1 1/2 cups brandy
3 teaspoonfuls soda
3 teaspoonfuls cinnamon
3 teaspoonfuls nutmeg
3 teaspoonfuls allspice
3 pounds white flour, sifted

Cream the butter; add the sugar and egg yolks. Mix in the flour, spices, and fruit. The stiffly beaten egg whites are last. Bake in a springform pan. Put a pan of water under the cake and bake in a moderate oven. Bake for 2 hours. Cover with brown paper and bake for 4 hours. Remove the water and bake 1 hour more.

Marriage

At sweet 16 I first began
To ask the good Lord for a man
At 17 I do recall
I wanted someone strong and tall
The Christmas I had reached 18
I fancied someone blond and lean
And then at 19 I was sure
I'd fall for someone more mature
At 20 I was sure I'd find
Romance with someone with a mind
I retrogressed at 21
And found the college boys most fun
My viewpoint changed at 22
When "one man only" was my cue
I broke my heart at 23
And asked for someone kind to me
Then begged at blasè 24
For anyone who wouldn't bore;
Now, Lord, that I am 25
Just send me someone who's alive.

Civil War Gingerbread

1/2 cup sugar
1/2 cup shortening
1 teaspoon salt
Blend in 1 cup molasses. Add 2 eggs and beat well. Add sifted dry ingredients alternately with 1 cup hot water. Blend well and bake in greased and floured 9 x 13 inch pan 30-35 minutes.
Sift together and set aside:
2 3/4 cups flour
2 teaspoonfuls baking powder
1/2 teaspoonful cloves
1/2 teaspoonful soda
1 teaspoonful ginger
2 teaspoonfuls cinnamon

1849 – Fort Wayne was named in honor of
General Anthony Wayne.

Olde Tyme 1-2-3-4 Cake

1 cup butter
2 cups sugar
3 cups flour
4 eggs
1 cup sour cream
1 teaspoonful soda
Spices

Cream butter and sugar; add eggs and stir until creamy. Add the sour cream and soda dissolved in cream and lastly the flour containing the spices. Pour into 2 pans and bake in moderate oven for 20-30 minutes.

Coffee Cake

One cup of brown sugar, one cup of butter, two eggs, one-half cup of molasses, one cup of strong, cold coffee, one teaspoonful of soda, two teaspoonfuls of cinnamon, one teaspoonful of cloves, one cup of raisins or currants, and five cups of sifted flour. Add the fruit last, rubbed in a little of the flour. Bake 1 hour.

Frostings & Fillings

Plain Chocolate Icing

Put into a shallow pan four tablespoonfuls of scraped chocolate, and place it where it will melt gradually, but not scorch; when melted, stir in three tablespoonfuls of milk or cream, and one of water; mix all well together, and add one scant teacupful of sugar; boil about five minutes, and while hot, and when the cakes are nearly cold, spread some evenly over the surface of one of the cakes; put a second one on top, alternating the mixture and cakes; then cover top and sides, and set in a warm oven to harden. All who tried recipe after recipe, vainly hoping to find one where the chocolate sticks to the cake and not to the fingers, will appreciate the above. In making those most palatable of cakes, "Chocolate Eclairs," the recipe just given will be found very satisfactory.

Chocolate Icing

2 squares chocolate
Confectioners' sugar
1/4 cup boiling water
1/2 teaspoonful vanilla

Melt chocolate, add boiling water, and mix well; add confectioners' sugar until of right consistency to spread; add vanilla and beat well. Coffee may be used in place of water.

Orange Filling

1/2 cup sugar
1/2 cup orange juice
2 tablespoonfuls flour
1 beaten egg
Grated rind 1/2 orange
1 teaspoonful butter

Mix sugar, flour, and rind in the top of double boiler, add orange juice, egg, and butter, and cook over hot water for twelve minutes, stirring often.

Cream Icing

1 1/4 cups confectioners' sugar
Heavy cream
1/4 teaspoonful vanilla

Sift sugar and add cream until the right consistency to spread (about two tablespoonfuls), add flavoring, and beat well.

Cream Eggs

Whip thoroughly three or four egg whites, adding slowly a cup of cream. Slightly flavor with nutmeg or vanilla. This makes a delicious sauce to use over any kind of crushed fruit or berries.

Frosting Without Eggs

An excellent frosting may be made without eggs or gelatine, which will keep longer, and cut more easily, causing no breakage or crumbling, and withal is very economical.

Take one cup of granulated sugar; dampen it with one-quarter cup of milk, or five tablespoonfuls; place it on the fire in a suitable dish, and stir it until it boils; then let it boil for five minutes without stirring; remove it from the fire and set the dish in another of cold water; add flavoring. While it is cooling, stir or beat it constantly, and it will become a thick, creamy frosting.

Cream Filling

1 1/2 cups milk
1/8 teaspoonful salt
1 cup sugar
1 egg slightly beaten
1/4 cup cornstarch
1 teaspoonful flavoring

Scald milk, mix sugar, cornstarch, salt, and egg; add to milk, and cook over hot water, stirring constantly until mixture thickens; cook 15 minutes, stirring occasionally. Cool and flavor before spreading.

Apple Filling

3 baked apples
White of 1 egg
1 cup confectioners' sugar

Press apples through a sieve; beat white of egg until stiff; add half of sugar, and beat well; add apple and remaining sugar gradually, and beat until very light. Spread between layers and on top of cake. Two tblespoons of tart jelly may be beaten with the apple.

Boiled Frosting

To one pound of finest pulverised sugar, add three wine-glassfuls of clear water. Let it stand until it dissolves; then boil it until it is perfectly clear and threads from the spoon. Beat well the whites of four eggs. Pour the sugar into the dish with the eggs, but do not mix them until the syrup is luke-warm; then beat all well together for one-half hour.

Season to your taste with vanilla, rose-water, or lemon-juice. The first coating may be put on the cake as soon as it is well mixed. Rub the cake with a little flour before you apply the icing. While the first coat is drying, continue to beat the remainder; you will not have to wait long if the cake is set in a warm place near the fire. This is said to be a most excellent recipe for icing.

Tutti Frutti Icing

Mix with boiled icing one ounce each of chopped citron, candied cherries, seedless raisins, candied pineapple, and blanched almonds.

Icing for Cakes

Beat the whites of two small eggs to a high froth; then add to them quarter pound of white sugar, ground fine, like flour; flavor with lemon extract, or vanilla; beat it until it is light and very white, but not quite fully stiff; the longer it is beaten the more firm it will become. No more sugar must be added to make it so. Beat the frosting until it may be spread smoothly on the cake. This quantity will ice quite a large cake over the top and sides.

Dresses for Boys
In the 18th century little boys wore dresses until they were toilet trained. There were no plastic pants for children to put over diapers to keep their clothes dry, and people did not wash their clothes or bodies very often.

Chocolate Frosting

The whites of 4 eggs
3 cups of powdered sugar
Nearly a cup of grated chocolate

Beat the whites a very little, they must not become white; stir in the chocolate, then put in the sugar gradually, beating to mix it well.

Gelatine Frosting

Soak one teaspoonful of gelatine in one tablespoonful of cold water half an hour, dissolve in two tablespoonfuls of hot water; add one cup of powdered sugar and stir until smooth.

Putting Up Butter
Butter was often preserved for use during the winter. In October and November, engage butter to be brought in fresh from the churn in rolls. Wrap each roll in a piece of old table cloth, and put in a sweet firkin or stone jar which has been washed with soda water, scalded and sunned for a month before using. Pour over it a clear strong brine, which also must have been prepared at least a week beforehand, by pouring off the settlings and repeated strainings. Have a nice flat rock washed and weight the butter down with it, being careful to keep it always under the brine.

Cookies

Flowers

To keep flowers fresh, stand them during the night in a cool, dark place in a tall vase so that the water reaches almost to the heads. Cut the stems a little every morning. Wild flowers should be put in boiling water as soon as they are picked. Allow the water to cool and keep the flowers in this water.

Cookies

3 eggs
1 cupful of butter or lard
2 cupfuls of sugar
6 cupfuls of sifted flour
1 nutmeg
1 teaspoonful of soda
2 teaspoonfuls of cream of tartar, sifted with flour

    Cream the butter with one cup of the sugar, beat the eggs separately and put into the yolks the remaining cup of sugar; add this to the butter, and put in whites and flour last. Roll thin and bake quickly.

Chocolate Cookies

2 squares chocolate
1/4 cup milk
1/2 cup shortening
2 cups flour
1 cup brown sugar
2 1/2 teaspoonfuls baking powder
1 egg well beaten
1/2 teaspoonful salt
1/2 teaspoonful cinnamon

    Put chocolate with shortening in mixing bowl and place over hot water until melted; add other ingredients in order given. Chill, roll thin, and cut with fancy cutter. Bake in a moderate oven about ten minutes.

Dinner Etiquette - 1852

If there are ladies, gentlemen offer their arms and conduct them to the dining-room, according to their age or the degree of respect to be shown them.

The lady of the house sits at the head of the table, and the gentleman opposite at the foot. The place of honor for gentlemen is on each side of the mistress of the house – for ladies on each side of the master. The company should be so arranged that each lady will have some gentleman at her side to assist her. Of course, it is every gentleman's duty, first of all to see that ladies near him are attended to.

When napkins are provided, they are at once carefully unfolded, and laid on the knees. Observe if grace is to be said, and keep a proper decorum.

If soup is served, take a piece of bread in the left hand and the spoon in the right, and sip noiselessly from the side of the spoon. Do not take two plates of the same kind of soup, and never tip up the plate.

If possible, the knife should never be put in the mouth at all, and if at all, let the edge be turned outward. Anything taken into the mouth not fit to be swallowed, should be quietly removed with the fingers of the left hand, to that side of the plate.

The teeth should be picked as little as possible, and never with fork or fingers. Carefully abstain from every act of observation that may cause disgust, such as spitting, blowing the nose, gulping, rinsing the mouth, etc.

Nutmeg Cookies

    One cup of butter, two cups of sugar, a small teacupful of sweet milk, half a grated nutmeg, and five cups of sifted flour, in which there has been sifted with it two teaspoonfuls of baking-powder; mix into a soft dough, and cut into round cakes; roll the dough as thin as pie-crust. Bake in a quick oven a light-brown. These can be made of sour milk and a teaspoonful of soda dissolved in it, or sour or sweet cream can be used in place of butter.

    Water cookies made the same as above, using water in place of milk. Water cookies keep longer than milk cookies.

Fruit Cookies

One cupful and a half of sugar, one cupful of butter, one-half cup of sweet milk, one egg, two teaspoonfuls of baking-powder, a teaspoonful of grated nutmeg, three tablespoonfuls of English currants or chopped raisins. Mix soft, and roll out, using just enough flour to stiffen sufficiently. Cut out with a large cutter, wet the tops with milk, and sprinkle sugar over them. Bake on buttered tins in a quick oven.

Sugar Cakes

Mix four cupfuls of sugar with eight cupfuls of flour and one large spoonful of coriander-seed; add one cupful of butter, one cupful of lard, six eggs, two tablespoonfuls of sour cream or milk, one teaspoonful of soda. Mix and roll out. Cut into small cakes. Sprinkle with sugar and bake in moderate oven until done.

Surprise Sugar Cookies

1 cup sugar
1/2 cup butter
1 egg
1 teaspoonful flavoring
1/2 cup milk
3 1/2 cups flour
2 teaspoonfuls cream of tartar
1 teaspoonful soda

Roll out thin. One large round cut with raisin filling covered by second round. Pierce top with fork. Bake in moderate oven until light brown.

Honey Cakes

2 eggs
1/2 cup sugar
1/4 cup honey
1 cup flour

Beat eggs. Add sugar and honey, mix well. Add flour gradually. Let stand for 45 minutes then spread on buttered pan and bake in quick oven a short time. Cut up while warm and let cool and harden. Keep in tight container.
Submitted by M. Humes.
100-year-old Hungarian family recipe.

Maple Butternut Sugar Cookies

1/4 cup butter, melted
1/2 cup maple syrup
1/2 cup flour
1/4 teaspoonful salt
1/8 teaspoonful baking soda
1/8 teaspoonful baking powder
1/2 cup chopped nuts

Combine butter and maple syrup. Sift flour with salt, soda and powder. Blend with first mixture, then add the nuts. Drop by teaspoonfuls onto greased cookie sheets three inches apart. Bake in moderate oven for ten minutes or until lightly brown. Remove from oven after baking. Cool on sheet. Remove to rack until cookies are cold and crisp.

Sour Cream Cookies

1 scant cup butter
2 cups sugar
1 cup sour cream
2 eggs
Pinch of salt
1 teaspoonful salt
1 teaspoonful soda

Flour enough to roll dough and cut the cookies. Cream the butter and sugar; add the eggs and salt. Stir the soda into the sour cream and add to the mixture. Add enough flour to roll out and cut the cookies (between 4 and 5 cups). Bake 10 minutes in hot oven.

White Cookies

2 cups sugar
1 cup lard
1 teaspoonful flavoring
1 cup sweet milk
7 cups flour
2 eggs
2 teaspoonfuls baking powder
1 teaspoonful soda
Salt

Mix together. Roll out. Cut in large rounds. Sprinkle with white sugar. Bake in hot oven. Submitted by Mary Ellen Busch. This is a German recipe from her grandmother, Elizabeth Doerr, and is at least 100 years old dating back to 1854. Originally baked in a wood stove and still a favorite of the Busch family.

This panoramic view of businesses located on Griswold Street in the early 1800's was made by Panoramic and Cabinet Sketches. The photographer was Jex Bardwell located at 31 Monroe Avenue. Many photographers of the era specialized in taking pictures of whole blocks of businesses.

Hard Tack

4 eggs
2 cups sugar
2 cups flour
2 cups dates, stoned
1 1/2 cups nut meats
1 tablespoonful water

Cream eggs, sugar and flour together, then add dates and nuts; also water. This makes a stiff batter. Spread over a waxed paper in a long biscuit pan, thin, and bake till it is a light brown all over. Turn out and cut in squares and dip in powdered sugar while hot.

Shortbread

1 cup butter
2 teaspoonfuls vanilla
1/2 cup confectionersí sugar
2 cups flour

Knead the butter, vanilla and sugar on a baking board and add the flour gradually. Pat into cakes 1/2-inch thick, place on cookie sheets, and prick each cake with a fork, as for pie crust. Bake in a moderate

Raisin Drop Cookies

3 tablespoonfuls shortening
2 teaspoonfuls baking powder
1/2 cup brown sugar
1 teaspoonful cinnamon
1 egg well beaten
1/2 cup raisins, seeded and chopped
2 tablespoonfuls milk
1 cup flour

Cream the shortening and sugar; add egg and milk, and beat well; add flour, baking powder, and cinnamon sifted together; add raisins; beat well, drop from a teaspoonful two inches apart on a greased baking sheet, and bake in a moderate oven about twelve minutes.

Pies

About Pastry

Pastry has fallen somewhat into disfavor, on account of its unwholesome properties, but as many persons still use it, we will give some directions for making it as wholesome and palatable as possible.

It is a great mistake to use what is called "cooking butter" and old lard for pastry. Only fresh butter and sweet lard should be employed for the purpose, and in summer these should be placed on ice before being used for pastry. Pastry, like cake, should be made in the cool of the morning, and it should be eaten fresh, as, unlike cake, it will not admit of being kept.

If a marble slab cannot be obtained, it is well to keep thick wooden board exclusively for rolling out pastry. Handle as little as possible, and if anything should prevent you from putting it on to bake as soon as it is rolled out, put it on ice in the interim, as this will make it nicer and more flaky. Sometimes there is a delay about getting the oven or fire ready, in which case the cook generally leaves the pastry lying on the kitchen table; but its quality would be much improved if it were put on the ice instead, whilst waiting to be baked.

Pastry (Paste)

1 pound fresh butter
1 quart flour

Make up the dough with ice water. Divide the butter into parts. Roll out, and cover quickly with one part of the butter. Continue till all is rolled, sifting flour each time. Don't handle much, or it will be heavy.

Lemon Pie

Grate the rind and squeeze the juice of two lemons. Stir two tablespoonfuls corn-starch into two teacups hot water, and boil, stirring well. Add three-quarters of a pound of granulated sugar. When cool, add the yolks of four eggs well beaten, then the lemon-juice and grated rind, stirring the whole well together. Line the plates with rich pastry, and pour the mixture in. Bake until the crust is done. Beat the whites of the eggs very light, add six ounces powdered sugar, pour over the pies, set them again in the oven, and slightly brown. This will make two pies.

Mock Cream Pie

Take three eggs, one pint of milk, a cupful of sugar, two tablespoonfuls of corn-starch, or three of flour; beat the sugar, corn-starch, and yolks of the eggs together; after the milk has come to a boil, stir in the mixture, and add a pinch of salt and about a teaspoonful of butter. Make crust the same as any pie; bake, then fill with the custard, grate over a little nutmeg and bake again. Take the whites of the eggs and beat to a stiff froth with two tablespoonfuls of sugar, spread over the top and brown in a quick oven.

Strawberry Short-Cake

Bake a rich paste in pie-plates. Have six ready. In these spread stewed strawberries well sweetened; lay one upon another, six deep. In winter, use preserved or canned berries.

An Apple Pandowdy

Make a good plain paste. Pare, core, and slice half a dozen or more fine large juicy apples, and strew among them sufficient brown sugar to make them very sweet; adding some cloves, cinnamon, or lemon-juice. Have ready a pint of sour milk. Butter a deep baking-pan, and put in the apples with the sugar and spice. Then, having dissolved, in a little lukewarm water, a small teaspoonful of soda, stir it into the milk, the acid of which it will immediately remove. Pour the milk, foaming, upon the apples, and immediately put a lid or cover of paste over the top, in the manner of a pie. This crust should be rolled out rather thick. Notch the edge all round, having made it fit closely. Set it into a hot oven, and bake it an hour. Eat it warm, with sugar.

For Cleaning Glass Bottles

Crush egg-shells into small bits, or a few carpet tacks, or a small quantity of gunshot, put into the bottle; then fill one-half full of strong soap-suds; shake thoroughly; then rinse in clear water. Will look like new.

Peach Mèringue Pie

Pare and stew ripe peaches. When nearly done, sweeten, take from the fire. Stir in a heaping teaspoonful fresh butter to each pie. Pour in a deep pie-plate, lined with paste. Bake; when done, remove from the oven and cover with the whites of three eggs beaten to a stiff froth, and sweetened with three tablespoonfuls powdered sugar. Set back in the oven to brown slightly. Apple mèringue pie made be made in the same way, only flavoring the fruit.

Peach Pie

Pare and stew a quart of peaches with a pint of sugar, stirring often; when boiled to look nearly as thick as marmalade, take from the fire and when nearly cool, add one tablespoonful fresh butter. Have ready three crusts, baked in shallow tin plates. Spread and pile up the fruit on each.

Apple Cream Pie

Pare and stew the apples till thoroughly done and quite dry. Rub through a colander and sweeten with powdered sugar. When cool add the whites of eggs – three eggs to a pint of apples – and a teacup of cream, whipped. Beat all the ingredients together with a patent egg-whip – one with a wheel if convenient. Spread upon crusts of rich paste, baked in shallow tin pie-plates. Grate nutmeg on each one and pile up three or four deep.

Molasses Pie

One teacup molasses, one teacup sugar, four eggs, four tablespoonfuls butter. Mix sugar and eggs together, pour in butter, and add molasses.

Rhubarb Pie

Cut the large stalks off where the leaves commence, strip off the outside skin, then cut the stalks in pieces half an inch long; line a pie-dish with paste rolled rather thicker than a dollar piece, put a layer of the rhubarb nearly an inch deep; to a quart bowl of cut rhubarb put a large teacupful of sugar; strew it over with a saltspoonful of salt and a little nutmeg grated; shake over a little flour; cover with a rich pie-crust, cut a slit in the centre, trim off the edge with a sharp knife, and bake in a quick oven until the pie loosens from the dish. Rhubarb pies made in this way are altogether superior to those made of the fruit stewed.

Mince Meat

4 cups cooked beef chopped, 1 pound citron shredded, 2 cups chopped suet, 2 tablespoonfuls salt, 8 cups chopped apples, 1 tablespoonful cinnamon, 1 cup brown sugar, 1 tablespoonful mace, 2 cups molasses, 1 teaspoonful clove, 1 glass tart jelly, 1 teaspoonful allspice, 1 1/2 pounds seeded raisins, 1/2 teaspoonful pepper, 1 pound washed currants, 1 quart boiled cider.

Mix, and cook slowly about two hours, stirring frequently. One cup of chopped cranberries may be substituted for the jelly. Store in jars or in a stone crock. If mince meat grows dry by standing, moisten with a little coffee.

Dinner Etiquette - 1850's

When the ladies leave the table, which they do together, at the signal of the mistress, the gentlemen rise and conduct them to the door and then return to the table. This is in formal parties.

If at dinner you are requested to help anyone to sauce, do not pour it over the meat or vegetables, but on one side. If you should have to carve and serve, do not load a person's plate – it is vulgar; also in serving soup, one ladleful to each plate is sufficient.

Eat peas with a dessert spoon; and curry also. Tarts and puddings are to be eaten with a spoon.

As a general rule, in helping any one at table, never use a knife where you can use a spoon.

Never pare an apple or a pear for a lady unless she desires you, and then be careful to use your fork to hold it; you may sometimes offer to divide a very large pear with or for a person.

At some tables, large colored glasses, partly filled with water, with a bit of lemon, are brought when the cloth is removed. You dip a corner of your napkin in the water, and wipe your mouth, then rinse your fingers and wipe them on your napkin.

The best general rule for a person unacquainted with the usages of society, is to be cautious, pay attention, and do as he sees others do, who ought to know what is proper.

Whipped Cream Pie

Line a pie-plate with a rich crust, and bake quickly in a hot oven. When done, spread with a thin layer of jelly or jam, then whip one cupful of thick sweet cream until it is as light as possible; sweeten with powdered sugar and flavor with vanilla; spread over the jelly or jam; set the cream where it will get very cold before whipping.

Cream Tarts

Make themsmall, of rich paste. Fll them after baking, with whipped cream, and drop a small spot of jelly in each one. The prettiest and most delicate of tarts.

Apple Butter Custard Pie

4 eggs
1 cup apple butter
1 cup sugar
1 tablespoonful allspice
4 cups milk
Pinch of salt
Pastry for 3 single-crust pies or 3 prepared pastry circles

Preheat oven to hot temperature. In large bowl beat together the eggs, apple butter, sugar and allspice. Stir in milk. Pour into prepared pie shells. Bake for 10 minutes, then reduce oven temperature to moderate and continue baking for 1 hour. Allow to cool slightly before serving. May also be served cold. Makes 3 pies.

Custard Pie

Beat together until very light the yolks of four eggs and four tablespoonfuls of sugar, flavor with nutmeg or vanilla; then add the four beaten whites, a pinch of salt and, lastly, a quart of sweet milk; mix well and pour into tins lined with paste. Bake until firm.

Cranberry Pie

Prepare as for sauce, stewing two pounds fruit to one pound sugar. Pour into a pie plate lined with paste, cover with a top crust and bake.

To Wash Corsets

Choose a clear, sunny day; make a strong solution of good soapsuds and a small amount of ammonia. Remove the stays and spread the corsets on a clean board or table and scrub with a good stiff brush until thoroughly clean. Apply clear water to rinse them. Do not wring out. Let them drip dry so the shape will not be changed.

Lemon Tarts

Chop or grate a lemon; add a cupful white sugar, a cupful water, one egg, one tablespoonful flour. Line small patties with paste, put a spoonful in each and bake.

Detroit Stoves

Wood burning stoves appeared in the 1850's after centuries of cooking over an open fire or the open hearth of the fireplace. Detroit was home to a popular maker of these beautiful cast iron stoves –
THE DETROIT STOVE WORKS.

Pineapple Pie

1 cup sugar
1/2 cup butter
1 cup sweet cream
5 eggs, separated
1 pineapple, grated or 2 20-ounce cans crushed pineapple, drained
1 prepared 9-inch deep-dish piecrust

Preheat oven to moderate temperature. Beat egg yolks and whites separately and set aside. Beat butter and sugar until creamy. Add egg yolks, pineapple and cream. Fold in egg whites. Pour into prepared 9-inch deep-dish piecrust. Bake for 45-60 minutes. Serve cold.

Makes 6-8 servings.

In the 19th century pineapples, like oranges and lemons, were considered exotic fruits and were saved for special occasions such as Christmas. They were shipped by rail to the Midwest for holiday cooking and gift-giving.

Pudding

Pudding Without Milk or Eggs

Put into a buttered baking-dish, alternate layers of grated bread, and finely chopped apples seasoned with brown sugar, bits of butter and allspice. Pour over it a pint of wine and water mixed. Let the top layer be bread crumbs, and bake one hour.

300 Years in the Same Spot

1701 – The City County Building rests on the site of Cadillac's landing and the first fort, called Pontchartrain, after Cadillac's patron. Detroit has been governed from the same spot since 1701.

Spanish Cream

Boil, till dissolved, one ounce of gelatine in three pints of milk. Then add the yolks of six eggs, beaten light, and mixed with two teacups sugar. Put again on the fire and stir till it thickens. Then set it aside to cool, and meantime beat the six whites very stiff and stir them into the custard when almost cold. Pour into moulds. Flavor to your taste, before adding the whites.

A Frenchman

1658, March 5 – Antoine de Lamothe Cadillac is born in St. Nicholas-de-la-Grave, France.

Molasses Pudding

1 cupful molasses
1/2 cupful butter and lard mixed
1 cup not quite full of buttermilk
3 eggs
1 teaspoonful soda

Flour enough to make it as thick as cake batter. If you wish to eat it cold, add another cup of sugar. Bake it quickly.

Baked Indian Pudding

Take nearly one pint sifted meal and make into a mush. Pour over it one quart of boiled sweet milk. Add onegill of molasses, onegill of sugar, six eggs beaten separately, half a pint chopped suet. If yo like, add a few currens, raisins, or a little citron. Bake nearly two hours. Eat with sauce.

Rice Pudding

3 cupfuls boiled rice
6 eggs
1 1/2 cupfuls sugar
1 1/2 pints milk
1 wine-glassful wine and brandy
1 tablespoonful melted butter
Flavor with nutmeg

Charlotte Russe

Sweeten one quart cream, flavor it with wine and whip it lightly. Dissolve half a box gelatine in a tablespoonful cold water and the same quantity of boiling water. Set over the steam of a kettle to dissolve. Then add half a pint of cream. When cold, stir it into the whipped cream. Beat the whites of four eggs very light, and stir into the cream. When it begins to stiffen, pour into a glass bowl, lined with thin strips of sponge cake. Whip, sweeten and flavor another pint of cream, and garnish the dish.

Baked Custard

Scald eight teacups milk. (Be careful not to boil it.) After cooling, stir into it eight eggs and two teacups sugar. Bake in a dish or cups. Set in a stove and surround with water, but not enough to boil into the custard cups. An oven for baking puddings is the right temperature. Bake when the custard is set, which will be in twenty minutes.

Tapioca Cream

Three tablespoonfuls tapioca, one quart milk, three eggs, one cupful sugar. Flavor with lemon or vanilla.

Soak the tapioca, in a little water, overnight. After rinsing, put it in milk and let it cook soft. Add sugar and yolks of eggs. Whip the whites stiff and pour on the tapioca, as you remove it from the fire. It should be cooked in a tin pail, set in a kettle of boiling water, to prevent the milk from scorching. Eat cold.

Mrs. Spence's Pudding

One pint grated bread crumbs put into one quart fresh sweet milk. Beat the yolks of five eggs very light. Add one teacup of sugar to them. Stir in the milk and crumbs and add three-quarters pound clipped raisins and one-quarter pound sliced citron. Season with mace. Bake nicely.

Whip the whites of the five eggs to a stiff froth. Add one teacup pulverized sugar and season with extract of vanilla. Put this over the pudding and set in the stove again to brown it slightly. Serve hot with a rich sauce made of sugar and butter seasoned with nutmeg and Madeira wine.

High-Neck Dresses

High-neck dresses are generally becoming, but not upon a very high-shouldered person. If the shoulders are not only moderately high, the neck may be covered, and a narrow piece of lace, instead of a collar, put around the throat.

Bavarian Cream

Sweeten one pint thick cream to your taste and flavor it with lemon or vanilla. Churn the cream to a froth, skim off the froth as it rises and put it in a glass dish. Dissolve one and a half tablespoonfuls gelatine in warm water, and when dissolved pour into the froth and stir fifteen minutes. Set in a cold place and it will be ready for use in a few hours.

Russian Cream

Boil, till dissolved, one ounce gelatine in three pints milk. Then add the yolks of four eggs, well beaten, and five ounces sugar. Mix the whole and let it cook. Then strain and set aside to cool. Beat the four whites to a stiff froth, and when the cream is nearly congealed, beat them in. Flavor to your taste, and mould.

French Pudding

Grate one pint stale bread. Pour over it one quart fresh milk, yolks of four eggs, rind of one lemon and part of juice, one teacup of sugar, piece of butter size of an egg. Mix all well, put in a pudding-dish and bake until it looks like custard. Then set it to cool, after which spread the top with jelly or preserves. Beat the whites of the four eggs to a stiff froth, adding the remaining juice of the lemon and three table-spoonfuls of sugar. Spread this on top of the preserves, then put the pudding again in the oven and bake a light brown.

Fruit Pudding

1 pint grated bread crumbs
1 pound raisins
3/4 pound suet, chopped fine
1/2 pound sugar
1/2 pint chopped apples
Yolks of 3 eggs, well beaten

Pour over the top the whites of the three eggs, frothed and sweetened. Bake an hour.

Teacup Pudding

1 teacup grated bread
1 teacup raisins
1 teacup chopped apples
1 teacup chopped suet
3 eggs
1 gill of cream
Wine glass of brandy

Strew the bread crumbs, the raisins, apples and suet into a dish. Mix eggs and cream and pour over. Add spice and sugar to taste. Pour on glass of brandy and bake a light brown.

Sewing in 1800's

Sewing machines and paper patterns appeared on the scene in the late 1800's.

Hard Sauce

Beat 1/2 cup margarine or butter, softened, 1 cup powdered sugar and 2 tablespoonfuls brandy until smooth.

Ye Olde Van Antwerpen Plum Pudding 1845

Prepare ahead of time.
Chop fine and coat with flour:
3 cups seeded raisins
1 cup currants
1/2 cup orange peel
1/2 cup lemon peel
1/2 cup citron
Mix with:
1/2 cup jamaica rum or cider
1/2 glass currant jelly
1/2 blanched almonds chopped fine
Combine:
6 cups day-old bread crumbs
1 teaspoonful cinnamon
1/2 teaspoonful nutmeg
1/2 teaspoonful ground cloves
1 1/2 teaspoonfuls salt
1 1/2 cups brown sugar
1 1/2 cups milk
Add:
8 eggs, one at a time
Steam in double cheesecloth on rack with 1 inch water in pot with tight cover for 5 or 6 hours adding water as necessary.
Serve with hard sauce rum or cider.
From Frances Van Antwerp
(Mrs. Eugene I. Van Antwerp)

Bread Pudding

3 cups bread
1 cup sugar
2 cups milk
2 eggs
Nutmeg or vanilla
Beat mixture and eggs together; add milk. Pour mixture over moistened bread and stir. Add flavoring to taste.
Sauce for Bread Pudding:
2 eggs
1 cup sugar
1/2 cup butter
1 teaspoonful vanilla
Beat eggs and sugar thoroughly; add vanilla and put in double boiler; add butter. Do not boil.

Whipped Cream

Thick sweet cream, whipped until stiff, slightly sweetened with powdered sugar makes a delicious dressing for salads, fruits and jellies and it is especially recommended for winter use. As an element of nutrition cream is very superior, easily digested and contributes to the body a large amount of heat.

Whip Cream Substitute

Put one teaspoonful of powdered gelatine into a basin. Dissolve in two tablespoonfuls boiling water. Whip until frothy, then add six tablespoonfuls ice cold rich cream, one tablespoonful sugar and flavor to taste.

Blueberry Pudding

1/2 cup sugar
4 tablespoonfuls oil
1 egg
1 cup water
2 cups blueberries
2 cups flour
4 teaspoonfuls baking powder
1/2 teaspoonful salt
1/2 teaspoonful mace
Cream sugar, oil and egg together; add water. Stir in the sifted dry ingredients and blueberries. Turn in to a greased mold; cover tightly and steam two and a half hours.

Canadian Pudding

1 cup copped suet
1 cup molasses
1 cup bread crumbs
1 cup brown sugar
1 cup seeded raisins
1 cup finely chopped apples
1 cup sweet milk
1 cup chopped nuts
1 teaspoonful each of cinnamon, cloves, nutmeg
2 teaspoonfuls of baking powder in 2 large cups of flour
Steam or boil three hours. Serve with hard sauce.

Drinks

Switchel

To a gallon cold water, add 3 cups molasses, 1 cup vinegar and 1 teaspoonful ginger.

This drink was often taken to the field during the haying season for the farmers would take their "nooning" (midday dinner) with them. The switchel washed the meal down. Although a switchel was usually straight, farmers have been known to spike it with hard cider or brandy, which Down Easters used to say got the hay in the barn in half the time.

Fine Milk Punch

Pare off the yellow rind of four large lemons, and steep it for twenty-four hours in a quart of brandy or rum. Then mix with it the juice of the lemons, a pound and a half of loaf-sugar, two grated nutmegs, and a quart of water. Add a quart of rich unskimmed milk, made boiling hot, and strain the whole through a jelly bag. You may either use it as soon as it is cold, or make a larger quantity (in the above proportions), and bottle it. It will keep several months.

English Eggnog

Beat separately the yolks and whites of six eggs. Stir the yolks into a quart of rich milk, or thin cream, and add half a pound of sugar. Then mix in half a pint of rum or brandy. Flavour it with a grated nutmeg. Lastly, stir in gently the beaten whites of three eggs.

It should be mixed in a china bowl.

Mint Flavored Punch 1825

President James Monroe's Favorite Summer Drink

2 cups water
2/3 cup sugar
1/2 cup fresh mint leaves, snipped
2 cups red grape juice
2 cups orange juice
3/4 cup lime juice

Combine sugar and mint in 2 cups boiling water. Chill and strain. Add remaining ingredients. Serve over crushed ice. Makes 13 4-ounce servings.

For a Summer Draught

The juice of one lemon, a tumblerful of cold water, pounded sugar to taste, half a small teaspoonful of carbonate of soda. Squeeze the juice from the lemon; strain, and add it to the water, with sufficient pounded sugar to sweeten the whole nicely. When well-mixed, put in the soda, stir well, and drink while the mixture is in an effervescing state.

Style of Bonnett - 1850's

A person of delicate pale complexion should wear a hat with pink lining. A person of dark complexion should have white lining, with rose trimming. A person with very red or yellow complexion should not wear high colors.

Lemon Cordial

12 lemons
2 cups sugar (approximately)
4 cups white brandy (approximately)

From one or more of the lemons, obtain 1 tablespoonful of peel; set aside. Juice the lemons and measure the juice. In large bowl combine the juice, lemon peel and 1/2 cup sugar for every cup of juice. Cover the bowl and let stand for 24 hours. After 24 hours, measure out liquid and pour into large glass bottle. Add an equal amount of brandy to the bottle. Seal tightly and let stand for a month, rotating the bottle from time to time to mix. After a month, strain the liquid through cheesecloth and bottle.

Makes 8 servings.

Lemons were considered exotic and a luxury, so this Lemon Cordial must have been quite a holiday treat.

Wassail

1 gallon fresh cider
1 clove
1/4 cup sugar
Pinch allspice
Pinch nutmeg

Put all of the ingredients into a pot and let simmer about one hour. Put it on just before the guests arrive - and they will be greeted with a heavenly aroma. Then add some rum.

Birch Beer

Gather 4 quarts of black birch twigs, cut them into short lengths, and put them in a 5-gallon crock. In a large vessel containing 4 gallons of water, stir 8 pounds of brown sugar until dissolved. Heat to the boiling point and continue boiling for 10 minutes. Immediately pour the bubbling liquid over the birch twig pieces in the crock.

Dissolve 1 yeast cake in 4 ounces of warm water. Stir this into the contents of the crock. Cover and allow to work for 10 days or until clear. Ladle into bottles and cap tightly. Birch beer is best when served chilled.

Old Time Home Brew

Recipe from the old country
1 can malt
4 gallons water
5 pounds sugar
3 small potatoes, diced
1 1/2 cakes yeast
1 pound raisins

Put malt in a large kettle and heat with sugar until dissolved. Add some water if necessary to keep from burning it. Add rest of water, stir well. When mixture is luke warm add yeast, potatoes and raisins. Set in a warm place to work. Ready to bottle in seven or eight days or when bubbles are gone.

Grape Wine

Pick the grapes from the bunch, mash thoroughly, and let them stand twenty-four hours. Then strain and add three pounds of sugar to every gallon of juice. Leave in a cask six months, and then bottle, putting three raisins in each bottle.

Russian Tea

1/2 cup sugar
1/2 cup water
1 stick cinnamon
1 teaspoon lemon & orange rind each
2/3 cup orange juice
º cup lemon and pineapple juice each
4 cups strong hot tea

Boil sugar, water, cinnamon and rinds together for 5 minutes. Add fruit juices and hot tea. Remove cinnamon stick and serve hot.

Anti Drink

1874 – The first temperance crusade is held in Detroit.

Dandelion Wine

Put 1 gallon flower heads into crock or enamel vessel. Pour over 3 quarts boiling water. After 7 days strain and wring out, then return to crock. Boil 1 1/2 pounds sugar in 1 pint of water; cool and add to liquor. Add 1 ounce yeast and the juice of 2 lemons; cover and ferment 7 days. Pour into gallon jar leaving sediment off. Boil 1 1/2 pounds sugar in 1 pint of water, cool and add to liquid. Cover and let it set until all fermenting has ceased. Bottle immediately.

Simple Root Beer
(yield: twelve 1-quart bottles)

1/3 ounce root beer extract
4 1/2 cups sugar
3 gallons lukewarm water
1/2 teaspoonful wine yeast

Thoroughly wash and rinse all equipment, bottles, and caps. Dry them.

Shake the bottled extract well. Mix the sugar and extract in the water, blending until the sugar dissolves. Blend the yeast in well until it dissolves. Fill the bottles to within 1 inch of their rim. Close with plastic or crown lids.

When using plastic lids, stand the bottles up in a box. If using crown tops, lay the bottles in the box on their sides. Cover against drafts. Put the box in a warm spot. Where the temperature is approximately 70°, (the root beer will carbonate within one to five days; carbonation will usually take place in one day where the temperature is above 80). To check for carbonation, refrigerate a bottle after one day. When it is chilled, slowly open it over the sink. Inspecting and tasting it will tell you whether the root beer is sufficiently carbonated. If it seems a little flat, allow it to stand another day or longer.

Soup

Game Soup – American

2 grouse or partridges, or, if you have neither, use a pair of rabbits
1/2 pound lean ham
2 medium-sized onions
1 pound of lean beef
Fried bread
Butter for frying
Pepper
Salt
2 stalks of white celery cut into inch lengths
3 quarts of water

Joint your game neatly; cut the ham and onions into small pieces, and fry all in butter to a light brown. Put into a soup-pot with the beef, cut into strips, and a little pepper. Pour on the water; heat slowly, and stew gently two hours. Take out the pieces of bird, and cover in a bowl; cook the soup an hour longer; strain; cool, drop in the celery, and simmer ten minutes. Pour upon fried bread in the tureen.

Venison soup made the same, with the addition of a tablespoonful of brown flour wet into a paste with cold water, adding a tablespoonful of catsup, Worcestershire, or other pungent sauce, and a glass of Madeira or brown sherry.

This picture is from a portion of a recent exhibit at the Detroit Historical Museum. The exhibit featured a wide variety of toys that children played with in the 1800's. All these dolls and toys are part of the Museum's collections.

Irish Potato Soup

Peel and boil eight medium-sized potatoes with a large onion, sliced, some herbs, salt and pepper; press all through a colander; then thin it with rich milk and add a lump of butter, more seasoning, if necessary; let it heat well and serve hot.

A Little Fire Truck

In 1798 the little town of Detroit acquired its first hand operated fire engine, which was a rather small vehicle. A number of cisterns were established around the village to supply water for the engine.

Squirrel Soup – American

Wash and quarter three or four good-sized squirrels; put them on, with a small tablespoonful of salt, directly after breakfast, in a gallon of cold water.

Cover the pot close, and set it on the back part of the stove to simmer gently, not boil. Add vegetables just the same as you do in case of other meat soups in the summer season, but especially good will you find corn, Irish potatoes, tomatoes and Lima beans. Strain the soup through a coarse colander when the meat has boiled to shreds, so as to get rid of the squirrel's troublesome little bones. Then return to the pot, and after boiling a while longer, thicken with a piece of butter rubbed in flour. Celery and parsley leaves chopped up are also considered an improvement by many. Toast two slices of bread, cut them into dice one half inch square, fry them in butter, put them into the bottom of your tureen, and then pour the soup boiling hot upon them.

Very good.

Pea Soup

Put a quart of dried peas into five quarts of water; boil for four hours; then add three or four large onions, two heads of celery, a carrot, two turnips, all cut up rather fine. Season with pepper and salt. Boil two hours longer, and if the soup becomes too thick add more water. Strain through a colander and stir in a tablespoonful of cold butter. Serve hot, with small pieces of toasted bread placed in the bottom of the tureen.

Pumpkin Soup – American

1/2 cup chopped onion
2 tablespoonfuls butter
3 1/2 cups chicken broth
1 cup potatoes, chopped
1 cup corn
1/2 cup chopped green or red pepper
2 cups pumpkin
1/2 teaspoonful salt
1/4 teaspoonful pepper
3 cups cream

Saute onion in butter until soft but not brown. Add chicken broth, potatoes, corn and pepper. Cover and simmer 15 minutes or until vegetables are tender. Stir in pumpkin and cream. Heat over low heat, stirring often until thoroughly heated. Serve warm garnished with green onions or chives, if desired.

Scotch Broth

2 pounds scrag end of mutton
3-4 parts water
2 ounces pearl barley
2 teaspoonfuls mixed dried herbs, tied in muslin bag
2 carrots
1 turnip, small
2 onions
2 leeks
1 teaspoonful chopped parsley
Seasoning

Wash the meat and chop it. Put it in a pan with water to cover, bring to a boil and skim, then continue to simmer with barley for 2 hours. Add the herbs and the vegetables which should be cut into pieces. Cook for a further hour. Remove the meat bones and the bag of herbs, cool the broth and remove the fat from the surface. Reheat it. Season to taste and serve sprinkled with parsley.

Tomato Soup

Place over the fire a quart of peeled tomatoes, stew them soft with a pinch of soda. Strain it so that no seeds remain, set it over the fire again, and add a quart of hot boiled milk; season with salt and pepper, a piece of butter the size of an egg, add three tablespoonfuls of rolled cracker, and serve hot. Canned tomatoes may be used in place of fresh ones.

Streetcars
Detroit's first streetcars appeared in 1863.

Cock-a-Leekie – English

2 1/2 pound broiler-fryer chicken, cut up
4 cups water
1 medium carrot, sliced
1 medium stalk celery, sliced
1/2 cup barley
2 teaspoonfuls salt
1/4 teaspoonful pepper
1 bay leaf
1 1/2 cups sliced leeks (with tops)

Heat all ingredients except leeks to boiling in Dutch oven; reduce heat. Cover and simmer 30 minutes. Add leeks. Heat to boiling; reduce heat. Cover and simmer until thickest pieces of chicken are done, about 15 minutes. Remove chicken from broth; cool slightly. Remove chicken from bones and skin; cut chicken into 1-inch pieces. Skim fat from broth; remove bay leaf. Add chicken to broth; heat until hot, about 5 minutes.

Fruit Soup – Polish

1 quart blueberries
2 or more medium green apples
2 soft peaches or pears
5 plums
Lemon juice
4 tablespoonfuls sugar
Water

Wash fruit and place in large pot. Add water to cover plus a little more. Cook until soft – about 10 minutes if fruit is not too hard. Strain fruit mixture. Add lemon juice and sugar to taste. Cook a few minutes longer. Serve cold.

Automobiles
The day after the first automobile ran on the streets of Detroit, March 7, 1896, the Detroit Free Press had this to say: "The first horseless carriage seen in this city was out on the streets last night. It is an invention of C. B. King, a Detroiter, and its progress up and down Woodward avenue about 11 o'clock caused a deal of comment, people crowding around it so that its progress was impeded. The apparatus seemed to work all right, and went at the rate of five or six miles an hour at an even rate of speed."

Pasta

Egg Noodles for Soup

Beat up one egg light, add a pinch of salt, and flour enough to make a very stiff dough; roll out very thin, like thin pie crust, dredge with flour to keep from sticking. Let it remain on the bread board to dry for an hour or more; then roll it up into a tight scroll, like a sheet of music. Begin at the end and slice it into slips as thin as straws. After all are cut, mix them lightly together, and to prevent them sticking, keep them floured a little until you are ready to drop them into your soup, which should be done shortly before dinner, for if boiled too long they will go to pieces.

Baked Macaroni

Break into pieces one inch long and put in the dish you wish to fill, filling it only one-third full. Wash well and boil in a covered stewpan until soft and tender, drain off all the water; cover with this the bottom of a baking dish. Sprinkle over pepper and salt, grated cracker, bits of butter and grated cheese; then another layer of macaroni, etc., in the same order. When the dish is filled, pour over fresh milk until all is barely covered. Sift over pounded cracker and set in the oven. If it becomes too brown, sift over more cracker before serving.

Settlers
1732 – Louis XIV directed the settling of all granted lands on pain of forfeiture.

Ham Dumplings

Chop some cold ham, the fat and lean in equal proportions. Season it with pepper and minced sage. Make a crust, allowing half a pound of chopped suet, or half a pound of butter to a pound of flour. Roll it out thick, and divide it into equal portions. Put some minced ham into each, and close up the crust. Have ready a pot of boiling water, and put in the dumplings. Boil them about three-quarters of an hour. You may use potatoe paste.
From Miss Leslie's Directions For Cookery 1851.

Egg Dumplings for Soup

To half a pint of milk put two well-beaten eggs, and as much wheat flour as will make a smooth, rather thick batter, free from lumps; drop this batter, a tablespoonful at a time, into boiling soup.

Cornmeal Dumplings

1/2 cup all-purpose flour
1/2 cup yellow cornmeal
1/4 cup milk
1 egg
1 small onion, finely chopped
2 tablespoonfuls vegetable oil
1 teaspoonful baking powder
1/2 teaspoonful salt
1/4 teaspoonful ground thyme

Mix all ingredients together. Drop by spoonfuls onto hot liquid or stew. Cover and simmer 20 minutes.

Macaroni

Mix a pint of milk, and a pint of water, and a teaspoonful of salt; put in two ounces of macaroni, and boil till the liquor is wasted and the macaroni tender. Put on butter, or pour over some gravy. Cut the macaroni in pieces of three or four inches, in order to help it out more conveniently.
From Miss Beecher's Domestic Receipt Book 1858

Salads & Dressings

Salads

In making salads, be careful to add the vinegar last. Where oil cannot be obtained, fresh butter, drawn or melted, is an excellent substitute and is indeed preferre to oil by some persons, epicureans to the contrary notwithstanding. Always use good cider vinegar in making salads, as chemical vinegar is sometimes very unwholesome. Much depends on the rotation in which you mix the ingredients for a salad, so I would call particular attention to the directions given.

Hyden Salad – 1875

1 gallon of finely chopped cabbage
1 1/2 gallons green tomatoes
1 pint green peppers – 1/2 pint will do
1 quart onions
1/2 pint horseradish
1 pound sugar
1/2 gallon vinegar
4 tablespoonfuls ground mustard
2 tablespoonfuls ginger
1 tablespoonful cloves
1 tablespoonful cinnamon
1 tablespoonful celery-seed
2 spoonfuls salt
    Beat the spice well, mix all together well, and boil fifteen minutes.

Dressing for Cabbage

The yolk of an egg
1 teaspoonful salt
1 teaspoonful mustard
2 teaspoonfuls sugar, mashed smooth
1 cup of cream
Vinegar to your taste

Entertainment

Theater was growing in Detroit and there were a number of theatrical centers on Jefferson, Gratiot, Woodward, Randolph, Fort, Shelby and Griswold to name a few in what is now the downtown area. In the 1890's there was a demand for Sunday theater as the city was acquiring a large foreign population.

Everyday Manners 1852

Ladies are allowed to consult fancy, variety, and ornament, more than men, yet nearly the same rules apply. It is the mark of a lady to be always well shod. If your feet are small, don't spoil them by pinching – if large, squeezing them makes them worse.

As you regard health, comfort, and beauty, do not lace too tightly. A waist too small for the natural properties of the figure, is the worst possible deformity, and produces many others. No woman who laces tight can have good shoulders, a straight spine, good lungs, sweet breath, or is fit to be a wife and mother.

The most elegant dresses are black or white. Common modesty will prevent indecent exposure of the shoulders and bosom. A vulgar girl wears bright and glaring colors, fantastically made; a large, flaring, red, yellow, or sky-blue hat, covered with a rainbow of ribbons, and all the rings and trinkets she can load upon her. Of course, a modest well-bred young lady chooses the reverse of all this. In any assemblage, the most plainly dressed woman is sure to be the most lady-like and attractive. Neatness is better than richness, and plainness better than display. Single ladies dress less in fashionable society than married ones, and all more plainly and substantially for walking or traveling, than on other occasions.

Ladies are not allowed upon ordinary occasions to take the arm of any one but a relative, or an accepted lover, in the street, and in the day time; in the evening – in the fields, or in a crowd, wherever she may need protection, she should not refuse it. She should pass her hand over the gentleman's arm, merely, but should not walk at arm's length apart, as country girls sometimes do. In walking with a gentleman, the step of the lady must be lengthened, and his shortened, to prevent the hobbling appearance of not keeping step. Of course, the conversation of a stranger, beyond asking a necessary question, must be considered as a gross insult, and repelled with proper spirit.

The Trumbull Avenue Congregational Church was built in 1868 on Trumbull Avenue, near Tiger Stadium. This picture was made for a stereopticon. A picture viewer that made pictures appear three-dimensional. They were popular through the 1930's. Jex Bardwell's Stereoscopic Gems.

Bubble and Squeak – English

Fry three strips bacon, cut up – remove from pan. Cook one medium-sized onion in bacon grease; add two cups or more of coarsely cut up cabbage. Return bacon to pan and stir often. When cabbage is wilted, add two cups left over potatoes. Pat down to make a large pancake, fry brown on one side, and turn and brown on other side.

Irish Potato Salad

Cut ten or twelve cold boiled potatoes into small pieces. Put into a salad bowl with –
4 tablespoonfuls vinegar
4 tablespoonfuls best salad oil
1 teaspoonful minced parsley
Pepper and salt to taste

Stir all well that they may be thoroughly mixed; it should be made several hours before putting on the table.

Throw in bits of pickle, cold fowl, a garnish of grated cracker, and hard-boiled eggs.

French Potato Salad

6 medium potatoes
1 garlic clove, cut
1/3 cup hot water
1/3 cup white wine
Tarragon Dressing (below)
3 tablespoonfuls parsley

Heat 1 inch salted water to boiling. Add potatoes. Heat to boiling; reduce heat. Cover and cook until tender, 30 to 35 minutes. Drain and cool.

Rub bowl with garlic; discard garlic. Cut potatoes into 1/4-inch slices; place in bowl. Add wine. Pour over potatoes. Cover and set on ice. Stir once or twice; drain.

Prepare Tarragon Dressing; gently toss with potatoes. Sprinkle with parsley. Garnish with tomato and sliced cooked meat if desired.

Tarragon Dressing

3 tablespoonfuls olive or vegetable oil
2 tablespoonfuls tarragon vinegar
2 teaspoonfuls snipped chives
1 teaspoonful salt
1 teaspoonful dark prepared mustard
1/2 teaspoonful dried tarragon leaves
1/8 teaspoonful pepper

Shake all ingredients in tightly covered jar.

Bottle Salad Dressing 1850

Put one tumbler of vinegar, and one lump butter, size of an egg, on to boil.

Beat up the yolks of three or four eggs, and pour the boiling vinegar over them, stirring all the time; return it to the fire and continue to stir, until it thickens liked custard. When it is perfectly cold add one tumblerful cream, into which has been mixed one tablespoonful salt, one tablespoonful mustard, two spoonfuls sugar, and one spoonful bruised celery-seed.

Bottle the dressing and it will keep for a month.

An old Church
The first Methodist Church in Detroit was built at Gratiot Avenue and Library Avenue South East.

Pickles & Preserves

Pickles and Catsups

For pickles and catsups, use the best cider vinegar, it being not only more wholesome than other kinds of vinegar, but the only sort that will keep pickles or catsup for any length of time.

In making catsup, or in scalding pickles in vinegar, if a brass kettle is used, it must be scoured with sand and ashes, washed and wiped dry, and then scoured with vinegar and salt. By attending to these directions, the brass kettle may be safely used – though the pickles or catsup must be poured from it the instant it is taken from the fire, or they will canker.

In making pickles, it is a good rule to allow two pounds of sugar to each gallon of vinegar for sour pickle, though a larger proportion must be allowed for sweet pickle.

Vinegar for pickling should be spiced and set to sun from spring to autumn. Never put pickle in a jar that has been used for butter or lard. Examine often to see if the pickle is well covered with vinegar, and if any of it has turned soft, remove it. Keep it in a dry, airy closet, and be careful not to let it freeze. Pickle is generally considered best when from six months to a year old. Some housekeepers use the same vinegar (with a slight addition) from year to year, by draining the pickle as they take it out of the jar.

Walnut Pickles

The walnuts must be quite green and tender. First soak them in fresh water, then rub off with a coarse towel. The walnuts must be kept in brine a week, and then soaked in clear water for several hours. Boil them in vinegar a little while – this time put water in the vinegar; then put them in good strong vinegar, a portion of which must be boiled and poured over them four successive mornings. Season with cinnamon, mace, cloves, and add two pounds of sugar to one gallon vinegar, or in proportion to quantity of pickle.

Sweet Cucumber Pickle

Slice cucumbers and soak in brine a week; then soak in salt water until the salt is extracted sufficiently. Boil in strong alum water half an hour, then in ginger tea half an hour. Make a syrup of one quart good vinegar, one pint water, three pounds sugar, to four pounds cucumbers; season with mace, cinnamon, cloves, and celery-seed. Put in the cucumbers and boil till the syrup is thick enough. Add some sliced ginger.

Piccalili

1 peck of green tomatoes
8 large onions, chopped fine, with 1 cup of salt well stirred in

Let it stand over night; in the morning drain off all the liquor. Now take two quarts of water and one of vinegar, boil all together twenty minutes. Drain all through a sieve or colander. Put it back into the kettle again; turn over it two quarts of vinegar, one pound of sugar, half a pound of white mustard seed, two tablespoonfuls of ground pepper, two of cinnamon, one of cloves, two of ginger, one of allspice, and half a teaspoonful of cayenne pepper. Boil all together fifteen minutes, or until tender. Stir it often to prevent scorching. Seal in glass jars.

A most delicious accompaniment for any kind of meat or fish.

Land

1707 – Cadillac gave the first known grants of land to settlers.

Pink Pickles

Boil fresh eggs half an hour, then put them in cold water. Boil red beets until tender, peel and cut in dice form, and cover with vinegar, spiced; shell the eggs and drop into the pickle jar.

Open Market

The central market, opened in the 1840's, was a place for produce growers, livestock dealers, harness makers and farmers to sell and or trade their products to city dwellers in an open-air marketplace. (Labor could also be purchased – wood sawers being found at the west end and white-washers and day laborers on the east end.)

Cranberry Jelly

Wash and pick the cranberries, put them in the preserving kettle with a very small quantity of water, cover closely and stew till done. Pour through a jelly bag or coarse towel, without squeezing, as this will prevent it from being clear. Measure and pour the liquid into the preserving kettle. Let it boil up and remove the scum, then add the sugar, cut or loaf, 1 pound to a pint. Boil about twenty minutes, or until it jellies. It preserves the color of fruit jellies to add the sugar as late as possible.

Raspberry Jam

Wash and pick the berries, boil with a little water, mashing and scraping from the bottom as they simmer. When reduced to a thick pulp, add one-half pound sugar to each pound berries. Stew till very thick, scraping constantly from the bottom. Cool in a large bowl, then put in a glass jar with screw top. Blackberry, Dewberry, and Whortleberry Jam may be made by the same recipe.

Apple Jelly

Take half a peck of pippin apples, wash them clean, slice them from the core, put them in a preserving kettle with a quart of water. Boil till entirely soft, then strain through a flannel bag. To each pint of juice add one pound white sugar and the juice of three lemons. Boil till jellied. Do not stir while boiling.

Coal Fire

If your coal fire is low, throw on a tablespoonful of salt, and it will help it very much.

Tomato Marmalade or Sauce for Meats

Scald and peel fully ripe tomatoes, then cut them up, if large. To twelve pounds add six pounds sugar, one tablespoonful beaten cloves, one tablespoonful spice and one tablespoonful cinnamon.

Boil all in a kettle until the syrup becomes the thickness of molasses. Then add one quart of strong vinegar and boil for ten minutes. Put away in quart jars.

Face Powder

Take of wheat starch, one pound; powdered orris-root, three ounces; oil of lemon, thirty drops; oil of bergamot, oil of cloves, each fifteen drops. Rub thoroughly together.

Preserved Apples for Winter Use

Pare and slice pippins. Put to each pound apples half a pound sugar, and to every eight pounds thus sweetened one quart water, a few cloves, the thin rind and juice of a lemon. Stew till clear, and eat with cream.

To Make Hard Soap

Put into an iron kettle five pounds each of unslacked lime and soda, and three gallons of soft water. Let soak over night; in the morning, pour off the water, then add three and one-half pounds of grease, boil till thick, turn into a pan until cool, and then cut into bars.

Cold Eggs For a Picnic

This novel way of preparing cold egg for the lunch-basket fully repays one for the extra time required. Boil hard several eggs, halve them lengthwise; remove the yolks and chop them fine with cold chicken, lamb, veal or any tender, roasted meat; or with bread soaked in milk, and any salad, as parsley, onion, celery, the bread being half of the whole; or with grated cheese, a little olive oil, drawn butter, flavored. Fill the cavity in the egg with either of these mixtures, or any similar preparation. Press the halves together, roll twice in beaten egg and bread-crumbs, and dip into boiling lard. When the color rises delicately, drain them and they are ready for use.

Sauces

Drawn Butter

Melted butter is the foundation of most of the common sauces. Have a covered sauce-pan for this purpose. One lined with porcelain will be best. Take one-fourth pound of the best fresh butter, cut it up, and mix with it about one tablespoonful of flour. When it is thoroughly mixed, put it into the sauce-pan, and add to it one half teacupful of hot water. Cover the sauce-pan and set it in a large tin pan of boiling water. Shake it round continually (always moving it the same way) till it is entirely melted and begins to simmer. Then let it rest till it boils up.

If you set it on too hot a fire, it will be oily.

If the butter and flour are not well mixed, it will be lumpy.

If you put too much water, it will be thin and poor. All these defects are to be carefully avoided.

In melting butter for sweet or pudding sauce, you may use milk instead of water.

White Sauce

Mix two tablespoonfuls of sifted flour with half a teacup of warm butter. Place over the fire a sauce-pan containing a pint of sweet milk and a salt-spoon of salt, and a dash of white pepper; when it reaches the boiling point, add the butter and flour, stirring briskly until it thickens and becomes like cream. Have ready three cold, hard-boiled eggs, sliced and chopped, add them to the sauce; let them heat through thoroughly, and serve in a boat. If you have plenty of cream, use it and omit the butter. By omitting the eggs, you have the same as "White Sauce."

Baby Medicine 1860

Never give medicine to a very young child. Many have thus lost darling children. It will, if not murdered, be permanently injured. It cries often on account of tight clothes or the pricking of pins. If medicine must be given at all, give it to the nurse.

Applesauce

Wash, pare, quarter and core eight juicy apples. Add 1/2 cup water and cook in heavy sauce pan covered until tender. Add 3/4 cup sugar and cook a few minutes longer. Serves 6. Cloves, cinnamon or nutmeg may be added.

Hollandaise Sauce

1/2 teacupful of butter
Juice of half a lemon
The yolk of 2 eggs
A speck of cayenne pepper
1/2 cupful of boiling water
1/2 teaspoonful of salt

Beat the butter to a cream, add the yolks of eggs one by one; then the lemon-juice, pepper and salt, beating all thoroughly; place the bowl in which is the mixture in a sauce-pan of boiling water; beat with an egg-beater until it begins to thicken which will be in about a minute; then add the boiling water, beating all the time; stir until it begins to thicken like soft custard; stir a few minutes after taking from the fire; be careful not to cook it too long. This is very nice with baked fish.

Bechamel Sauce

Put three tablespoonfuls of butter in a sauce-pan; add three tablespoonfuls of sifted flour, quarter of a teaspoonful of nutmeg, ten pepper-corns, a teaspoonful of salt; beat all well together; then add to this, three slices of onion, two slices of carrot, two sprigs of parsley, two of thyme, a bay leaf and half a dozen mushrooms cut up. Moisten the whole with a pint of stock or water and a cup of sweet cream. Set it on the stove and cook slowly for half of an hour, watching closely that it does not burn; then strain through a sieve. Most excellent with roast veal, meats and fish.

Making Fine Butter - 1880's

To make fine butter you must have fine milk; the making of fine butter must begin with the cows. They will give just as they receive. Good food and good care will give good milk, poor food and careless keeping will give poor milk, and the result will be poor butter; but it often happens poor butter is made of good milk, and to avoid this observe the following simple rules:

1st. Set the milk in the pans as near its natural heat as possible, 98°, if the room is very cold; if not very cold, set the milk 85° to 90°.

2nd. Don't let it stand too long before the cream is taken off – 24 hours in a cool place.

Chili Sauce

Boil together two dozen ripe tomatoes, three small green peppers, or a half teaspoonful of cayenne pepper, one onion cut fine, half a cup of sugar. Boil until thick; then add two cups of vinegar; then strain the whole, set back on the fire and add a tablespoonful of salt, and a teaspoonful each of ginger, allspice, cloves and cinnamon; boil all five minutes, remove and seal in glass bottles. This is very nice.

Making Your Own Laundry Soap

6 pounds clean grease, strained
1 can lye
5 cups soft water
2 tablespoonfuls borax
2 tablespoonfuls sugar
1/2 cup ammonia

Melt fat in a large iron or enamel pan. (Not aluminum) Should be 6 pints. Cool to 80° and combine 13-ounce can of lye with 5 cups of water in enamel pan, stirring slowly with long wooden paddle. Long paddle is necessary to keep from splashing hands. Cook to 70°. Add lye water gradually to fat, stirring slowly for 10 minutes. Stir until mixture is creamy, then add borax, sugar and ammonia. Mix well and pour into shallow pans or cardboard box. Cool slowly for 24 hours. Remove from mold and cut with string into bars. Stack and let dry for 2 weeks. If properly dried, soap should be white and will float.

Egg Sauce

Chop six hard-cooked eggs and mix with one cup cream. Heat in a double boiler, add one tablespoonful butter, pinch of salt and a little paprika. Cook for ten minutes. Remove from flame, add a little chopped parsley and serve hot over asparagus, Brussels sprouts or fish.

Cranberry Sauce

One quart of cranberries, two cupfuls of sugar, and a pint of water. Wash the cranberries, then put them on the fire with the water, but in a covered sauce-pan. Let them simmer until each cranberry bursts open; then remove the cover of the sauce-pan, add the sugar and let them all boil for twenty minutes without the cover. The cranberries must never be stirred from the time they are placed on the fire. This is an unfailing recipe for a most delicious preparation of cranberries. Very fine with turkey and game.

The Dover Egg-Beater

Is indispensable to housekeepers. It froths eggs in less than a fourth of the time a spoon or an ordinary egg-beater requires to froth them.

Baby Food

It should receive its food at regular hours, three or four times a day, and it should not be permitted to take so much as to cause vomiting. The stomach of new-born infant is very small, not larger than a common-sized thimble, so that there is great danger of giving it too much food.

Wild Game

Cooking Cool

It is important to remember that no meat should be cooked until it has thoroughly cooled – that is, until all the natural heat has been withdrawn after the animal has been killed; otherwise, it is likely to make you ill. To hasten the bleeding of fresh meat, cover with a layer of salt for a couple of hours. Rinse well in cold water before freezing or cooking. Incidentally, black pepper, finely ground and dusted on the surface of meat, is an excellent repellent for flies. Use it freely, especially in and about folds in the meat.

Squirrel

They are cooked similar to rabbits, are excellent when broiled or made into a stew, and, in fact, are very good in all the different styles of cooking similar to rabbit.

There are many species common to this country; among them the black, red, gray and fox. Gophers and chipmunks may also be classed as another but smaller variety.

Detroit's Central Market

A public market was established in the middle of Woodward Avenue just below Jefferson Avenue which consisted of a long narrow building, with stalls on each side. No produce was to be sold at any other place than the market. Doing so meant a $5 fine. The big market days in Detroit were Tuesdays and Saturdays.

Brunswick Stew

Take two chickens or three or four squirrels, let them boil in water. Cook one pint butter-beans, and one quart tomatoes; cook with the meat. When done, add one dozen ears corn, one dozen large tomatoes, and one pound butter.

Take out the chicken, cut it into small pieces and put back; cook until it is well done and thick enough to be eaten with a fork.

Season with pepper and salt.

Barbecued Squirrel

Put some slices of fat bacon in an oven. Lay the squirrels on them and lay two slices of bacon on the top. Put them in the oven and let them cook until done. Lay them on a dish and set near the fire. Take out the bacon, sprinkle one spoonful of flour in the gravy and let it brown. Then pour in one teacup of water, one tablespoonful of butter, and some tomato or walnut catsup. Let it cool, and then pour it over the squirrel.

Venison

The horned family of animals such as deer, elk, moose, roebuck, antelope, reindeer, and caribou provides the meat that we call "venison." Gourmets agree that there are few dishes superior to venison that has been properly processed and prepared, and served with its traditional currant jelly.

As is the case with all meat animals, the young provide the tender cuts, toughness increasing with age. The meat from animals between eighteen and thirty months is at its savory best. The hoofs of young venison are slightly opened; those of older venison have a wide spread. Unlike beef, pork, lamb, and veal, however, venison must be hung for a period varying from two days to two weeks, depending on the climate. To remove the gamy odor, after the flesh has been hung, cleaned, and trimmed, soak the meat in water for several days. The saddle, rack, and tenderloin are lean and therefore require larding or additional fat in cooking. The haunch and quarters may be marinated a few days before larding. Fresh meat from young animals needs no marination.

Roast 'Coon

The raccoon should be first soaked in strong salt and water from 8 to 10 hours, and it is also desirable to have the carcass frozen. It should be par-boiled from 1 to 1 1/2 hours, and a dessertspoon of soda or saleratus should be put into the water. The time required for roasting, both in the case of the opossum and the raccoon, depends somewhat on circumstances, and the judgment of the cook must determine when they are ready for the table. Irish potatoes are a good accompaniment to the raccoon.

The season, both for the opossum and raccoon, is from about the 1st of November to the 1st of March.

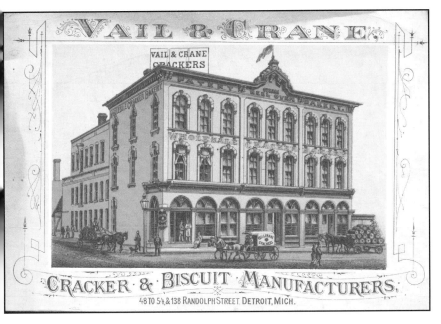

Stewed Venison

Slice cold venison in a chafing dish and add:

A cup of water
A small teacup of red wine
A small teacup of currant jelly
A tablespoonful of butter
A teaspoonful of made mustard
A little yellow pickle
A little chopped celery
A little mushroom catsup
Salt and cayenne pepper to the taste

The same receipt will answer for cold mutton.

Cholera

Asiatic cholera appeared again in June, 1854, and continued its scourge through the middle of August; the death toll averaged about three a day.

Roast Hare or Rabbit

A very close relationship exists between the hare and the rabbit, the chief difference being in the smaller size and shorter legs and ears of the latter. The manner of dressing and preparing each for the table is, therefore, pretty nearly the same. To prepare them for roasting, first skin, wash well in cold water and rinse thoroughly in lukewarm water. If a little musty from being emptied before they were hung up, and afterward neglected, rub the insides with vinegar and afterward remove all taint of the acid by a thorough washing in lukewarm water. After being well wiped with a soft cloth put in a dressing as usual, sew the animal up, truss it, and roast for 1/2 or 3/4 of an hour, until well-browned, basting it constantly with butter and dredging with flour, just before taking up.

To make a gravy, after the rabbits are roasted, pour nearly all the fat out of the pan, but do not pour the bottom or brown part of the drippings; put the pan over the fire, stir into it a heaping tablespoonful of flour, and stir until the flour browns. Then stir in a pint of boiling water. Season the gravy with salt and pepper; let it boil for a moment. Send hot to the table in a tureen with the hot rabbits. Serve with currant jelly.

Haunch of Venison

Rub the venison over with pepper, salt, and butter. Repeat the rubbing. After it has been put in the oven, put in as much cold water as will prevent burning and draw the gravy. Stick five or six cloves in different parts of the venison. Add enough water to make sufficient gravy. Just before dinner, put in a glass of red wine and a lump of butter rolled in flour, and let it stew a little longer.

Venison Pie or Pastry – French

The neck, breast and shoulder are the parts used for a venison pie or pastry. Cut the meat into pieces (fat and lean together) and put the bones and trimmings into the stew-pan with pepper and salt, and water or veal broth enough to cover it. Simmer it till you have drawn out a good gravy. Then strain it.

In the meantime make a good rich paste, and roll it rather thick. Cover the bottom and sides of a deep dish with one sheet of it, and put in your meat having seasoned it with pepper, salt, nutmeg and mace. Pour in the gravy which you have prepared from the trimmings, and a glass of port wine. Lay on the top some bits of butter rolled in flour. Cover the pie with a thick lid of paste and ornament it handsomely with leaves and flowers formed with a tin cutter. Bake two or more hours according to the size. Just before it is done put it forward in the oven, and brush it over with beaten egg; push it back and let it slightly brown.

Roast Wild Shoat (young pig) – French

When roasted whole, a pig should not be under four nor over six weeks old. In town, the butcher prepares for roasting, but it is well to know, in the country, how this may be done. As soon as the pig is killed, throw it into a tub of cold water, to make it tender; as soon as cold, take it by the hind leg, and plunge into scalding, not boiling water (as the last cooks the skin so that the hair can with difficulty be removed), shake it about until the hair can be removed by the handful. When all that is possible has been taken off in this way, rub from the tail up to the end of the nose with a coarse cloth. Take off the hoofs, scrape and wash the ears and nose until perfectly clean. The nicest way to dress it is to hang it by the hind legs, open and take out the entrails; wash well with water, with a little soda dissolved in it; rinse again and again, and leave hanging an hour. Wrap in a coarse cloth wrung out of cold water and lay on ice or in a cool cellar until next morning, when, if the weather is warm, it must be cooked. It should never be used the same day that it is killed.

First prepare the stuffing of the liver, heart and haslets of the pig, stewed, seasoned, and chopped. Mix with these an equal quantity of boiled potatoes mashed; add a large spoonful of butter, with some hard-boiled eggs, parsley and thyme, chopped fine, pepper and salt.

Scald the pig on the inside, dry it and rub with pepper and salt, fill and sew up. Bend the fore legs under the body, the hind legs forward, under the pig, and skewer to keep in position. Place in a large baking-pan, pour over one quart of boiling water. Have a lump of fresh butter tied up in a clean rag; rub it all over the pig, then sprinkle over pepper and salt, putting some in the pan with a bunch of herbs; invert over it a baking-pan while it simmers, and steam until entirely done. Underdone pork, shoat, or pig, is both unpalatable and unwholesome. Remove the pan, rub over with the butter and baste often. When of a fine brown, cover the edges of a large dish with a deep fringe of curled parsley; first sift over the pig powdered cracker, then place it, kneeling, in the green bed. Place in its mouth an orange or a red apple; and, if eaten hot, serve with the gravy in a tureen or sauce-boat. It is much nicer cold; served with little mounds of grated horseradish amongst the parsley.

Nice Wooden Furniture

Crude furniture was made by workmen with the use of a few simple pioneer tools. Many houses had hard-packed clay floors. A few floors were made of slabs of basswood or pine, smoothed on one side.

Broiled Bear Chops

Lay the bear chops cut thick, in salt water for two days, wipe dry, grease with butter and sprinkle with pepper and a little salt. Lay on the gridiron, turning often so that they may cook through and through, without becoming hard and dry. When brown, lay on a hot dish. Cook some onions in butter until soft and brown and serve with chops.

For Bear Pot Roast follow recipe for Venison Stew.

The Ingle-Nook

The ingle-nook was made by building a partition out from the wall of the house on each side of the fireplace and placing a high-backed bench called a "settle" on each side of the fireplace. Grandparents usually claimed this warm winter seat.

Rabbit Pie – English

1 rabbit
1 onion
2 bay leaves
Flaky pastry

Wash and cut up the rabbit and season with salt and pepper and roll in flour. Sear in fat to which the onion and bay leaves have been added. Cover with water and cook until tender. Place in a baking dish and cover with gravy made from the fat in which the rabbit was cooked. Cover the meat with a rich pastry, trim the edges, and cut small openings in the top to allow steam to escape. Bake in a hot oven.

Beefsteak and kidney pie is prepared in the same way.

Opossum

The savoriness of the opossum depends largely on the nature of its dining during the period immediately preceding its preparation for the table. Possums' unrestricted menu may include such items as mice, insects, rabbits, and birds. Consequently, some authorities recommend taking the animal alive and feeding it on a diet of milk, bread, and table scraps so that it will be "sweetened up" before eating. Hang to freeze for a night or so; remove the kernels at the back of the neck and the armpits. Marinate the meat, then cook as you would rabbit.

Roast Opossum

1 winter possum
2 pods red pepper
2 teaspoonfuls salt
1/4 teaspoonful black pepper
1/8 teaspoonful sage
2 tablespoonfuls lemon juice
4 large cooked yams, peeled and quartered
1/4 cup brown sugar
1/2 teaspoonful cinnamon
1/8 teaspoonful ginger

Place dressed possum in a kettle with pepper pods; cover with cold water. Bring to a boil and simmer for 1 hour. Remove from the pot and place on a trivet in a Dutch oven or roasting pan. Add 1 cup water. Sprinkle with salt, pepper, sage, and lemon juice. Place yams around the roast. Combine sugar, cinnamon, and ginger, and sprinkle on top of yams. Cover. Cook with very low heat on top of the stove or in the oven for 2 hours or until the meat is crisp and brown. Transfer opossum and yams to a hot platter to serve. Serves 4 to 6.

Porcupine, raccoon, muskrat, woodchuck, and even beaver are cooked by this same method.

Stewed Duck

Prepare them by cutting them up the same as chicken for fricassee. Lay two or three very thin slices of salt pork upon the bottom of a stew-pan; lay the pieces of duck upon the pork. Let them stew slowly for an hour, closely covered. Then season with salt and pepper, half a teaspoonful of powdered sage, or some green sage minced fine; one chopped onion. Stew another half hour until the duck is tender. Stir up a large tablespoonful of brown flour in a little water and add it to the stew. Let it boil up, and serve all together in one dish, accompanied with green peas.

Stuffed Duck

Truss the ducks and stuff them with bread, butter, and onion. Flour them and brown them in lard. Have prepared slips of bacon, giblets, onion, water, pepper, salt, and a little clove or mace, if you like. Put in the ducks and let them stew gently but constantly for two hours. Then add the juice of green grapes or of a lemon, or else a little lemon pickle. Flour the ducks each time you turn them, and thicken with butter rolled in flour.

A Small House

Detroit houses were one-story high, with a loft under the roof. There was not a pane of glass available in town for many years. The doors were mostly "Dutch doors," with the upper half open to let in light and air.

Wild Turkey

If the turkey is old, after it is dressed wash it inside thoroughly with soda and water. Rinse it and plunge it into a pot of boiling water for five minutes. Make a stuffing of bits of pork, beef, or any other cold meat, plenty of chopped celery, stewed giblets, hard-boiled eggs, pounded cracker, pepper, and salt, and a heaping spoonful of butter. Work this well and fill the turkey. With another large spoonful of butter grease the bird, and then sprinkle salt and pepper over it. Lay in a pan, with a pint of stock or broth in which any kind of meat has been boiled. Place in a hot oven. When it begins to brown, dredge with flour and baste, turning often, so that each part may be equally browned. Put in a buttered sheet of paper over the breast, to prevent dryness. When thoroughly done, lay on a dish, brown some crackers, pound and sift over it, and serve with celery or oyster sauce.

Broiled Partridges

Place them in salt and water, an hour or two before boiling. When taken out, wipe them dry, and run them all over with fresh butter, pepper and salt. First broil the under or split side on the gridiron, over bright, clear coals, turning until the upper side is of a fine, light brown. It must be cooked principally from the under side. When done, rub well again with fresh butter and if not ready to serve them immediately, put them in a large shallow tin bucket, cover it and set it over a pot or kettle of boiling water, which will keep them hot without making them hard or dry and will give time for the many "last things" to be done before serving a meal. When served, sift over them powdered cracker, first browned.

Fish

About Fish

Fish must be perfectly fresh and firm and must be kept cool. Wrap fish in a damp cloth, then in paper and keep on ice. Thaw frozen fish in cold water and use at once.

Clean a fish in cold water and sprinkle it with salt and pepper to bring out its flavor.

Trout, mackerel, whitefish, perch, pike, and bass are in season throughout the year.

Pan Fish

Place them in a thick bottom frying-pan with heads all one way. When they are fried quite brown and ready to turn, put a dinner plate over them, drain off the fat; then invert the pan, and they will be left unbroken on the plate. Put the lard back into the pan, and when hot slip back the fish. When the other side is brown, drain, turn on a plate as before, and slip them on a warm platter. Leaving the heads on and the fish a crispy-brown, in perfect shape, improves the appearance. Garnish with slices of lemon.

Pretty Flowers
This lovely floral medallion was created by the Calvert Litho Co. for a box of cigars. Detroit was a leading manufacturer of tobacco products from 1840 through 1922.

German Fish Stew

Put the fish in a kettle to boil. Stew together in a saucepan one onion chopped fine and a wine-glass of sweet oil; when well done, pour them in with the fish. Then mix yolks of three eggs, juice of two lemons strained, one tablespoonful sifted flour. Beat these well together, and pour upon the fish when nearly done. Then add ginger, pepper, and salt to taste; stew three or four minutes, after mixing all the ingredients. Oysters may be cooked by the same receipt, only substituting one quart oysters for the fish.

Detroit Entertains a President - 1817
Early on the morning of Wednesday, August 13, 1817, the men, women and children of Detroit dressed in their very best attire, and the carriages, carts and saddles were readied to make the three-mile journey to Springwells to greet President James Monroe. However, the Presidential barge landed instead five miles further at the mouth of the Ecourse River.

Excerpted from an essay by Henry D. Brown and based on articles that appeared in the Gazette on August 1817. Detroit Historical Society Minutes

To Fry Perch

Sprinkle with salt and dredge with flour; after a while dredge with flour the other side. When the lard boils hard, skim it well and put in the fish. Serve hot.

Ladies Helping
The Ladies' Aid Society of Detroit, later called the "Soldier's Aid Society," was founded in November 1861 in order to provide supplies to the soldiers fighting in the Civil War. In a letter to Mrs. Cyrus Smith from her husband, an assistant surgeon of the Ninth Infantry Regiment, he explained that quilts, night caps and other materials were lacking for the soldiers. The army had come together so quickly that the Government had been unable to provide promptly the usual supplies for the sick and wounded.

Parsley Butter

1 tablespoonful butter
1 teaspoonful chopped parsley
1 teaspoonful lemon juice
1/4 teaspoonful salt
Pepper
Paprika

Cream the butter, add seasoning and lemon juice. Spread over fish directly after it is removed from fire.

Baked Fish – 1858

Walleye, pike, muskelunge, and bass are good for baking. Stuff them with a seasoning made of bread crumbs or crackers, butter, salt, pepper, and, if you like, spices. Put the fish in a bake-pan, with a teacup of water, and a bit of butter, and bake from 45 to 60 minutes.

Fish Baked on a Campfire

Build a hot fire of twigs and dry wood. Use when embers are red hot.

Remove head and entrails of fish, also its large fins but not the tail. Wrap in heavy paper and place in the hot embers.

Let bake for half an hour unless fish is very large.

Rake out the fish, unwrap, sprinkle with pepper and salt and serve. The scales and skin will cling to the wrapping paper.

Stuffing for Baked Fish

Beat one egg and use to moisten one and one-half cups bread crumbs. Add four tablespoons melted butter, season and mix well. Put the stuffing into the cleaned washed fish and sew in with thread.

Planked Fish

Use a hickory or oak plank. Have the fish boned and sprinkle with salt and pepper. Broil for five minutes on skin side. Then place on a heated, greased plank, skin side down. Paint with melted butter and put in a hot oven.

Bake until the fish is browned, then reduce the flame. Bake for fifteen minutes or until fish is quite tender. Press mashed potatoes through a pastry bag to form a trimming around the fish; brown well in the oven, pour on melted butter, sprinkle with parsley and serve on the plank placed on a platter.

To Cook Turtle

Kill the turtle at daylight in summer, the night before in winter, and hang it up to bleed. After breakfast, scald it well and scrape the outer skin off the shell; open it carefully, so as not to break the gall. Break both shells to pieces and put them into the pot. Lay the fins, the eggs and some of more delicate parts by – put the rest into the pot with a quantity of water to suit the size of your family.

Add two onions, parsley thyme, salt, pepper, cloves and allspice to suit your taste.

About half an hour before dinner thicken the soup with brown flour and butter rubbed together. An hour before dinner, take the parts laid by, roll them in brown flour, fry them in butter, put them and the eggs in the soup; just before dinner add a glass of claret or Madeira wine.

Detroit Printer

Fr. Richard brought the first printing press to Michigan and printed the first books and the first newspaper published in Detroit. He died of cholera September 13, 1832, at the age of 65.

Turtle Soup

To one turtle that will weigh from four to five pounds, after being dressed, add one-half gallon water, and boil until the turtle will drop to pieces, then add:
2 tablespoonfuls allspice
1 tablespoonful black pepper
2 tablespoons butter, and salt to the taste

When nearly done, put in a small handful of pot marjoram, thyme and parsley tied together, and two large onions; when ready to come off, add two sliced lemons, one pint good wine, and a small quantity of curry powder; thicken with flour.

Terrapin Stew

After they are well cleaned, parboil the meat, then pick it to pieces. Season highly with pepper, salt, cayenne pepper, hard-boiled egg, spices, lemon, and champagne or other wine.

Stew until well done.

Stains on Marble

Iron-rust stains on marble can usually be removed by rubbing with lemon-juice. Almost all other stains may be taken off by mixing one ounce of finely-powdered chalk, one of pumice stone, and two ounces of common soda. Sift these together through a fine sieve, and mix with water. When thoroughly mixed, rub this mixture over the stains faithfully and the stains will disappear. Wash the marble after this with soap and water, dry and polish with a chamois skin, and the marble will look like new.

Broiled Fish

Clean and bone the fish. Sprinkle with pepper and salt and dot with butter. Place as near flame as possible on broiling rack, flesh side up. As soon as flesh starts to brown, reduce flame and cook until white and firm. Turn on skin side with aid of pancake turner and broil until brown and crisp.

Remove to hot platter, garnish with parsley and lemon and serve with parsley butter poured over the fish.

Fish Soup

Almost any kind of fish fillets can be used for this great tasting soup. Commonly used were pan fish because the lakes were full of them.
Cook:
Two cups fish fillets – several minutes or until fish turns white. With a slotted spoon transfer to a large plate to cool.

Brown two strips of bacon cut up fine; pour off grease leaving enough to sauté one-half of an onion; add to broth. Add three diced potatoes, one-quarter cup fresh parsley and cook until potatoes are tender. Cut fish into small pieces and add to the soup. Season with salt and pepper; add three cups milk. Mix three tablespoonfuls and two tablespoonfuls flour; add to soup and boil gently several minutes.

Fish Chowder

Fry a few slices of salt pork, cut the fish in small pieces, pare and slice the potatoes, add a little onion chopped fine.

Place all in layers in the kettle; season with salt and pepper. Stew over a slow fire 30 minutes.

Old School

Detroit School District No. 1 had a school over Col. Nathaniel Prouty's grocery, which stood on piles over the river on the south side of Woodbridge Street near Shelby. The rent was $100 a year. School was used until 1842.

Beef

Meats

All meats are better in winter for being kept several weeks, and it is well, in summer, to keep them as long as you can with out danger of their being tainted. If it is not in your power to keep meat in an ice-house, in summer, keep it in a cool dark cellar, wrapped around with wet cloths, on top of which lay boughs of elderberry. The evaporation from the cloth will keep the meat cool and the elderberry will keep off insects.

If you should unfortunately be obliged to use stale meat or poultry, rub it in and out with soda, before washing it. Tough meats and poultry are rendered more tender by putting a little vinegar or a few slices of lemon in the water in which they are boiled. The use of an acid will save time and fuel in cooking them and will render them more tender and digestible.

If possible, keep the meat so clean that it will not be necessary to wash it, as water extracts the juices. When it is frozen, lay it in cold water to thaw, and then cook quickly, to prevent its losing its moisture and sweetness.

In roasting or boiling, use but little salt at first, as it hardens meat to do otherwise. In roasting, baste frequently, to prevent the meat from hardening on the outside, and try to preserve the juices. If possible, roast the meat on a spit before a large, open fire, after using salt, pepper, butter or lard, and dredging with flour. Where an open fire-place cannot be obtained, however, the meat may be well roasted in a stove or range. Mutton, pork, shote and veal should be well done, but beef should be cooked rare.

Fricassèed Beef

Take any piece of beef from the fore quarter, such as is generally used for corning, and cook it tender in just water enough to have it all evaporate in cooking. When about half done, put in salt enough to season well, and half teaspoonful pepper. If the water should not boil away soon enough, turn it off, and let the beef fry fifteen minutes – it is better than the best roast beef. Take two tablespoonfuls flour, adding the fat – when mixed, pour on the hot juice of the meat. Serve with apple sauce.

Presidential Visit

When President Monroe visited Detroit, August 13, 1817, he still dressed in the style of Washington's time, with knee breeches, silk hose, low-cut shoes fastened with silver buckles, a sash with brass buttons, flare coat, buff vest with a frilled ruffle of his shirt fluttering in the breeze.

Beef Stew

This is best when made of slices cut from an underdone roast, and simmered in any liquor in which meat has been boiled, but if none is at hand, use water instead – just covering the beef.

To a half dozen slices of the usual size, add:

2 tablespoonfuls pepper vinegar
1 tablespoonful of made mustard
1 tablespoonful of acid fruit jelly
1 tablespoonful of butter
1 teaspoonful salt
1 teaspoonful celery-seed
1 saltspoonful black pepper
1 raw turnip, grated or scraped fine
1 mashed Irish potato

Add minced onions and parsley. Boil up and serve.

Cold beefsteak or mutton chops, which are always unfit to appear upon the table a second time, are delicious cut up in small pieces and mixed or stewed separately in this way.

Woodworth's Steamboat Hotel

Benjamin Woodworth came to Detroit in 1806 and had a hotel built on the northwest corner of Woodbridge and Randolph Streets. He built a new one on the same site in 1818. This hotel was the main stop for steamboat and stage-coach lines.

To Cure Beef Ham

Divide the ham into three parts; rub on one-half-pint molasses; let it remain in this molasses a day and two nights, turning it over occasionally during the time. Rub on then one handful salt and put it back in the vessel with the molasses; turn it over, morning and night for ten days. Hang it up to dry for one week, then smoke a little. It is an excellent plan, after sufficiently smoked, to put each piece of beef in a bag, to protect from insects, and keep hanging till used.

Dining Etiquette 1800

Never transfer the fork from one hand to the other.

Never drink with the spoon in the cup.

Do not leave the spoon in the cup after stirring coffee or tea, but place it in the saucer.

Do not rest the elbow on the table.

The knife should be taken by the handle only, resting the forefinger on the upper part of the blade.

The fork should be used for mashing and eating potatoes. Never touch potato with a knife, except to butter it.

Ice cream may be eaten with either a spoon or ice-cream fork.

Pass anything which you see is desired, even to a stranger.

When through dinner the napkin should be left unfolded, unless at home.

Ladies should always be served before gentlemen.

Veal Birds – Italian

1 slice veal steak
1/2 cup parsley, minced
1 clove garlic, chopped
1/2 cup chopped or ground ham
A pinch of grated cheese

Cut the steak into 4-inch squares and sprinkle with the parsley, the garlic, the ham, salt, pepper, and the cheese. Roll the squares and pin them together with toothpicks. Brown in a frying pan and serve with gravy or vegetables.

Presidential Dinner

August 13, 1817 – A wonderful banquet was held at Woodworth's Steamboat Hotel that evening, which was followed by a grand ball, to honor the five-day visit of President James Monroe.

Beef a la Stroganoff – Russian

3 onions, chopped
3 tablespoonfuls butter
1/2 cup tomatoes
1/2 pound mushrooms
1 pound beef tenderloin, cubed
1/2 cup sour cream

Brown the onions slightly in butter. Add the tomato. Cook slowly, stirring constantly for 5 minutes. To this add the beef stock and cook until it thickens. Add the mushrooms and beef cubes, which have been browned in hot fat. Cook 15 minutes and just before serving stir in the sour cream.

Veal Stew – Hungarian

2 tablespoonfuls lard
2 or 3 onions, chopped
1/4 cup paprika
3 or 4 tablespoonfuls, tomatoes
1 pound veal or beef, cut into small pieces
3 or 4 medium potatoes

Heat the lard in a skillet. When hot, add the onions, salt and paprika, the tomatoes, and the veal or beef. Let the mixture cook for a few minutes and then add enough water to cover. Cover tightly and cook for about 1 hour. Add the potatoes, cut into small squares, and cook until tender.

French Boiled Dinner

1 1/2 pounds beef
1 teaspoonful salt
1 teaspoonful thyme
1 bay leaf
4 cups water
1 1/2 pounds chicken drumsticks
10 carrots, cut up
3 onions, cut up
3 turnips, cut up

Bring beef, salt, thyme, bay leaf and water to a boil. Simmer one hour then add chicken and simmer one hour longer. Add vegetables, salt and pepper to taste. Cook 45 minutes. Slice beef before serving.

Roast Beef Pie

Cut up roast beef, or beef steak left from a previous meal, into thin slices, lay some of the slices into a deep dish which you have lined on the sides with rich biscuit dough, rolled very thin, (say a quarter of an inch thick); now sprinkle over this layer a little pepper and salt; put in a small bit of butter, a few slices of cold potatoes, a little of the cold gravy, if you have any left from the roast. Make another layer of beef, another layer of seasoning, and so on, until the dish is filled; cover the whole with paste, leaving a slit in the centre, and bake half an hour.

Steak and Kidney Pie – English

1 1/2 pounds steak (beef or veal)
1/2 pound kidney
Flour
Salt and pepper
1 tablespoonful chopped onion
1 tablespoonful minced parsley
1/2 pound mushrooms, sliced
Water or stock
Pastry

Cut steak and kidney into 1/2-inch cubes and dredge with flour. Season with salt and pepper. Arrange meat in greased pan and add onions, parsley, mushrooms and sufficient water to cover meat. Cover pan and cook in a moderate oven one hour or until meat is almost tender. Remove cover and replace it with pastry, pricking crust to allow steam to escape. Return to a very hot oven and bake for 15 minutes or until crust is browned. Serves 4.

Detroit Stoves

Stove manufacture was begun in Detroit during the 1830's. By 1870 there were five stove manufacturers: the Michigan Stove Company, the Detroit Stove Works, the Peninsular Stove Company, the Detroit Vapor Stove Company and the Art Stove Company. The first cast-iron cook stoves were sold in Detroit by a house to house solicitation.

Cornish Pastries

1/4 pound beef
1/4 pound potatoes
1 small onion, chopped fine
1/2 pound flour
6 tablespoonfuls lard
1 teaspoonful baking powder
A pinch of salt

Cut the meat and potatoes into small pieces, add the onion, pepper and salt to taste, and mix well together. Rub the lard into the flour and add the baking powder and salt. Mix the whole into a stiff paste with water and roll out into a square. Cut into 8 pieces, put a tablespoonful of the mixture on each, wet the edges and draw the opposite corners together, and then press the edges and crimp them with the thumb and finger. Place on a greased tin and bake in a quick oven for one-half hour.

Detroit Travellers

Travellers disembarking from lake packets at the foot of Randolph Street had a full view of the leading hotel of the time – the Woodworth Hotel. Stage lines maintained offices and the owner operated lines of his own from the door to Mount Clemens, Pontiac, Ypsilanti, and Monroe.

Beef Liver with Onions

Slice the liver rather thin, and throw into salt and water. Meantime slice the onions and put into a deep frying-pan, just covered with water, and boil until done, keeping it closely covered. When the water has all boiled away, put in a heaping spoonful of sweet lard, and fry until the onions are a light brown. Take them up in a deep plate; set them on the back of the stove or range to keep hot, and fry the liver in the same pan, adding more lard if there is not enough. Season all with salt and pepper, cutting the liver in slices suitable to help one person. Make a little mound of fried onions on each piece, grate pounded cracker on the top, and serve.

FALL SEASON . . .

1894.

The Detroit News Company.

Meat Pies

Early pies were baked in large black Dutch ovens. These kettles were placed on trivets over hot coals which had been raked out onto the hearth; additional coals were then piled on top of the lid to provide more even heat. The pies were really more steamed than baked; as a result, the crusts were often soggy. Early meat pies were not very glamorous by modern standards, but they were nourishing and could be easily adapted to make use of whatever meats or vegetables were available.

Detroit Entertainment

The March 8, 1833, issue of the Detroit Journal and Michigan Advertiser in an editorial urged the "stimulation of wholesome entertainment" in Detroit citing the fact that in Germany, Italy and France some of the poorest and most ignorant classes have a decided taste for music, painting, statuary, dancing and theatre that provided for the relaxation of its citizens.

Pork

Roast Loin of Pork

Score the skin in strips about a quarter of an inch apart; place it in a dripping-pan with a very little water under it; cook it moderately at first, as a high heat hardens the rind before the meat is heated through. If it is very lean, it should be rubbed with fresh lard or butter when put into the pan. A stuffing might be made of bread-crumbs, chopped sage and onions, pepper and salt, and baked separately on a pie dish; this method is better than putting it in the meat, as many persons have a great aversion to its flavor. A loin weighing about six pounds will roast in two hours; allow more time if it should be very fat. Make a gravy with flour stirred into the pork drippings. Serve with apple sauce and pickles.

Pieces of Eight
The currency used in Detroit was mostly in the form of Spanish gold milled dollars. There was no fractional currency available, so the people took their gold dollars to the blacksmith shops and chiseled them into halves, quarters, and eights as best they could.

Scrappel

Scrappel is a most palatable dish. Take the head, heart and any lean scraps of pork, and boil until the flesh slips easily from the bones. Remove the fat, gristle and bones, then chop fine. Set the liquor in which the meat was boiled aside until cold, take the cake of fat from the surface and return to the fire. When it boils, put in the chopped meat and season well with pepper and salt. Let it boil again, then thicken with corn-meal as you would in making ordinary corn-meal mush, by letting it slip through the fingers slowly to prevent lumps. Cook an hour, stirring constantly at first, afterwards putting back on the range in a position to boil gently. When done, pour into a long, square pan, not too deep, and mold. In cold weather this can be kept several weeks. Cut into slices when cold, and fried brown, as you do mush, is a cheap and delicious breakfast dish.

Need Change
Makeshift coinage in Detroit was carried around in a leather pocket because of the ragged edges, and sharp corners. People were constantly cutting their fingers when reaching for coin.

Leg of Pork Stuffed

Make deep incisions in the meat parallel to the bone, trim it so as to leave the skin longer than the flesh; then boil some potatoes, and when they are done, mash them with a piece of butter, cayenne pepper and salt, an onion finely chopped, and a little rubbed sage.

With this dressing fill the incisions, draw the skin down and skewer it over to keep the dressing from falling out. Season the outside of the meat with salt, cayenne pepper and sage.

Roast it slowly; when done, pour the gravy in a pan, skim off the fat and add some browned flour wet in a little cold water, and boil up once.

Serve with apple or cranberry sauce.

Currency Problems
The citizens, tired of using makeshift coinage, petitioned the government to meet their needs. Subsequently, a grand jury in Detroit on May 10 declared the money a nuisance, formalizing the public protest.

Fried Ham

The slices are always taken from a raw ham, but are most delicate when first simmered a short time: five minutes in a stewpan, dried with a clean cloth and put in a hot frying-pan, first removing the skin. The pan must be hot enough to scorch and brown both ham and gravy quickly. Lay the slices on a hot dish, pour into the gravy one-half teacup new milk, pepper, and minced parsley; boil up and serve.

Spare-Ribs

Put them on in a small quantity of water and boil for fifteen or twenty minutes. Gash them with a knife; sprinkle with pepper and put them on a hot gridiron as near the fire as possible; broil quickly, but not too brown. Have some butter melted and pour over the meat and shut it up in the dish. These are good for breakfast.

"Shinplasters"

Some years after Fr. Richard arrived in Detroit, there was a currency crisis, wherein coinage was not readily available. So Fr. Richard as well as other reputable citizens issued "shinplasters," a paper type of coinage, available in small denominations of 3, 5, 25, and 50 cents. The issuers were prepared to back up the value of this paper currency.

Sausage Cakes Baked with Apple

1 pound sausage meat
4 apples

Shape meat into small flat cakes, and put in the center of a dripping pan; core apples, cut into one-half-inch slices, and put around sausage. Bake in a hot oven until brown, basting frequently with the fat from the sausage.

Toad-in-the-Hole

1 pound pork sausage
1 cup all-purpose flour
1 cup milk
2 eggs
1/2 teaspoon salt

Cook sausages and place in single layer in baking dish. Beat flour, milk, eggs and salt with hand beater until smooth; pour over sausages. Bake uncovered until puffed and golden brown. Cut into squares.

Postal Change

Early Detroit settlers tried using postage stamps for small change. But the stamps had glue on them and they would stick together. Shopkeepers had to keep basins of water handy so customers could separate their stamps to pay the odd change on a purchase.

To Cure Bacon

Pack the meat in salt and allow it to remain five weeks. Then take the hams up, wash off, and wipe dry. Have some sacks made of about seven-eighths shirting, large enough to hold the hams and tie above the hock. Make a pot of sizing of equal portions of flour and corn meal, boil until thick, and dip each sack until the outside is well coated with sizing. Put the hams in bags, and tie tight with a strong twine and hang by the same in the smoke-house.

This is a photo of an original "shinplaster" issued by Gabriel Richard. At the beginning of the Civil War "fractional currency" disappeared from circulation. Shinplasters were issued in small denominations, usually by reputable individuals who were able to back them up with real gold or silver. Often Detoiters would find they had no value and were not redeemable.

Whipping Post

In 1818 a whipping post was built at the upper end of the market building. It was about five feet high. Deadbeats, thieves, wife-beaters, brawlers and other minor offenders occasionally received 39 lashes on their bare backs. This practice was discontinued in 1830.

Tourtière – Traditional French Dish

1 pound lean ground pork
1 cup water
1/2 cup finely chopped onion
1/2 cup fine dry bread crumbs
1 teaspoonful salt
1/8 teaspoonful ground sage
Dash pepper
Dash ground nutmeg
Pastry for 2-crust, 9-inch pie

Brown ground pork in skillet; drain off excess fat. Stir in water, onion, bread crumbs, salt, sage, pepper, and nutmeg. Cover and cook slow till onion is tender, stirring often. Line a 9-inch pie plate with pastry; fill with meat mixture. Adjust top crust; seal and flute. Cut slits in top. Bake till golden brown.

On April 9, 1872 this monument to the Soldiers and Sailors from the Civil War was unveiled in front of the new city hall at Woodward and Cadillac Square. It was designed by Randolph Rogers of Ann Arbor.

Sausage Casings

Casings can be made from the intestines of beef, hogs, or sheep, the sheep casings being used for small sausage, like wiener-wurst, and hog casings for link sausages, and beef for bologna sausage, ham sausage, and blood sausage. Empty as soon as possible, turn inside out and scrape and clean first the in and then the outside. The cleaning is easy where one has running water. Soak 24 hours in lime water or lye water, turn, scrape and rinse again, then salt down and use when needed. When one cannot clean the casings, good substitutes can be made by stitching up tubes of new unbleached muslin, 1 1/2 or 2 feet long, and 2 or 3 inches in diameter, when filled. When ready to hang away, rub the outside well with melted lard, to exclude all air, and sprinkle with pepper.

Filling Sausage

Sausage meat should be finely ground, as it keeps and holds together better. Beef alone, or pork alone can be used, but better two-thirds fat and lean pork, and one-third beef. Vary the seasoning by using pepper, onions, sage, nutmeg or clovesóthe latter two are not very common. For filling the skins a piece of bone two or three inches long is most serviceable, but a piece of tin, shaped into a funnel, smallest end a trifle smaller than skins, will do very nicely. Insert this funnel into one end, hold in left hand, and proceed to fill, using the thumb to force the meat down. Prick the casings often with a hatpin, to let out any air. To have a change make some with cooked barley and some with potato (raw), finely chopped or ground. Use the proportion of one-fourth of barley or potatoes. This is fine.

Theater in Detroit

Benjamin Woodworth, proprietor of the Steamboat Hotel, turned his barn into a theater in the 1830's. Other theaters were located at the northeast corner of Jefferson and Woodward avenues, the Methodist Church at Gratiot and Farrar St., even old City Hall on Cadillac Square was occasionally used.

Stuffed Cabbage – Russian

2 pounds ground pork
1 cup rice, uncooked (partially)
1 teaspoonful salt
1 large can tomato sauce
1 medium onion, chopped fine
2 eggs, beaten
1/2 teaspoonful pepper
1 large head cabbage

Parboil cabbage, separate leaves when they reach the point of being parboiled enough to roll them – cut off hard outer edge of each leaf.

Mix all ingredients together except tomato sauce. Place spoonful of filling on each cabbage leaf and roll, tucking in edges. Pour tomato sauce diluted with 1/2 can of water over top and bake in moderate oven for about 2 hours or until done.

Poultry

Poultry

In summer, kill and dress the poultry the day before-hand, except chicken for frying, which is not good unless killed the same day it is eaten.

The best way to kill a fowl is to tie it by its legs, hang it up, and then cut off its neck. In this way, it dies more quickly, suffers less, and bleeds more freely.

It is best to pick fowls dry; though, if you are pressed for time, you may facilitate the picking of chickens, as well as of partridges and other small birds, by putting them first into water, hot, but not boiling. Then take off the feathers carefully, so as not to break the skin. Never scald a turkey, duck or goose, however, before picking.

To draw the crop, split the skin of all poultry on the back of the neck. Pull the neck upward and the skin downward, and the crop can be easily pulled out. Then cut off the neck close to the body, leaving the skin to skewer at the back of the neck after the dressing has been put in. Make an incision under the rump lengthwise, sufficient to allow the entrails to be easily removed. Be careful not to break the gall, and to preserve the liver whole. Cut open the gizzard, take out the inner skin, and wash both carefully. Wash the bird inside several times, the last time with salt and water. Some persons object to using water inside or outside, but I consider it more cleanly to wash the bird first and then wipe it dry with a clean towel. It should then be hung with the neck downwards till ready to cook.

The Back Log

The foundation of a fire was a heavy hardwood log a foot or more in diameter hauled in and rolled to the rear wall of the fireplace. This was termed the "back-log." The fire was built against it with successive rows of kindling and wood in front of it.

Fried Chicken

Kill the chicken the night before, if you can, and lay on ice, or else kill early in the morning. When ready, wipe dry, flour it, add pepper and salt, and fry in a little lard. When nearly done, pour off the lard, add one-half teacup water, large spoonful butter, and some chopped parsley. Brown nicely and serve. Meal mush fried is nice with the chicken.

Roast Turkey

Wash nicely in and out. Plunge into boiling water 10 minutes. Have ready a dressing of
Bread crumbs
Hard-boiled eggs, chopped fine
1 tablespoonful butter
Minced parsley, thyme and celery

After rubbing the cavity well with salt and pepper and putting in a slice of pork or bacon, fill with the above dressing. Do the same also to the crop, so as to make the turkey look plump. Rub the turkey well with butter and sprinkle salt and pepper over it. Dredge with flour. Lay in the pan with a slice of pork or bacon and a pint of boiling water. Lay the liver and gizzard in the pan with it. Put in a hot oven, basting and turning frequently till every part is a beautiful brown. When the meat is amber color, pin a buttered sheet of writing paper over it to keep it from becoming hard and dry. Cook three or four hours. Season the gravy with minced parsley and celery and serve with cranberry sauce.

Famous Inventor

Elijah McCoy, a black inventor who settled in Michigan in the 1880s, is one whose railroad inventions were first called "the real McCoy" by the public.

Roast Goose

A goose must never be eaten the same day it is killed. If the weather is cold, it should be kept a week before using. Before cooking let it lie several hours in weak salt and water, to remove the strong taste. Then plunge it in boiling water, for five minutes, if old. Fill the goose with a dressing made of:
Mealy Irish potatoes, boiled and mashed fine
A small lump of butter
A little salt or fresh pork, chopped fine
A little minced onion
Parsley, thyme, and a pinch of chopped or powdered sage

Grease with sweet lard or butter. Lay in a pan with the giblets, neck, etc. Pour in two teacups of boiling water, set in a hot oven, and baste frequently. Turn so that every part may be equally browed. Serve with gravy or onion sauce.

Early Detroit Fireplaces

The opening of the fireplace was wide enough to use four-foot logs. It was built of stones and clay and later of stones and mortar, until bricks began to be manufactured.

Lamp Wicks
To insure a good light, wicks must be changed often, as they soon become clogged, and do not permit the free passage of the oil. Soaking wicks in vinegar twenty-four hours before placing in lamp insures a clear flame.

Chicken and Maccaroni

Boil a chicken until very tender, take out all the bones, and pick up the meat quite fine. Boil half a pound of maccaroni until tender, first breaking it up to pieces an inch long. Butter a deep pudding-dish, put on the bottom a layer of the cooked macaroni, then a layer of the minced chicken, bits of butter, pepper and salt, then some of the chicken liquor, over this put another layer of maccaroni, and so on, until the dish is filled. Pour a cup of cream over the whole, and bake half an hour. Serve on a platter.

Pollo Alla Cacciatora – Italian

3 to 4 pounds chicken
1 cup tomatoes
1 medium onion, chopped fine
4 teaspoonfuls olive oil
1/2 pound mushrooms
1/4 cup white table wine
Salt and pepper to taste

Cut and wash the chicken as for fricassee. Heat the oil in a pan, add the chicken, and brown; add the onion, and let cool for 5 minutes. Increase the heat and pour on the wine; cook briskly for a few minutes. Then decrease the heat, add the tomatoes (strained if desired). Salt, pepper, cover and cook slowly till the chicken is tender. Add mushrooms 20 minutes before serving.

Chicken Pudding

10 eggs beaten very light
1 quart rich milk
1/4 pound melted butter
Pepper and salt to the taste

Stir in enough flour to make a thin, good batter. Put four young chickens, nicely prepared and jointed, in a saucepan, with some salt and water and a bundle of thyme or parsley. Boil till nicely done, then take up the chickens and put in the batter. Pour all in a deep dish and bake. Serve with gravy in a boat.

Ukrainian Chicken a la Kiev

6 very small chicken breasts, deboned
1/4 pound butter, unsalted
2 eggs, beaten with pinch of salt
1/2 cup bread crumbs
1 1/2 teaspoonfuls dill or chives, minced
1 sprig fresh parsley, minced
Salt and pepper to taste

About an hour or more before starting the recipe, place half the butter on ice. Preheat the oven to a moderate temperature. Flatten chicken breasts and sprinkle lightly with salt. Divide butter into 6 long, slender pieces and insert one into the pocket of each chicken breast with the chopped dill, chives and parsley. Tuck ends of breasts in with care and secure openings with toothpicks. Dip chicken breasts in beaten eggs, then in bread crumbs. Heat half the remaining butter in frying pan and brown chicken breasts rapidly in the hot (but not burning) butter, adding more butter as necessary. Put well-browned breasts in an open pan in moderate oven until tender. Remove toothpicks and skewers. Serve with a mushroom, or white dill sauce.

The feat in preparing this dish is to get the chicken browned and cooked before the butter inside begins to seep out.

Table Etiquette - 1852
Never lift a glass by the rim; take goblets by the stem and tumblers near the bottom.

Never ask whether any one will have some meat, but whether he will have roast beef, beefsteak, or whatever kind of meat is served.

When asking for anything at the table mention the party's name when you speak.

Do not give any one at the table the trouble of waiting upon you if there be a servant in the room.

Do not, when at a private table, leave until all have finished.

Gentlemen remaining for cigars, rise when the ladies do, and remain standing until they have left the room.

Gentlemen allow the ladies to pass out first en masse, if all leave the dining room.

Wear evening dress at a formal dinner party. Wear gloves and do not take them off until seated at the table.

Chicken Paprikas – Hungarian

4 tablespoonfuls lard
1 chicken
2 cups tomatoes or tomato soup
4 tablespoonfuls paprika
4 tablespoonfuls flour
2 cups milk or sour cream

Heat the lard. Add the chicken, cut into pieces and seasoned with salt and pepper, and cook until the chicken browns. Add the tomatoes or tomato soup and enough hot water to cover the chicken. When the chicken is tender make a gravy by adding the flour, paprika, and milk or sour cream. Veal may also be prepared in this way.

Keep the Child Clean
Wash it every morning in warm water, and never, as some have done, plunge it in cold water.

Chicken with Almond/Raisin Dressing – Polish

1 small young roaster
1 cup milk
1 egg, slightly beaten
1 hard-boiled egg
2 bread rolls
2 bunches chopped fresh parsley
1/3 cup almonds, coarsely chopped
1/2 cup golden raisins
1/4 cup dry bread crumbs
1/4 cup butter

Scald milk, add bread rolls and let soak. Chop hard-boiled egg and add to above mix. Add raw egg, parsley, raisins and almonds, bread crumbs and 1/8 pound butter. Mix and stuff into salted cavity of chicken. Bake in moderate oven for about 1 hour or until done. Dot chicken with remaining butter before putting into oven.

The mayor, aldermen and other dignitaries marched across Woodward Avenue on July 4, 1871 to their beautiful and new city hall. In 1884 Bela Hubbard donated four statues of famous people, that were placed in the corner niches which made it even more striking. In 1967 the "new" city hall building was torn down.

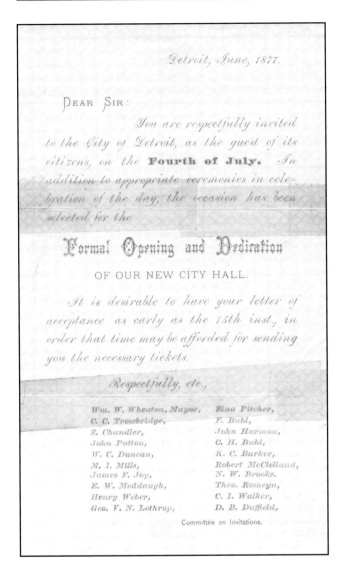

Invitation to Dedication of Detroit's New City Hall

For Weak Back
Two tablespoonfuls finely powdered rosin, four tablespoonfuls white sugar, whites of two eggs, one quart best whiskey. Dose, a tablespoonful three times a day, either before or after meals. Excellent also for colds or weak lungs; will stop an irritating cough. Taken half a teaspoonful at a time.

Chicken Fricassee – French

1 carrot
1 onion
6 tablespoonfuls butter
1 chicken, cut up
2 cups water
1 cup white wine
1/2 teaspoonful salt
16 small white onions
1/2 pound sliced mushrooms
1 tablespoonful lemon juice
2 egg yolks
1/2 cup thick cream
2 tablespoonfuls parsley
1/2 bay leaf
1/8 teaspoonful rosemary

Cook vegetables and 4 tablespoons butter in Dutch oven until onions are soft. Add chicken; cook until light brown. Add water, wine and salt and herbs. Cover and simmer until chicken is done. Heat 16 onions, 2 tablespoonfuls parsley, 1/2 bay leaf, 1/8 teaspoonful rosemary, in 2 tablespoonfuls butter and cook until onion is tender. Remove chicken and onions. Discard other vegetables. Heat broth, mushrooms and lemon juice to boiling. Simmer. Mix egg yolks and whipping cream slowly into broth. Heat to boiling, stirring constantly. Boil and stir 1 minute. Pour over chicken and onion. Serve with rice.

Roast Chicken

Chicken should never be cooked the same day it is killed. Wash well with cold water, then pour boiling water over it and into the cavity. Rub the latter with salt and pepper, and fill with a dressing made of bread soaked in water and squeezed out, a tablespoonful butter, a little salt, pepper and parsley.

Rub the chicken well with butter. Sprinkle pepper and salt over it and dredge with flour. Lay it into a pan with a slice of pork or bacon and a pint of water. Let it simmer slowly 2 hours, basting and dredging frequently. Turn the chicken so each part may be equally browned. Add chopped thyme and parsley to the gravy.

Some persons think ground ginger a more delicate flavoring for the dressing than pepper.

Vegetables

Vegetables

If possible, use vegetables gathered early in the morning, with the dew on them. It is even better to gather them late the evening before, with the evening dew on them (setting them in the ice-house or some cool place), than to gather them after the morning sun has grown hot. If you are living in the city, get your vegetables from market as early in the morning as possible.

As soon as gathered or brought from market, all vegetables should be carefully picked over, washed, placed in fresh water, and set in a cool place till the cook is ready to put them on for dinner.

To Stew, Fry, or Broil Mushrooms

After you have peeled them, sprinkle with salt and pepper and put them in a stewpan with a little water and lump of butter. Let them boil fast for ten minutes and stir in a thickening of flour and cream. They may be broiled on a gridiron, and seasoned with butter. Fry them also in butter. The large mushrooms are used for the two latter modes of cooking them.

Fried Cauliflower

Boil the cauliflowers till about half done. Mix two tablespoonfuls of flour with two yolks of eggs, then add water enough to make a rather thin paste; add salt to taste; the two whites are beaten till stiff, and then mixed with the yolks, flour and water. Dip each branch of the cauliflowers into the mixture, and fry them in hot fat. When done, take them off with a skimmer, turn into a colander, dust salt all over, and serve warm. Asparagus, celery, egg-plant, oyster plant are all fine when fried in this manner.

Rice and Vegetables – Italian

1 onion, chopped fine
1 cup rice
3 cups chicken or beef stock or soup
1/2 cup grated cheese

Cook the onion slowly in a little butter; do not allow it to brown. Add the rice, stir, and cook for a few minutes. Add the stock or soup, and salt. Cook 15 or 20 minutes, stirring often to prevent sticking. Just before serving add butter and grated cheese.

Egg yolk may be added to the onion and butter. If it is used, stir into the rice a little at a time, so that the egg will not be cooked at this time.

Scene on Ferry Seed Farm

Sour-Crout

Barrels having held wine or vinegar are used to prepare sour-crout in. It is better, however, to have a special barrel for the purpose. Strasburg, as well as Alsace, has a well-acquired fame for preparing the cabbages. They slice very white and firm cabbages in fine shreds with a machine made for the purpose. At the bottom of a small barrel they place a layer of coarse salt, and alternately layers of cabbage and salt, being careful to have one of salt on the top. As each layer of cabbage is added, it must be pressed down by a large and heavy pestle, and fresh layers are added as soon as the juice floats on the surface. The cabbage must be seasoned with a few grains of coriander, juniper berries, etc. When the barrel is full it must be put in a dry cellar, covered with a cloth, under a plank, and on this heavy weights are placed. At the end of a few days it will begin to ferment, during which time the pickle must be drawn off and replaced by fresh, until the liquor becomes clear. This should be done every day. Renew the cloth and wash the cover, put the weights back, and let stand for a month. By that time the sour-crout will be ready for use. Care must be taken to let the least possible air enter the sour-crout, and to have the cover perfectly clean. Each time the barrel has to be opened it must be properly closed again. These precautions must not be neglected.

This is often fried in the same manner as fried cabbage, excepting it is first boiled until soft in just enough water to cook it, then fry and add vinegar.

To Peel Tomatoes

Put the tomatoes into a frying-basket, and plunge them into hot water for three to four minutes. Drain and peel. Another way is to place them in a flat baking-tin and set them in a hot oven about five minutes; this loosens the skins so that they readily slip off.

Scalloped Tomatoes

Butter the sides and bottom of a pudding-dish. Put a layer of bread-crumbs in the bottom; on them put a layer of sliced tomatoes; sprinkle with salt, pepper and some bits of butter, and a very little white sugar. Then repeat with another layer of crumbs, another of tomato, and seasoning until full, having the top layer of slices of tomato, with bits of butter on each. Bake covered until well cooked through; remove the cover and brown quickly.

Stuffed Pumpkin – Native American

1 large pumpkin, 10-12 inches in diameter
2-3 tablespoonfuls butter
Salt and pepper to taste
2 cups corn, canned or frozen
1 pound ground beef, browned and drained
2 cups green beans, canned or frozen
3 onions, chopped
1 cup cooked chicken, cubed
1 cup sunflower seed kernels
1/2 cup chicken broth

Preheat oven to moderate temperature. Prepare the pumpkin by cutting a wide lid from the top and scooping out the seeds and pulp. Coat the inside with butter, salt and pepper. Put remaining ingredients into pumpkin. Place pumpkin in shallow pan and bake in moderate oven for 3-4 hours or until pumpkin is soft on the outside and stew bubbles on inside, adding more chicken broth if stew becomes too dry. To serve, cut wedges of pumpkin and top with stew.

Makes approximately 8 servings

The pumpkin seeds would have been saved, and would have either been baked for ìsnackingî or planted in the spring. Similar recipes are found in the foodways history of the Native American culture, using whatever small game is in season instead of the ground beef.

Extinct River

The Savoyard River was located where Congress and Woodward Avenue intersect. It was 25 feet wide and from 3 to 8 feet deep. In March, 1817, a new bridge was built across it at a cost of $104.80.

Onions Baked

Use the large Spanish onion, as best for this purpose; wash them clean, but do not peel, and put into a sauce-pan, with slightly salted water; boil an hour, replacing the water with more boiling hot as it evaporates; turn off the water, and lay the onions on a cloth to dry them well; roll each one in a piece of buttered tissue paper, twisting it at the top to keep it on, and bake in a slow oven about an hour, or until tender all through; peel them; place in a deep dish, and brown slightly, basting well with butter for fifteen minutes; season with salt and pepper, and pour some melted butter over them.

Boston Baked Beans

3 pounds dry pea beans or navy beans (6 cups)
1 1/2 cups dark molasses
1 tablespoonful dry mustard
1/2 pound salt pork, diced
1 large onion, chopped

Rinse beans; in a large kettle combine beans and 24 cups (6 quarts) cold water. Bring to boiling; simmer 2 minutes. Remove from heat. Cover; let stand 1 hour. (Or, add beans to water and soak overnight.) Bring to boiling; simmer till beans are tender, about 1 hour. Drain, reserving liquid. Combine molasses, mustard, 1 teaspoonful salt, 1/2 teaspoonful pepper, and 3 cups reserved cooking liquid. In 6-quart bean pot, mix beans, salt pork, and onion. Stir in molasses mixture. Cover; bake in moderate oven for 3 1/2 to 4 hours, stirring occasionally. Add more reserved cooking liquid, if needed. Serves 15.

Cold Slaw

Wash your cabbage and lay in cold water some hours. Have a seasoning of egg, mustard, oil, pepper, salt, celery-seed, and vinegar, and pour over it. In winter the slaw will keep a day or two.

Scalloped Potatoes – Kentucky Style

Peel and slice raw potatoes thin, the same as for frying. Butter an earthen dish, put in a layer of potatoes, and season with salt, pepper, butter, a bit of onion chopped fine, if liked; sprinkle a little flour. Now put another layer of potatoes and the seasoning. Continue in this way till the dish is filled. Just before putting into the oven, pour a quart of hot milk over. Bake 3/4 of an hour.

Cold boiled potatoes may be cooked the same. It required less time to bake them; they are delicious either way. If the onion is disliked, it can be omitted.

Potato Pie – English

A savory potato pie is made thus: A layer of mashed potatoes placed in a pie dish and then slices of any cold meat (if chicken or veal, slices of tongue or ham may be added), and herbs, pepper and salt, sprinkled over to taste. Continue these layers alternately till the dish is full; the potatoes must well cover the top, which should have some butter added, and be brushed over with the yolk of an egg, and put into the oven till done through. A little butter on each layer is needed if the meat is not fat, and it should not be too fat.

Scene on Ferry Seed Farm

To Fry Cymlings (Squash)

Steam or boil the cymlings (unpeeled), till tender. When cool, slice and butter them, sprinkle pepper and salt and pour over them a spoonful of eggs, lightly beaten. Sift over it cracker, pounded fine, and fry a light yellow brown. Take from the frying pan, prepare the other side the same way. Return to the pan and fry it a pale brown.

Wrinkles in the Skin

White wax, one ounce; strained honey, two ounces; juice of lily-bulb, two ounces. The foregoing melted and stirred together will remove wrinkles.

Stuffed Eggplant – Italian

1 eggplant
1 tomato
1 tablespoonful parsley
2 tablespoonfuls onion
1 tablespoonful olive oil

Cut the top from the eggplant and remove the center. Stuff with a mixture of the chopped center, the tomato, parsley, onion, seasoned with salt, pepper and olive oil. Replace the top of the eggplant. Place in an upright position in a baking dish and bake in hot oven for about 1 hour.

Table Etiquette - 1850's

Never shove dishes on the table; always pass them.

Never shove yourself from the table.

Never touch the face or head at the table or fuss with the hands.

Never suck an orange.

Never spit seeds of fruit on the plate, but take them out of the mouth with a spoon and lay them on the plate.

Never take a larger mouthful than will allow you to speak with ease.

Never hold the spoon so that the handle rests in the palm of the hand.

Never loll back in your chair or lean against the table, but sit upright.

Never make introductions after the guests are seated.

Fried Corn – Native American

12 ears fresh corn
1/4 cup lard or bacon grease
Salt and pepper to taste

Cut the corn off the ears, scraping the cob to get all the milk and kernel. Put in a frying pan over medium heat with melted grease or lard. Turn the corn every 5 minutes or so until some of the corn starts to brown. Turn down heat and cover, stirring regularly to make sure the corn doesn't scorch. Add salt and pepper.

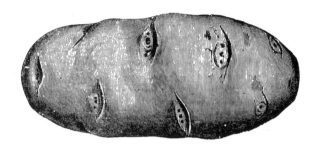

Pommes de Terre Potatoes – French

2 pounds potatoes
1 1/2 pounds tomatoes
2 or 3 large onions
1/4 pound grated Gruyere cheese
2-3 tablespoonfuls butter
Salt
Pepper
Thyme

Potatoes can be partially cooked in their skins the day before. They can then be peeled and sliced thick. If potatoes are raw, slice thinner and place in 2 rows.

Cut the potatoes into pieces. Chop the onions. In an ovenproof dish that has been covered with butter, slice a layer of onions, one layer of potatoes, a layer of tomatoes, another layer of onions, cheese, thyme all over. Salt and pepper to taste. Finish with a layer of tomatoes. Cover with grated cheese and thyme. Sprinkle the oil over the dish. Place in hot oven and bake until all the cheese is melted and the potatoes are done.

Kindness

Father Richard was a very lovable man. Often when there was not a Protestant minister in Detroit he would, on request, preach to the Protestant population in the Council House, and conduct a religious service as well.

Potato Puff

One pint of hot mashed potatoes, seasoned with salt, pepper, celery salt, chopped parsley and butter. Moisten if needed with a little hot milk or cream. Beat 1 egg lightly and add part of it to the potatoes. Shape into smooth round balls. Brush over with the remainder of the egg and bake on a buttered tin until brown. (Be careful not to get them too moist.)

Wild Rice – Native American

Wild rice, a native American delicacy, is not rice at all but the seed of a tall aquatic grass. It is literally wild – efforts to farm it have been failures. It is harvested from canoes, mostly by Native Americans in Minnesota. Considering all this, itís hardly surprising that it costs a fortune!
1 1/2 cups wild rice
6 cups water
1 1/2 teaspoonfuls salt

Rinse the rice thoroughly. Combine rice, boiling water and salt in a saucepan. Boil, without stirring, until rice is tender, about 40 minutes. Drain well. Makes about 5 cups of rice.

New Parish Priest

Reverend Gabriel Richard arrived in June, 1798, to become a parish priest at old Ste. Anne's Church, and to supervise the Native American missions.

Apples and Potatoes – German

4 medium potatoes, cut into 1-inch cubes (about 4 cups)
2 tart apples, sliced
1 tablespoonful sugar
4 slices bacon, cut into 1-inch pieces
1 medium onion, sliced
1 tablespoonful margarine or butter, softened
Dash of ground nutmeg

Heat 1 inch salted water (1 teaspoonful salt to 1 cup water) to boiling. Add potatoes, apples and sugar. Heat to boiling; reduce heat. Cover and cook until tender, 10 to 15 minutes; drain.

Fry bacon until crisp; drain on paper towels. Cook and stir onion in bacon fat until tender. Place potatoes and apples in serving bowl. Dot with margarine; sprinkle with nutmeg. Top with onion and bacon.

Colcannon – Irish

1/2 cup finely chopped onion, leek, green onion or scallion
1/4 cup butter
1/4 cup milk
1 pound cooked mashed potatoes
1 1/2 cups cooked cabbage

Melt the butter in a large skillet. Add the onion and fry gently until softened. Add the milk and the mashed potatoes and stir until heated through. Mince the cabbage finely and beat into the mixture over a low heat until the mixture is pale green and fluffy.

Potato and Egg Casserole – Hungarian

1/2 cup bread crumbs
6 potatoes, cold boiled
3 eggs, hard-boiled, sliced
1 cup sour cream

Butter a baking dish and dust the sides and bottom with the bread crumbs, finely ground. Fill with alternate layers of potatoes and eggs. Pour over the sour cream, and bake 1/2 hour.

Sweet Potato Pudding – American

Boil one and a half pounds potatoes very tender. Add half a pound butter, and rub both together through a sieve. Then add a small cupful milk, six eggs, one and a half cupfuls sugar. Beat all together and add a little salt, the juice and rind of a lemon. Then beat again, and prepare pastry. Bake twenty minutes. It may be baked without pastry. Irish potato pudding may be made by the same recipe.

Brush Park

In 1850 about 300 homes were built on farmland in Brush Park. About 70 of these were Victorian Mansions built for the city's elite, such as lumber baron David Whitney Jr., and J. L. Hudson, the owner of the Department Store. At the time Brush Park was bounded by Woodward, Mack, Beaubien and the now Fisher Freeway.

Electric Park stood at the corner of Jefferson and Belle Isle Bridge in 1920. It had a roller coaster, many rides and a dance hall called the Pier Ballroom. It was one of the most popular places in town with the young people.

This view of Electric Park is from the wooden Belle Isle Bridge which was under construction about 1920.

Shoppers strolling through the vegetable stalls at Eastern Market with buggies and children in 1905.
Horse drawn carts are parked nearby. See this scene in 2001 on page 224.

Opposite page:
In 1840 the Detroit Central Market was located on the east side of Woodward,
behind the old, old city hall, which can be seen in the center background with
the white cupola. Tuesdays and Saturdays were the busiest days at the market.

These boys were having some fun fooling around at their Eastern Market produce stall when a photography student from Center for Creative Studies, a
downtown art school, took their picture in 1972.

Bob-Lo cruise ship "Ste. Claire" transporting hundreds of fun-seekers to the popular island amusement park. The dock was at the foot of Woodward and Jefferson. The Columbia was one of the two boats that each day made three round trips to Bob-Lo Island and an extra trip Saturdays, at 10 pm called the "Moon Light Cruise".Both ships are now in the process of being restored. The Columbia staying in Detroit and the Ste. Claire going to Cleveland.

Bicycle riding was another popular pastime in 1920-30's. It gave women more independence, they could now ride alone or with a companion. It also forced clothing styles to change to meet the needs of the sport and corsets began to disappear.

The most famous of the steamship companies was the Detroit and Cleveland Navigation Company which operated a fleet of fast and luxurious side-wheelers between Detroit, Buffalo, Cleveland, and Mackinac Island, offering overnight service. It was organized in 1850 with their Detroit terminal at the foot of Third Street. They stopped operation in 1950.

In 1969 Berry Gordy established the *Motown* record label and signed entertainers to record contracts. Three years later the *Mototown Revue* singers left Detroit on tour. From then on there was a series of Number 1 songs on the pop chart. Motown moved to Hollywood, California in 1972 leaving a branch office and museum in Detroit on West Grand Boulevard called "Hitville, U.S.A." Photo courtesy of Fox Theatre Archives.

"ParadiseValley" flourished as a group of entertainment spots and black-owned businesses in the African American neighborhoods. Beginning in about 1910 the area was home to a number of famous lounges including the *606 Horseshoe Bar*. Sunnie Wilson can be seen in the front row left.

Thousands of Detroiters celebrated the end of World War I by showing up for a celebratory parade.
The plaster "Statue of Liberty" was stationed on Woodward Avenue for this *Stars and Stripes Forever* –
Peace Celebration, November 11, 1918.

The military Red Arrow regiment was made up of Michigan residents. They had a reunion gathering and parade in
Detroit in 1921, three years after the end of W. W. I.

Joseph L. Hudson opened his first store in rented quarters at the Detroit Opera House in 1881. The J. L. Hudson company grew and continued to serve the Detroit population at this site until it closed in 1983 after 102 years in downtown Detroit.

Opposite page:
A scene from the world-famous annual Hudson's Thanksgiving Parade in the 1930's. In 2001 Hudson's became Marshall Field. The parades began in 1924 and continue with local sponsorship.

Christmas shoppers in 1942 urged to buy U. S. War Savings Bonds by J. L. Hudson's.

Fred Sanders opened up his confectionery business in 1875. In 1965, two new stores opened at Macomb mall and Livonia mall featuring the latest décor.

Opposite page:
A successful black business, Friars Ale, located in Paradise Valley. c.1920.

James Vernor began his drugstore business when he returned from the army in 1862. He sold soft dinks as a sideline and his ginger ale beverage soon became the chief source of income. Vernor's Gingerale became a major Detroit business, first with the riverfront bottling plant then at the Woodward site in the 1950's. The family-owned business was sold to a major bottling company in 1966.

General Motors was involved in the W. W. II production of the M4 and M5 tanks displayed in front of the General Motors Building in March 1943.

In the 1890's high-speed inter-urban lines began to connect Detroit with other Michigan towns. This train ran from Detroit to Port Huron. The inter-urban terminal was located at Bates and Jefferson. They ceased operation in 1934

Cars rolled off the assembly line one each minute in the early 1960's, including this one at a Chrysler plant. Demand was great for the latest model.

The Greyhound Bus and Air Lines Terminal was located on Washington Boulevard at Grand River. Hundreds of people arrived every day to work in Detroit auto plants during the 1940's and 50's. You could also get a bite to eat at Cunningham's Drug Store.

Mayor Van Antwerp personally congratulates 169 DSR employees from the steps of the City Hall in June, 1949. They all have received letters of commendation for courtesy and were given shoulder patches to be worn on their uniforms.

Replica of the 1896 J. B. King car; first car in Detroit. Pioneer Days at Fort Wayne 1975. From the Detroit Historical Museum Collections.

Detroit Historical Society Guild Members churning butter at Fort Wayne Old Pioneer Days.

Military muster on the parade ground. Pioneer Days at Fort Wayne 1975.

This happy looking Polish bride and groom are following the band in their wedding parade. They are on their way, probably , to the wedding breakfast, with bridal party, family and friends following them. Wedding breakfasts following the church service were common in this era. c. 1950.

There will be an exhibit about Polish culture at the Detroit Historical Museum in October 2001.

Part 3

CAST IRON STOVES TO MICROWAVE OVENS

1901 to 2001

HISTORICAL HIGHLIGHTS OF 1901 TO 2001

The Twentieth century saw Detroit grow to maturity, becoming the nation's fourth largest city, with a population peaking at around two million people; all of this by mid-century. The second half of the century saw Detroit caught up in a nationwide pattern of population shifting from core city to surrounding suburbs. Changing political patterns in the world, such as the fall of communism, opened up opportunities for new cultures and language groups to move into the area. By the end of the century Detroit's population hovered around one million, dropping the city to tenth largest in the nation.

In 1901, Detroit celebrated its Bi-Centennial by holding two parades, re-creating Cadillac's landing and erecting a "Chair of Justice" in Cadillac Square. Detroit's prosperity was apparent in many areas. There were forty-four millionaires in the city in 1902; the Penobscot building was completed. Twenty thousand cars were produced in Detroit in 1904. The Detroit Edison Company and Burroughs Adding Machine Corporation began their operations about the same time. Perry and Ben Feigenson opened the Faygo soft drink company and in 1908 Henry Ford introduced the classic Model T car and sold 17,500 of them the first year.

By 1910, more than 465,766 people lived in Detroit, making it the ninth largest U.S. city. The entertainment market was growing and the Paradise Valley area on Hastings Street became an entertainment hot spot with its many clubs. They thrived for the next forty years. The city wanted to develop a zoo for the residents, so they established the Detroit Zoological Society with Horace Rackham as its first president to work toward that goal.

Ford inaugurated the first movable assembly line at the Highland Park Plant. In order to secure more workers, he offered to pay five dollars a day in 1914 with some restrictions.

John and Horace Dodge founded Dodge Brothers Company. In 1917, Detroit auto production topped more than one million vehicles.

This was a very active period for immigration and soon Detroit became the fourth largest city in the U.S. with 993,078 residents in 1920; double what it was in 1910. As a growing metropolitan area with industry, department stores and shops, it was time for Detroit to establish a radio broadcasting system, so WWJ, WJR and WYXZ began broadcasting within a few years of one another.

Automobile sales were booming and production increased to more than one million Model-T Fords in one year. The J. L. Hudson Department Store was experiencing strong growth in sales; everyone wanted to shop at Hudson's. Hudson's became an integral part of the community in many ways, and to show their involvement they had a huge American flag made to hang on the side of the store on November 11, 1923, to mark Armistice Day. The flag was 90 feet by 123 feet. The following year they began the tradition of the Thanksgiving Day Parade.

Detroit continued to annex new areas, and by 1927 it reached its current size of 139 square miles; six times larger than in the year 1900.

The stock market crash of 1929 and the depression that followed hit industrial Detroit especially hard. Prohibition had become the law in 1920 but it did not seem to have much effect on the availability of alcohol. Smugglers just began to bring it across the Detroit River in a variety of creative ways. Thus, Detroit led the nation in violations of the Prohibition, because at least 60% of all illegal alcohol entered the United States through Canada. After they built the Ambassador Bridge it became just another route to smuggle alcohol into Detroit. Smuggling and gangsterism became so bad in Detroit that in 1932 Michigan repealed its state prohibition laws.

In 1935 Detroit became the city of champions as the Tigers, Lions, and Red wings ALL won championships.

The radio stations were doing well, and in 1937 some popular new programs were being aired. Everyone enjoyed The Lone Ranger, The Green Hornet, and Challenge of the Yukon on WXYZ. That same year Joe Louis, "The Brown Bomber," became the heavyweight champion of the boxing world.

By the end of 1941 the whole U.S. went to war as we became involved in WWII. Auto production was stopped everywhere, as auto plants retooled for the war effort and began to manufacture army tanks, airplanes and other weapons. Detroit became known as the Arsenal of Democracy. Fort Wayne served as an Army induction center for Detroit and the Belle Isle Bridge was named after the war hero General Douglas McArthur. When the war ended in 1945, the country gradually returned to normal, and Henry Ford II took over the control of Ford Motor Co. from his grandfather, who died two years later in 1947 at age 83.

With the influx of returning soldiers, a reactivated economy, and a building boom to provide housing for families, there were thousands of cars on the roads. A network of freeways was proposed that would provide the rapid movement of traffic throughout the city. No longer needed as an induction center, Fort Wayne was deactivated and became a Military Museum.

The Detroit Historical Society was founded in 1922 and eventually was able to build or acquire three local museums. At the present, it operates four museums: Fort Wayne, Moross House on east Jefferson, Dossin Museum on Belle Isle, and the Detroit Historical Museum. The Detroit Historical Museum celebrated the opening of its new building in 1951, as the city celebrated its 250th Birthday with a grand parade down Woodward Avenue. Later that evening on July 24, thousands of Detroiters gathered downtown to light a giant Birthday Cake in Grand Circus Park. The city held a great many other wonderful celebratory activities throughout the year.

Downtown Hudson's was thriving, with 12,000 employees and $100,000 in sales per day. It operated five restaurants throughout the facility, and was serving 14,000 meals every day.

A beautiful, new City-County building was built at the corner of Woodward and Jefferson. It opened in 1955 and Detroit City Hall moved into the new facility. Marshall Fredericks had been selected to sculpt a new figure for the front of the new building. He designed a spectacular 25-foot-high bronze figure called the "Spirit of Detroit." Surrounded by a beautiful garden it is one of the highlights of Woodward Avenue.

In the 1950's, some local people and businesses were in the news. Charlesetta Waddles opened her "Perpetual Mission" which offered food, clothing and transportation to the needy in Detroit; Berry Gordy, Jr., founded Motown records; and the Ernst Kern Department store closed its doors.

Detroit's population slipped in 1960 to 1,670,144 which placed it fifth largest in the nation. Following World War II, veterans had been able to go to school on the G.I. Bill and also obtain low-interest home loans from the Veterans Administration. All across the country these young men were moving their families to the burgeoning new suburbs, reversing a century-old trend of steadily increasing city population.

Civil unrest in 1967 led to the founding of New Detroit, the nation's first urban coalition to improve education, employment, housing and economic development in the city.

In 1919 the Detroit Symphony moved into its beautiful new Orchestra Hall on Woodward Avenue and Orchestra Place. In 1939, after the Depression, the Symphony was forced to move to a more economical setting, the smaller Music Hall. In 1941 Orchestra Hall was reopened as the Paradise Theater and became a home for many famous black performers in jazz, blues and vaudeville. But in 1951, the hall closed again and fell into disrepair. Orchestra Hall was scheduled to be demolished in 1970, but was saved from the wrecking ball, added to the National Register of Historic Places and reopened in 1989 after complete restoration.

Coleman A. Young was elected in 1973 as the first mayor of African descent and went on to serve five terms. During his tenure as mayor, the Renaissance Center, championed by Henry Ford II, opened in 1977. This was the first major downtown renewal project in several years. Then in 1979, the Joe Louis Arena was completed, as well as Hart Plaza with the lovely Isamu Noguchi Fountain (Dodge Fountain) set in the center of the open-air plaza.

Downtown Detroit suffered a loss when the J. L Hudson Store closed its doors in 1983 after having been in operation for 102 years, and gained with the opening of the third incarnation of the African-American Museum, the Charles H. Wright Museum of African-American history as it opened at its new location on Warren Avenue in 1997. Detroit gained an opera house in 1995 as the Michigan Opera Theatre opened in the extensively renovated old Broadway-Capitol Theater.

As Dennis Archer became mayor in 1994 he appealed to the suburbs to work with the city for the mutual benefit of each. The Gem Theatre and the Elwood Bar and Grill, two famous Detroit landmarks, were moved, intact, to a new location. New stadiums were to be built for the Tigers and Lions, and the Red Wings won two consecutive Stanley Cups in 1997 and 1998. Tiger Stadium closed with the final game in the 1999 season and moved to their new home, Comerica Park.

The Census of the year 2000 saw Detroit's population fall below one million for the first time in seventy-five years. As we celebrate the Tri-Centennial of Detroit, it is good to remember the past, but exciting to contemplate the future.

CAST IRON STOVES TO MICROWAVE OVENS

Detroit in the 1900's started with a bang! The population was 285,700 and growing. Immigrants were pouring into Detroit! They came from Armenia, Syria, Greece, Italy, Hungary, Poland, Germany and many other countries to work in Detroit. They lived two and three or even more, to a room in boarding houses, private homes, hotels and anywhere else. In 1930 30% of Detroit's population was foreign born. All these people had to be fed.

Grocery stores provided canned goods, meat came from the butcher shop, and peddlers sold fresh fruits and vegetables from their wagons as they circled the neighborhoods. The women tended to the arduous task of cooking on the cast-iron stove. They cooked breakfast and dinner and provided bag lunches for their families. If they ran a boarding house they cooked meals for twenty to thirty people or more, each day. The recipes they used were the ones they brought with them from their homelands. All of the recipes mentioned are found in Part III.

They cooked bread, cornbread, biscuits, pancakes, eggs and bacon, Jewish coffee cake, Greek Walnut Cake, Polish Poppy Seed Cake, Scotch Shortbread, and Italian Pudding. They made Turkish Coffee, Polish Dill Pickle Soup, German Spaetzle, Irish Stew, Swedish Meatballs, and Pigs Feet. An endless stream of meals were prepared from recipes that represented the ethnic backgrounds of Detroit's residents. Immigration continued sporadically throughout the 1900's. Today, in 2001, we still have a large influx of Hispanic and Middle Eastern peoples and smaller numbers from other lands.

Bread

Jalapeño Bread

2 loaves (1 pound each) frozen bread dough, thawed
1 can (8-3/4 ounces) whole kernel corn, drained
1 egg beaten
1 can (3-1/2 ounces) whole jalapeños, chopped
2 tablespoons taco seasoning mix
1 jar (2 ounces) sliced pimientos, drained
1 1/2 teaspoons vinegar

Cut bread dough into 1-inch pieces. Place all ingredients in a large bowl and toss to mix well. Spoon into two greased 8-inch x 4-inch x 2-inch loaf pans. Cover and let stand for 15 minutes. Bake at 350° for 35-40 minutes. Cool in pan 10 minutes before removing to a wire rack. Serve warm if desired.

Makes 2 loaves.

Remove the seeds from the jalapeños before chopping for a milder bread.

Evie's Apple Kuchen
Contributed by: Evie Douglas

1/2 cup (1 stick) softened butter or margarine
1 package yellow cake mix
1/2 cup flaked coconut
1 can sliced apples
1/2 cup sugar
1 teaspoon cinnamon
1 cup sour cream
2 egg yolks or 1 egg

Heat oven to 350°. Cut butter into dry cake mix until crumbly. Mix in coconut. Pat mixture lightly into 9 x 13-inch pan and bake 10 minutes. Arrange apple slices on warm crust. Mix sugar and cinnamon and sprinkle on apples. Blend sour cream and egg (or egg yolks) and drizzle over apples. (Topping will not cover all the apples.) Bake 20-25 minutes or until edges are light brown. Do not overbake. Serve warm.

Irish Soda Bread

Contributed by Linda Humes

Traditional. Irish Soda Bread is one of the specialties of the country and is still baked in countless farmhouses and homes all over Ireland. It is made in white or brown loaves, the latter being made from whole wheat flour. It is very easy to make.

White:

1 1/2 pounds (6 cups) plain flour
1 teaspoon bicarbonate of soda
1 teaspoon salt
1/2 pint (1 cup) buttermilk, sour milk or fresh milk; if the last, 1 teaspoon cream of tartar is added to dry ingredients

Mix all the dry ingredients together in a basin and make a well in the centre. Add enough milk to make a thick dough. Stir with a wooden spoon; the pouring should be done in large quantities, not spoonful by spoonful. The mixture should be slack but not wet and the mixing done lightly and quickly. Add a little more milk if it seems too stiff. With floured hands, put onto a lightly floured board or table and flatten the dough into a circle about 1 1/2 inches thick. Put onto a baking sheet and make a large cross over it with a floured knife. (This is to ensure even distribution of heat.) Bake in a moderate to hot oven (375°-400°) for about 40 minutes. Test the centre with a skewer before removing from the oven. To keep the bread soft, it is wrapped up in a clean tea-towel. This quantity will make 1 large loaf or 2 small ones.

Brown:

Exactly the same as above, but use 1 pound (4 cups) whole wheat flour and 1/2 pound (2 cups) plain white flour. A little more milk is used to mix the dough. If a brittle texture is required, add 1 tablespoon of melted butter to the above quantity.

This bread should not be cut until it is quite cold and "set." This takes 4-6 hours.

Big Auto Plant

The Dodge Hamtramck plant was large enough in the mid-1920's to have its own laundry, post-office, fire department, print shop, weather bureau, restaurant, barber shop and police force of 125.

Cinnamon Rolls Made from Frozen Bread Dough – 1990

Use dough from 1 loaf of bread. Pat into a large square. Butter generously. Sprinkle with a mixture of 6 tablespoons brown sugar and 1 teaspoon cinnamon. Roll up like a jelly roll and cut into 1-1/2 inch pieces. Place into a pan prepared with a generous greasing of fat and brown or white sugar. Place rolls into pan and let rise till double in bulk. Bake in 350° oven. Top rack may be needed in oven to prevent bottom from burning. Remove from oven and place pan upside down on clean towel for a few minutes. Remove pan and let rolls cool before eating.

This photo of Boerth's Quick Lunch was taken in 1908. There were many places in downtown Detroit where business men, and shoppers, could have a quick lunch. Boerths was located at 108 Woodward Avenue. The Cadillac Café at the Detroit Historical Museum in the Streets of Detroit is loosely modeled after the décor in Boerth's.

Wheat vs Corn

The first Detroit settlers planted a little patch of wheat in October of 1701, which they reaped in disappointment in the following July, for the soil of Detroit was not suitable to wheat. The ground needed better preparation so in 1704 Cadillac brought three horses and 10 head of oxen to Detroit to plough the ground. Eventually, they were able to harvest a modest crop. Corn was still the predominant grain.

Fried Bread Puffs – India

1 cup whole-wheat flour
1 cup all-purpose flour
1/2 teaspoon salt
3 tablespoons vegetable oil
1/2 to 3/4 cup water
Vegetable oil

Mix flours, salt and oil until mixture resembles fine crumbs. Stir in just enough water to make a very stiff dough. Turn dough onto lightly floured surface; knead until smooth and elastic, 5 to 8 minutes. Cover; let rest 20 minutes.

Shape dough by rounded teaspoonfuls into 1-inch balls. Roll into 3- to 4-inch circles 1/8 inch thick on lightly floured surface. (Cover to prevent drying.)

Heat oil (1 1/2 to 2 inches) to 370°. Fry 1 to 3 puris at a time, turning once, until golden brown and evenly puffed, 1 1/2 to 2 minutes. (Press flat portions into hot oil with spoon if necessary to insure even puffing.) Drain on paper towels. Makes 24.

Cranberry Bread – Early American

2 cups flour
1 cup sugar
1 1/2 teaspoons baking powder
1/2 teaspoon soda
1/2 teaspoon salt
1 1/2 cups fresh cranberries
1 cup chopped walnuts
3/4 cup orange juice
2 teaspoons melted butter
1 egg, slightly beaten

Sift dry ingredients together. Add and mix thoroughly the cranberries and walnuts. Heat and add the orange juice, butter and egg. Blend into dry ingredients. Pour into greased 9x5 inch loaf pan. Bake at 350° for 1 hour.

Quick Bread Sticks

2 packages hot dog buns
2 sticks margarine
1/2 teaspoon garlic salt
1/2 teaspoon celery salt
1/2 teaspoon parsley flakes
1 tablespoon Wish-Bone Italian dressing
Parmesan cheese

Split buns into quarters. Melt next 5 ingredients and brush on buns. Sprinkle with Parmesan cheese and bake in slow oven (250° to 275°) for 45 minutes, until golden.

Serve with dip:
1 pint sour cream
1 package Four Seasons Italian dressing mix

Standard Yeast Rolls

Milk, 2 cups
Shortening (part or all butter or margarine), 1/4 cup
Sugar, 1/4 cup
Salt, 2 teaspoons
Yeast, 2 packages
Water, warm, 1/4 cup
Enriched flour, sifted, 5 to 6 cups

Bring milk to a boil, add shortening, sugar and salt; cool to lukewarm.

Sprinkle yeast over warm water. After 5 minutes, stir and combine with cooled milk mixture; add about half the flour; beat well. Add enough of the remaining flour to make a soft dough; mix thoroughly.

Turn out on lightly floured board, cover with mixing bowl and let rest 10 minutes. Then knead about 10 minutes, until smooth and satiny.

Place dough in a warm greased bowl; brush surface very lightly with melted fat; cover and let rise in a warm place (80° to 85°) about 2 hours or until doubled in bulk. Do not punch down. Turn out on board and shape into rolls as directed below.

Place on a greased baking sheet; cover and let rise 1/2 to 3/4 hour or until doubled in bulk.

Brush with milk, melted fat, diluted egg white or diluted egg yolk. Bake in a moderate oven (375°) 15 to 20 minutes.

Biscuit Rolls: Roll 1/2 inch thick; cut into 2-inch rounds with a biscuit cutter.

Bowknots: Roll pieces of dough into ropes about 1/2 inch in diameter and 6 to 8 inches long; tie each length loosely into a knot.

Cloverleaf Rolls: Shape dough into tiny balls; dip in melted fat and place 3 balls in each section of a greased muffin pan.

THE AVENUE SERVSELF
84 WOODWARD AVENUE
DETROIT

As the name implies, this was another cafeteria-style diner located in downtown Detroit. Located at 84 Woodward Avenue. ca. 1909

Buttermilk Biscuits

2 cups flour
1/2 teaspoon soda
2 teaspoons baking powder
1 teaspoon salt

Cut in 1/4 cup cold shortening and mix with 1 cup buttermilk, or sour milk.

Sour Cream Coffee Bread

1 cup butter
2 cups sugar
2 eggs
1 cup dairy sour cream
1/2 teaspoon vanilla
2 cups sifted all-purpose flour
1 teaspoon baking powder
1/4 teaspoon salt
4 teaspoons sugar
1 teaspoon cinnamon
1 cup chopped pecans

Cream butter and sugar. Beat in eggs. Mix thoroughly. Add sour cream and vanilla. Add flour mixture. Mix sugar, cinnamon and pecans.

Spoon about one third of batter into a well-greased 9-inch tube pan. Sprinkle with about three-quarters of pecan mixture. Spoon in remaining batter and sprinkle with remaining pecan mixture.

Bake in moderate oven (350°) 1 hour, or until done. Remove from pan and cool on wire rack. Makes 10 servings.

Jesuit College
The Jesuit order of priests founded Detroit College in 1877. It was located on Jefferson between St. Antoine and Hastings. SS. Peter and Paul's Church is still there, but the college became so large it moved in 1927 to West Six Mile and Livernois. Six Mile Road was renamed McNichols in honor of Fr. John McNichols, long-time President of Detroit College.

Old Fashioned Molasses Bread – African American

1/2 cup shortening
Black sorghum (molasses)
Ginger
1 3/4 cups sugar
3 cups flour
Cinnamon
2 eggs
Buttermilk

Mix shortening and sugar until creamy. Add eggs and continue to cream. (Use mixer if you have one), then add milk and flour alternately. When ingredients are mixed, add cinnamon and ginger to taste and black molasses. Grease baking pan and bake at 350°. May be served plain or iced with your favorite icing.

Old Fashioned Northern Cornbread

Contributed by Christopher Humes

1 cup cornmeal
1 cup flour
4 teaspoons baking powder
1/4 cup sugar
1/2 teaspoon salt
1/4 cup shortening
1 cup milk
2 eggs, beaten

Combine dry ingredients and mix thoroughly. Add milk, eggs and shortening. Mix together just well enough to combine into batter. Pour into a greased 8 x 8 pan and bake at 425° for 25-30 minutes.

On Fire

Detroit's most notable fire started June 11, 1805, in John Harvey's bakeshop. Fanned by a strong wind, it spread rapidly, and within a few hours every building in the city had been destroyed. Thus the ancient French town vanished in one appalling conflagration.

Buttermilk Corn Meal Muffins – African-American

1 cup of corn meal
1 cup of buttermilk
2 teaspoons of baking powder
1/3 teaspoon of baking soda
1/2 teaspoon of salt
3/4 cup of flour
2 tablespoons of sugar
2 eggs
4 tablespoons of melted shortening

Mix corn meal, baking powder, baking soda, salt, sugar and flour. Add the eggs, milk and melted shortening. Preheat the muffin tins and grease. Do not fill to top, just over half. Bake in the oven at about 375° for about 20 minutes. Makes about 1 dozen.

Burned Cooking

When your cooking has been scorched, lift the vessel holding the food quickly from the fire, and stand it in a pan of water for a few minutes, and the scorched taste will entirely disappear.

Yorkshire Pudding – English

1 cup sifted flour
1/4 teaspoon salt
3 eggs
1 cup milk

Sift flour and salt together. Beat eggs until light and add sifted ingredients, mixing well. Add milk gradually and beat 2 minutes with rotary egg beater. Prepare pudding in time to pour into pan 30 minutes before beef has finished roasting. Place beef to one side of roasting pan. Pour off all fat except 1/4 cup and pour in pudding to depth of 1/2 inch. Return to hot oven (400°) to cook 30 minutes. Cut into squares and serve at once. Serves 6.

Yorkshire pudding may be baked separately in oblong pan heated very hot and well greased with beef drippings.

New Fireman

Although the volunteer fire companies added much to the life of the City, they were far from efficient as fire fighters. Brimful of spirit and energy, they would rush madly to the scene, where as likely as not they would fall to fighting a rival company, while the building burned down unhindered. The townsmen became tired of these madcap riots and in 1860 established a paid fire department.

Crusty Oatcakes – Scottish

2 cups rolled oats
2 cups flour
6 tablespoons sugar
1 teaspoon salt
1/2 teaspoon baking soda
1/3 cup coconut (optional)
1/3 cup currants
2/3 cup shortening
4 tablespoons butter (not margarine)
1/2 cup water
Juice of 1 lemon
Confectioners' sugar

Combine first 7 ingredients. With a pastry blender or fingers, work in shortening and butter. Add water as needed to form dough. On a floured surface roll dough out to 1/8 inch thickness. Cut into rounds. Bake at 375° for 10 minutes. Combine enough lemon juice and sugar to make thin frosting. Frost oatcakes while still warm.

Breakfast

Daisy's Baked Pancake

3 eggs
1/2 teaspoon salt
1/2 cup all-purpose flour
1/2 cup milk
2 tablespoons butter or margarine, softened
Confectioners' sugar
Lemon wedges

In a mixing bowl, beat eggs until very light. Add salt, flour and milk; beat well. Thoroughly rub bottom and sides of a 10-inch cast-iron skillet with butter. Pour batter into skillet. Bake at 450° for 15 minutes. Reduce heat to 350° and bake 5 minutes more or until set. Remove pancake from skillet and place on a large hot platter. Dust with confectionersí sugar and garnish with lemon. Serve immediately. Makes 4-6 servings.

Sunday Supper Waffles

1 cup sifted all-purpose flour
2 teaspoons baking powder
1/4 teaspoon salt
2 eggs, separated
1 cup milk
1/4 cup butter or margarine, melted

Into large bowl, sift together flour, baking powder and salt; set aside.

In small bowl, using mixer at high speed, beat egg whites until stiff, but do not let dry peaks form; set aside.

Add milk, melted butter and egg yolks to dry ingredients. Using mixer at medium speed, beat just until well blended. Do not overbeat. Gently fold beaten egg whites into batter, leaving a few puffs of egg white showing.

Bake batter in preheated waffle baker.

Egg, Cheese, Sausage Bake

1 pound pork sausage
1 onion
8 ounces grated sharp cheese
1 pound frozen hash browns
6 eggs
3 cups milk

Fry sausage and onion together. Mix eggs and milk together. Layer in baking dish; potatoes, sausage, cheese; repeat again and pour milk and egg mix over all. Bake 350° one hour. 6 to 8 servings.

Banana Nut Pancakes

Flour, 1 1/2 cups
Baking powder, 2 1/2 teaspoons
Salt, 3/4 teaspoon
Sugar, 3 tablespoons
Egg, well beaten, 1
Milk, about 1 1/4 cups
Shortening, melted, 3 tablespoons

Sift flour; measure; add baking powder, salt and sugar; sift again.

Combine egg, milk and melted shortening (slightly cooled); the amount of milk to use will depend upon thickness of pancakes desired; 3/4 cup milk will give thick cakes, 1 1/4 cups milk will make them quite thin. Pour into flour mixture and stir just enough to moisten the dry ingredients. Do not beat.

Bake on a hot griddle. Serve hot with butter and sirup, honey or sweet preserves. Makes 1 to 1 1/2 dozen cakes.

Apple Pancakes: Increase sugar to 1/4 cup; add 2 tablespoons of the sugar to 1 cup chopped apples; let stand a few minutes. Sift remaining sugar and 1/8 teaspoon cinnamon with the dry ingredients. Fold sweetened chopped apples into batter before baking. Serve with honey.

Banana-Nut Pancakes: Fold in 1 large banana, mashed or thinly sliced, and 1/4 cup chopped walnuts.

Blueberry Pancakes: Increase sugar to 1/4 cup; add 2 tablespoons of the sugar to 1 cup blueberries; let stand a few minutes. Sift remaining sugar with dry ingredients. Fold sweetened blueberries into batter before baking.

Sour Cream Blueberry Pancakes

Light, fluffy pancakes with that interesting flavor sour cream adds.

1 cup sifted all-purpose flour
3 teaspoons baking powder
1/4 teaspoon salt
1 tablespoon sugar
1 egg
1 cup milk
1/4 cup dairy sour cream
2 tablespoons melted butter
1/2 cup blueberries

Sift together flour, baking powder, salt and sugar.

Beat together egg, milk and sour cream.

Pour milk mixture over dry ingredients and blend with rotary beater until batter is just smooth. Stir in butter. Fold in blueberries.

Shirley's Scrambled Eggs, Peppers and Tomatoes

Contributed by Shirley Hartert

2 medium green peppers, sliced
1 medium onion, sliced
1 clove garlic, chopped
1/2 teaspoon salt
1/2 teaspoon dried thyme leaves
3 tablespoons olive oil or margarine
2 medium tomatoes, coarsely chopped
8 eggs
1/2 cup milk
1/2 cup 1/4 inch strips fully cooked smoked ham
1 1/2 teaspoons salt
1/4 teaspoon pepper

Cook and stir green peppers, onion, garlic, 1/2 teaspoon salt and the thyme in 1 tablespoon of the oil in 10-inch skillet over medium heat until green peppers are crisp-tender, about 8 minutes. Add tomatoes; heat until hot, about 2 minutes. Drain excess liquid from vegetables, place vegetables on platter. Keep warm.

Heat remaining oil in same skillet over medium heat until hot. Mix remaining ingredients; pour into skillet. Cook uncovered over low heat stirring frequently until eggs are thickened throughout but still moist, 3 to 5 minutes. Mound scrambled eggs in center of vegetables. Sprinkle with snipped parsley if desired, and/or paprika.

Familia

3 cups quick oats, uncooked
1 1/2 cups wheat germ
1 cup chopped dried apricots
1 cup chopped pecans or walnuts
2 cups raisins

Mix ingredients together. Store in airtight container. Serve with milk. Delicious cold cereal.

Black Fruit Salad

1 cup black cherries, pitted
1 cup black grapes
1/2 cup blueberries or black currants
1/3 cup light brown sugar
Juice of 1 lemon
1 cup dairy sour cream
Fresh mint sprigs

Combine fruits and sprinkle with brown sugar and lemon juice. Let stand for 2 hours, tossing several times.

Lift out fruit with slotted spoon and divide equally among 4 balloon wine glasses.

Stir sour cream into collected juices in bowl.

Serve fruits topped with a dollop of the sour cream sauce and a sprig of fresh mint.

4 portions.

Variation: We also like a combination of green grapes, kiwis and green apples. You can also use a mixture of just grapes.

Applesauce Puffs

2 cups packaged biscuit mix
1/4 cup sugar
1 teaspoon cinnamon
1/2 cup applesauce
1/4 cup milk
1 slightly beaten egg
2 tablespoons cooking oil
1/4 teaspoon cinnamon
1/4 cup sugar
2 tablespoons melted butter

Combine biscuit mix, 1/4 cup sugar, 1 teaspoon cinnamon. Add applesauce, milk and butter. Beat for 30 seconds. Fill greased muffin pans 2/3 full. Bake at 400° oven for 12 minutes or until done (golden). Remove from pans. Mix second 1/4 cup sugar and 1/4 teaspoon cinnamon. Dip tips of muffins in melted butter then in the sugar mixture.

Frank Hibbler, a longtime member of the Detroit Historical Society, was the artist who produced a wonderful series of six drawings, after the exhibits of the time located in the "Streets of Detroit." These drawings will appear in various places in this cookbook.

Conversation - 1901

The object of conversation is to entertain and amuse. To be agreeable, you must learn to be a good listener. A man who monopolizes a conversation is a bore, no matter how great his knowledge.

Never get into a dispute. State your opinions, but do not argue them. Do not contradict, and, above all, never offend by correcting mistakes or inaccuracies of fact or expression.

Never lose temper – never notice a slight – never seem conscious of an affront, unless it is of a gross character.

You are not required to defend your friends in company, unless the conversation is addressed to you; but you may correct a statement of fact, if you know it to be wrong.

Never talk at people, by hints, slurs, inuendoes, and such mean devices. If you have any thing to say, out with it. Nothing charms more than candor, when united with good breeding.

Do not call people by their names, in speaking to them. In speaking of your own children, never "Master" and "Miss" them – in speaking to other people of theirs, never neglect to do so.

It is very vulgar to talk in a loud tone, and indulge in hoarse laughs. Be very careful in speaking of subjects upon which you are not acquainted. Much is to be learned by confessing your ignorance – nothing can be by pretending to knowledge which you do not possess.

Never tell long stories.
Avoid all common slang phrases, and pet words.

Of all things, don't attempt to be too fine. Use good honest English – and common words for common things.

Janet's Buttermilk Pancakes – 1920

1 cup buttermilk
1/2 teaspoon salt
1 tablespoon shortening, melted
2 eggs
1 tablespoon sugar
1 teaspoon soda
Some flour to thicken
Mix and fry on greased griddle.

Brown Sugar Sirup

Boil one cup of brown sugar and one-half cup of water until the consistency of thick maple sirup. Serve hot or cold.

Cutting Bottles for Cups or Jars

A simple, practical way is to take a red-hot poker with a pointed end; make a mark with a file to begin the cut; then apply the hot iron and a crack will start, which will follow the iron wherever it is carried. This is, on the whole, simple, and better than the use of strings wet with turpentine, etc.

Coconut French Toast – Philipines

6 slices white bread (or 6 halves of small French rolls)
3 eggs
1/2 cup coconut milk (or more as needed to soak bread)
2 tablespoons sugar
3 tablespoons margarine or butter
1/3 teaspoon salt
1/2 teaspoon Accent
Cinnamon
Syrup (maple or honey)

Increase or double recipe as needed. Beat 3 eggs until fluffy; add coconut milk, sugar, salt and Accent. Soak slices of bread and turn each to coat well. Heat butter in skillet. Cook over medium heat until each side is golden brown.

Pina Colada Pancakes

Contributed by Shirley Hartert

2 cups Bisquick
2 eggs
3/4 cups milk (approximately)
4 tablespoons Coco Lopez (cream of coconut)
2 teaspoons vanilla or 2 tablespoons Kahlua
3 tablespoons coconut
1/2 cup diced pineapple, fresh or cannd
1 diced banana
1 orange sliced for garnish

Make pancakes with Bisquick, eggs, Coco Lopez, Kahlua and enough milk to make a firm consistency. Heat and butter griddle. Spoon enough batter for 4-inch pancakes, Turn and remove when both sides are browned. Place on hot platter and keep warm.Continue process until all batter is used. Sprinkle with diced fruit and coconut. Serve with warm syrup. Garnish with orange slices.

Syrup: equal amounts of Coco Lopez and Maple Syrup. Serves 4-6.

Cakes

Greek Baklava

1 1/4 cups all-purpose flour
3/4 cup sugar
1 teaspoon baking powder
1 teaspoon ground cinnamon
1/2 teaspoon salt
1/4 teaspoon ground cloves
3/4 cup milk
1/3 cup shortening
1 egg
1 cup finely chopped walnuts
Honey Syrup (below)

Heat oven to 350°. Grease and flour pan, 9 x 9 x 2 inches. Beat all ingredients except walnuts and Honey Syrup in small mixer bowl on low speed 30 seconds. Beat on high speed, scraping bowl occasionally, 1 minute. Stir in walnuts. Pour into pan. Bake until wooden pick inserted in center comes out clean, 35 to 40 minutes.

Cool cake in pan about 30 minutes. Prepare Honey Syrup. Cut top of cake into diamond pattern; pour syrup evenly over top of cake.

Honey Syrup

1/4 cup sugar
1/4 cup water
1/4 cup honey
1 teaspoon lemon juice

Heat sugar and water to boiling: reduce heat. Simmer uncovered 5 minutes. Stir in honey and lemon juice.

Danish Raisin Cake

1/2 pound butter
2 small cups sugar
4 eggs
5 cups flour
1 cup milk
3 teaspoons baking power
Raisins as desired
Fruit peels can also be used

Mix all ingredients together. Put into a buttered loaf pan, bake 1 1/4 hours at 350°.

Poppy Seed Cake – Polish

3 cups all-purpose flour
2 cups sugar
1/2 teaspoon salt
1 1/2 teaspoons baking soda
1 jar or can regular poppy seed
1 1/2 cup salad oil
4 eggs
1 teaspoon vanilla
1 can evaporated milk
Powdered sugar

Sift together flour, sugar, salt and baking soda. Add poppy seed, salad oil, 4 eggs, vanilla, evaporated milk. Mix well. Bake at 350° for approximately 1 hour and 10 minutes in 9-inch tube pan. Cool in pan before removing. Dust with powdered sugar.

Good News
Before there were newspapers in Detroit, one of the acolytes at St. Anne's Church would stand at a platform by the church door and read the news of the week. There were many activities going on such as dances during the week and horse racing after dinner on Sunday afternoon.

Jewish Coffee Cake

1/2 pound butter
2 cups sugar
6 eggs
4 cups flour
1 teaspoon baking soda
1 1/2 teaspoons baking powder
1/2 teaspoon salt
1 pint sour cream
1 teaspoon vanilla

Mix and beat in order given, creaming shortening and sugar, adding eggs, then flour. Mix well. Add the sour cream and vanilla. Pour half of the batter into a greased 10-inch tube pan and then put 3/4 of the filling on this batter, put the rest of the batter in pan and top with the rest of the filling. Bake at 350° until done, about 45 minutes. Test for doneness.

Filling:
1 cup ground nuts
1/2 cup brown sugar
1/2 teaspoon cinnamon
Mix well. If you like more cinnamon, use more than 1/2 teaspoon.

Pound Cake – German

Cream 1 pound margarine and 1 pound confectioners' sugar. Add 6 eggs, one at a time, and 1 teaspoon vanilla. Add 3 cups sifted cake flour. Bake in greased and floured tube pan, 350° – 1 hour.

Landlord / Tenants

When Fort Pontchartrain was laid out, the lots for the houses were marked out at 25 feet square. With smaller lots Cadillac could collect more rents. Houses were made of small oak logs set perpendicular into the ground about four feet, chinked with grass or mud and roofed with bark.

Canada War Cake (Without Butter, Eggs or Milk) – 1940's

1 cup brown sugar
1 teaspoon cinnamon
1/4 cup shortening
1/2 teaspoon mace
1 cup boiling water
1/4 teaspoon clove
2 cups seeded raisins
1 teaspoon soda
1/2 teaspoon salt
2 cups flour

Mix sugar, shortening, water, raisins, and salt; boil five minutes; cool, and add spices, soda, and flour sifted together, beat well; pour into a greased, paper-lined pan, and bake in a slow oven 1 hour.

(The amount of soda in these recipes is based upon the use of old-fashioned jug molasses; canned molasses varies greatly in acidity and, especially when freshly opened, requires little or no soda. If canned molasses is used, therefore, baking powder should wholly or partly take the place of soda.)

Odd Name

The original name of Kelly Road was "Pumpkin Hook Road."

Apple Sauce Cake (Without Butter, Eggs or Milk)

1 cup unsweetened apple sauce
2 cups flour
1/4 cup melted shortening
1/4 teaspoon salt
1 cup sugar
1 teaspoon cinnamon
1 teaspoon soda
1/2 teaspoon nutmeg
1 cup raisins seeded and chopped
1/4 teaspoon clove

Mix in order given, sifting dry ingredients together, beat well, pour into a deep pan, and bake about one hour in a slow oven.

Orange-Glazed Poundcake – French

Contributed by Shirley Hartert

1 cup butter
2 1/2 cups sugar
6 large eggs
3 cups sifted flour
1/2 teaspoon salt
1/4 teaspoon baking soda
1 cup sour cream
1 teaspoon grated orange rind
1 teaspoon vanilla

Preheat the oven to 350°. Grease the bottom of a 10-inch tube pan, and line with wax paper. Beat the butter until it is soft and fluffy. Add the sugar and beat until blended. Add the eggs, one at a time, beating well after each addition. Sift the flour with the salt and the soda. Then, alternately, add the flour mixture and sour cream to the butter and sugar. Beat batter until smooth after each addition. Stir in the orange rind and the vanilla. Spoon the batter into the prepared cake pan. Bake for one hour and 30 to 40 minutes, or until a cake-tester comes out clean. Place the cake in the pan on a cake rack; let it stand for five minutes. Then pour the hot orange glaze over the entire cake. The glaze will be absorbed into it. Let the cake sit for one hour before removing it from the pan.

Orange Glaze

1 cup orange juice
3/4 cup sugar
1/4 cup butter
1 tablespoon lemon juice

Combine ingredients in a small saucepan. Bring to a boil, lower heat, simmer for 10 minutes. Pour over the cake.

Rich Devil's Food Cake – 1950

1/2 cup cocoa
2 cups sifted flour
2 cups sugar
1 teaspoon salt
1 1/4 teaspoons baking soda
3/4 teaspoon double-acting baking powder
1/8 teaspoon cinnamon (optional)
1/2 cup vegetable shortening, at room temperature
3/4 cup milk
1 teaspoon vanilla
4 eggs, beaten
1/2 cup milk

    Preheat oven to 350°. Grease and generously flour 2 9-inch layer cake pans. Combine cocoa, flour, sugar, salt, soda, baking powder, and cinnamon together in a sifter. Stir shortening just to soften; sift in cocoa mixture. Add the 3/4 cup milk and vanilla. Mix until flour is dampened. Beat for two minutes at medium speed, or 300 vigorous strokes by hand. Scrape bowl frequently. Add the eggs and 1/2 cup milk; blend thoroughly and beat one minute longer in mixer or 150 vigorous strokes by hand. Pour into prepared pans and bake for 30-35 minutes or until done. Cool and frost with Fluffy Cream Frosting, or as desired.

Fast Ride in Detroit - 1700 Style

A hardy breed of ponies were imported to Detroit from the St. Lawrence Valley. They were very fast and when farmers came into town they drove them at breakneck speeds through town yelling at pedestrians to move out of the way.

Mexican Fruitcake

2 cups flour
2 cups sugar
2 teaspoons baking soda
1 20-ounce can crushed pineapple (juice and all)
1 cup chopped walnuts
2 eggs

    Stir ingredients with wooden spoon. Pour in 9-inch x 13-inch (floured and greased) cake pan. Bake 350° 30-40 minutes.
    Frosting:
1 8-ounce Philadelphia Cream Cheese
1 stick oleo
1 teaspoon vanilla
2 cups powdered sugar
    Beat together.

Scripture Cake

Contributed by Shirley Hartert

4 1/2 cups I Kings 4:22
1 1/2 cups Judges 5:25 (last clause)
2 cups Jeremiah 6:20 (sugar)
2 cups I Samuel 30:12 (raisins)
2 cups Nahum 3:12
1 cup Numbers 17:8
2 tablespoonfuls I Samuel 14:25
Season to taste II Chronicles 9:9
Six Jeremiah 17:11
A pinch of Leviticus 2:13
1/2 cup Judges 4:19 (last clause)
2 teaspoonfuls Amos 4:5 (baking powder)
    Prepare according to any good fruit-cake recipe.

Chunky Apple Walnut Cake – American

1 1/2 cups vegetable oil
2 cups granulated sugar
3 eggs
2 cups unbleached, all-purpose flour, sifted
1/8 teaspoon ground cloves
1 1/4 teaspoons ground cinnamon
1/4 teaspoon ground mace
1 teaspoon baking soda
3/4 teaspoon salt
1 cup whole-wheat flour, sifted
1 1/4 cups shelled walnuts, coarsely chopped
3 1/4 cups coarse chunks of peeled and cored Rome Beauty apples
3 tablespoons Calvados or applejack (optional)
Apple Cider Glaze

    Preheat oven to 325°.
    In a large bowl, beat vegetable oil and sugar until thick and opaque. Add eggs, one at a time, beating well after each addition.
    Sift together all-purpose flour, cloves, cinnamon, mace, baking soda and salt, then stir in whole-wheat flour. Add to oil and egg mixture and mix until well blended.
    Add walnuts, apple chunks and Calvados all at once and stir batter until pieces are evenly distributed.
    Pour batter into a greased 10-inch round cake pan. Bake for 1 hour and 15 minutes, or until a cake tester inserted in the center comes out clean.
    Let cake rest for 10 minutes, then unmold.
    One 10-inch cake, 10 to 12 portions

Trying to figure out how to operate the 19th century coffee mill is Nancy Jean Thomas. This charming little lady celebrated her fifth birthday on July 24, 1951, the same day Detroit celebrated its 250th Birthday and also the day the Detroit Historical Museum was dedicated. A joint birthday party was celebrated for Nancy Jean and the Museum as she turned five years old, and the city 255 years old. She was named the "Princess of Detroit." Her mother-in-law is Margaret Link.

Millennium Cake – 2000

Sugar, 2 cups
Milk, scalded, 1 1/2 cups
Cake flour, 3 cups
Baking powder, 4 teaspoons
Salt, 3/4 teaspoon
Shortening, 3/4 cup
Eggs, 4

Caramelize 1 cup of the sugar by beating in a heavy pan over low heat until liquefied and golden brown, stirring constantly. Stir slowly into hot milk; cook over low heat until smooth, stirring constantly. Measure (there should be 1 3/4 cups; add more milk if necessary to make this amount); cool thoroughly. Sift flour; measure, add baking powder and salt; sift again. Cream shortening; add remaining 1 cup sugar gradually; cream together until light and fluffy. Add unbeaten eggs one at a time beating thoroughly after each addition. Add dry ingredients alternately with caramel milk, stirring only enough after each addition to blend thoroughly. Do not beat. Pour into 2 greased 9-inch layer pans or 3 greased 8-inch layer pans. Bake in a moderate oven (375°) 25 to 30 minutes. When cool put layers together and frost top and sides with caramel butter frosting.3 cups all purpose flour

Horse Race on the Detroit River - 1830

The French, British and early Americans were horse racing enthusiasts. Their race tracks were the frozen surfaces of the Detroit River, the River Rouge and the Grand Marais, (a swampy Grosse Pointe area). The first race track was built in 1836 near Jefferson and Connor.

Southern Delight Loaf Cake – 1920

3 cups all purpose flour
1 teaspoon baking powder, heaping
1 teaspoon salt
2 cups sugar
1 cup vegetable shortening
4 whole eggs
1 cup milk
1 teaspoon vanilla
1 teaspoon lemon flavoring

Mix all ingredients on number 3 speed on electric mixer for seven to eight minutes. If speeds are not numbered, use medium speed. Bake at 350° for one hour. After cake has cooled slightly, melt 1/2 stick of butter or margarine and brush on cake and sprinkle generously with confectioners' sugar. Makes 2 medium loaves.

Rennie's Italian Cream Cake

Contributed by Rennie Hughes

Cream 1 cup shortening and 2 cups sugar. Mix 5 egg yolks, one at a time. Mix 1 cup buttermilk, 1 teaspoon baking soda, 1 teaspoon vanilla, 1/2 teaspoon salt and 2 cups flour.
Mix well!
Stir in 2 cups coconut and 1 cup chopped nuts. Fold in 5 egg whites, stiffly beaten. Pour into 3 cake pans. Bake 30 minutes at 350°.

Frostings & Fillings

Butter-Cream Frosting – 1940

Here's a "not-so-sweet" frosting –
1/4 cup butter or margarine
3 tablespoons enriched flour
3/4 cup milk
1 1/2 teaspoons vanilla
1/2 cup butter or margarine
3/4 cup sugar

Melt 1/4 cup butter in saucepan over low heat. Blend in flour. Gradually stir in milk. Cook and stir till mixture thickens and comes to boiling. Cool to room temperature. Add vanilla. Cream remaining butter with sugar till fluffy; gradually add milk mixture, beating till frosting is fluffy and of spreading consistency, about 5 minutes. Frosts tops and sides of two 9-inch layers.

In hot weather, chill frosting before spreading on cake.

Whipped Cream Frosting

1 pint heavy cream, well chilled
1 cup confectioners' sugar
1 teaspoon vanilla

In a chilled bowl with cold beaters, beat cream until frothy. Gradually add sugar and vanilla. Continue beating until thick enough to spread. Use at once or refrigerate. Cakes served with whipped cream should be served within a few hours.

"Sanders'" Butter Cream Frosting

1/2 cup of Crisco
1/2 cup of butter
1 cup granulated sugar (better with powdered sugar)
1/2 cup of scalded milk
1 beaten egg white – stiff
Flavoring

Cream shortening and sugar, add beaten egg alternately with scalded milk. Beat until thick.

Cool scalded milk.

Rattlesnake Isle

Belle Isle was originally infested with rattlesnakes. Hogs were permitted to run wild until they had exterminated the snakes.

Butter Frosting

1/3 cup butter
4 cups sifted confectioners' sugar
1 egg yolk
1 1/2 teaspoons vanilla
About 2 tablespoons light cream

Cream butter; gradually add about half the sugar, blending well. Beat in egg yolk and vanilla. Gradually blend in remaining sugar. Add enough cream to make of spreading consistency. Frosts two 8- or 9-inch layers.

Orange Frosting: Add 2 teaspoons grated orange peel to butter in Butter Frosting. Stir in orange juice instead of cream to make of spreading consistency.

Mocha Frosting: Add 1/4 cup cocoa and 1/2 teaspoon instant coffee to butter in Butter Frosting.

Chocolate Butter Frosting: In Butter Frosting, add two 1-ounce squares unsweetened chocolate, melted and cooled, with the egg yolk and vanilla; blend well.

The Active Child - 1910

The child whose body and brain is most active, who is into everything, who gives the mother most trouble, as a rule, gives back more comfort when it is grown, for the childish mischief is merely a bubbling over of surplus energy that makes civilization and history in later years.

Easy Chocolate Frosting

1 1/4 cups sugar
6 tablespoons butter
6 tablespoons milk
1/2 cup chocolate chips

Mix sugar, butter and milk in a saucepan. Bring to a boil and cook 1 minute. Remove from heat and stir in chocolate chips. Beat until chips melt and cool before using. If too thick, add a few drops more milk. This frosts a 9 x 13 inch flat cake.

Quick Strawberry Preserve Frosting

Combine:
1 egg white
1/8 teaspoon salt
1 cup strawberry preserves

Beat till frosting stands in peaks.

Coconut Pecan Frosting

1 6-ounce can (2/3 cup) evaporated milk
2/3 cup sugar
1/4 cup butter or margarine
1 slightly beaten egg
Dash salt
1 teaspoon vanilla
1 3 1/2-ounce can (1 1/4 cups) flaked coconut
1/2 cup chopped pecans

In saucepan combine milk, sugar, butter, egg, and salt. Cook and stir over medium heat till mixture thickens and begins to boil, 12 to 15 minutes. Remove from heat. Add vanilla, coconut, and pecans. Cool thoroughly. Frosts two 8- or 9-inch layers.

Broiled Coconut Frosting

2/3 cup brown sugar
1/2 cup melted butter or margarine
1/4 cup light cream
1 3 1/2-ounce can (1 1/4 cups) flaked coconut
1/2 teaspoon vanilla

Thoroughly combine ingredients; spread over warm cake. Brown lightly in broiler. Frosts one 9-inch square cake.

Caramel Butter Frosting

Melt 1/2 cup butter; add 1 cup brown sugar. Bring to a boil; stir 1 minute or until slightly thick. Cool slightly. Add 1/4 cup milk; beat smooth. Beat in about 3 1/4 cups sifted confectioners' sugar till of spreading consistency. Frost tops and sides of two 8-inch layers.

Chocolate Glaze

In small saucepan combine one 6-ounce package (1 cup) semisweet chocolate pieces and one 6-ounce can (2/3 cup), evaporated milk. Cook and stir over low heat till blended and mixture comes to a boil. Lower heat; cook gently and stir 3 to 5 minutes till thick. Cool, stirring occasionally.

White Lines

Edward N. Hines is credited with the idea of using white lines to divide roadways. According to legend, Hines was inspired by watching a pail leak from the back of a milk wagon as it bounced along a road. 1900–30

Chocolate-Cream Cheese Fluff

2 3-ounce packages cream cheese
1 egg
1 teaspoon vanilla
Dash salt
5 cups sifted confectioners' sugar
3 1-ounce squares unsweetened chocolate, melted

Have cheese at room temperature. Blend in egg, vanilla, and salt; gradually beat in sugar. Blend in slightly cooled chocolate. Frosts tops and sides of two 9-inch layers.

Orange Icing

Juice of 1/2 orange
Grated rind of 1/4 orange
Confectioners' sugar

Mix sugar with orange juice and rind until icing is firm enough to spread.

Top Off

Fillings can be used to top off a plain cake when you are in a hurry. Then add a spoonful of whipped topping. Can also be spread between layers of a cake and the top, or to make a surprise filling inside a cupcake.

Crystallized Flowers and Fruits

Give flowers and fruits an elegant look. They can be used to decorate cakes, fruit platters, meats, dessert trays, etc. Here's how:

Separate two egg whites into a bowl and stir very gently to break up. Do not over-stir or whip the egg whites as this will create air bubbles With a delicate, clean paint brush, lightly paint the petal with the egg whites. Hold the painted petals by the stem over a clean plate. Gently sprinkle superfine sugar with your fingertips over the petals so the excess sugar falls back on the plate. Do not drip or drag the petals directly in the sugar or clumping will occur. Gently lay the petals or fruit on waxed paper and put in cool place to dry. Then refrigerate until needed, preferably the same day. When ready to use, gently arrange flowers or fruit as you like. Fruits also look lovely stacked in glass bowl as a centerpiece. Powdered egg whites are also available in baking stores for use.

Pineapple Filling

Sugar, 1/2 cup
Cornstarch, 2 tablespoons
Pineapple juice, 2/3 cup
Lemon juice, 1 tablespoon
Crushed pineapple, canned, well drained, 1/2 cup

Combine sugar and cornstarch; stir in pineapple juice drained from crushed pineapple. Cook until clear and thickened, stirring constantly.

Remove from heat; add lemon juice and pineapple; cool. Makes enough filling for a 2-layer cake.

Cream Filling

1/2 cup sugar
1/3 cup enriched flour
1/2 teaspoon salt
2 cups milk
2 slightly beaten eggs
1 teaspoon vanilla

Mix sugar, flour, salt; slowly stir in milk. Cook and stir over medium heat till mixture boils and thickens; cook 2 minutes longer. Stir a little of hot mixture into eggs; stir into remaining hot mixture; stirring constantly, bring just to boiling. Add vanilla; cover surface with waxed paper; cool. Makes 2 1/3 cups.

Butterscotch Filling: In above recipe, use 2/3 cup brown sugar in place of granulated sugar. Add 1/4 cup butter with vanilla.

Chocolate Filling: In Cream Filling, add 1 1/2 1-ounce squares unsweetened chocolate, cut up, with milk; increase sugar to 3/4 cup.

Lemon Filling

3/4 cup sugar
2 tablespoons cornstarch
Dash salt
1 slightly beaten egg yolk
3/4 cup water
3 tablespoons lemon juice
1 teaspoon grated lemon peel
1 tablespoon butter or margarine

Mix sugar, cornstarch, and salt; add egg yolk, water, and lemon juice; cook in double boiler till thick, stirring occasionally. Remove from heat and add lemon peel and butter. Cool. Makes 1 1/2 cups.

Orange Filling

3/4 cup sugar
2 tablespoons cornstarch
Dash salt
1 teaspoon grated orange peel
3/4 cup orange juice
1 tablespoon lemon juice
1 to 2 beaten egg yolks
1 tablespoon butter or margarine

Combine sugar, cornstarch, and salt. Add peel and juices gradually; blend well. Cook over medium heat, stirring constantly till thick an clear.

Add small amount of hot mixture to egg yolks, stir into remaining hot mixture. Cook about 2 minutes longer. Remove from heat; add butter. Cool. Makes about 1 cup.

French Custard Filling

1/3 cup sugar
1 tablespoon enriched flour
1 tablespoon cornstarch
1/4 teaspoon salt
1 1/2 cups milk
1 beaten egg yolk
1 teaspoon vanilla
1/2 cup heavy cream, whipped

Combine sugar, flour, cornstarch, and salt. Gradually stir in milk. Cook and stir till mixture thickens and boils; cook and stir 2 to 3 minutes longer. Stir a little of hot mixture into egg yolk; return to hot mixture. Stirring constantly, bring just to boiling. Add vanilla. Cover entire surface with clear plastic wrap or waxed paper; cool. Beat smooth; fold in whipped cream. Makes 2 cups.

Lemonade Filling

Melt 2 tablespoons butter or margarine; blend in 1/4 cup sugar, 2 tablespoons cornstarch and 1/4 teaspoon salt. Gradually stir in 3/4 cup water. Cook, stirring constantly, till mixture thickens.

Combine 2 beaten egg yolks with 1/3 cup frozen lemonade concentrate. Stir a small amount of hot mixture into yolk mixture; return to hot mixture and, stirring constantly, bring just to a boil. Tint with a few drops yellow food coloring, if desired. Cool. Makes about 1 cup.

Fruit Dessert

Fresh Fruit Flan

Contributed by Shirley Hartert

1 cup sifted flour
1 teaspoon baking powder
1 pinch salt
1/4 cup softened butter
1/2 cup sugar
2 large egg yolks, beaten
1/3 cup + 1 tablespoon milk
1/2 teaspoon vanilla
1/4 teaspoon lemon rind
Fluted flan cake pan
Fresh fruits like kiwi, bananas and strawberries
    Filling:
1 cup milk
1 cup Cool Whip
1 small package instant vanilla pudding
    Glaze:
Melted apple jelly

Grease and flour flan pan well. Cream butter until light and add sugar, beat in yolks until fluffy. Combine flour, baking powder, salt, and add alternately with milk until combined. Add vanilla and rind and pour into pan and bake for 20 minutes at 350°. Remove from pan a few minutes after taking from oven and cool. Prepare filling while baking cake by combining all ingredients. Fill the indented center of cake with filling when cake is cooled. Let set before arranging fruit on top. Once set, arrange cut fruit in an attractive pattern such as bananas diagonally sliced over most of 2/3 top. In the 1/3 remaining section make a ring of overlapping kiwi slices. Then cut 1 heart-shaped large strawberry lengthwise and arrange as a flower in center of kiwi slices. Glaze with warm jelly. Leftovers freeze well. A truly elegant and attractive dessert. Serves 6-8.

Detroit Drinks

Detroit is responsible for the invention of four well-known drinks: in 1875 a clerk at Sanders Confectionery accidentally concocted the Ice Cream Soda; in 1884, the Vernor's Company was established and along with this oak-aged beverage came the famed "Boston Cooler"; in the 1960's the Pontchartrain Wine Cellars introduced Cold Duck to its patrons; and the London Chop House concocted the Hummer.

Hot Fruit Compote

Contributed by Meg Humes

1 large can pineapple chunks
1 20-ounce jar of chunky applesauce
1 8 3/4 ounce can sliced peaches
1 8 3/4 ounce can apricot halves
1 11-ounce can mandarin oranges
1 large can cherry pie filling
1/2 cup brown sugar
1 teaspoon cinnamon
Spread applesauce in 10 x 13-inch pan.

Drain remaining fruit well. Layer fruit and top with pie filling. Mix brown sugar and cinnamon and sprinkle on top. Bake 300° 1 hour or 10 minutes in microwave or until it bubbles.

French Peach Cobbler

Contributed by Lorene Rever

1 cup all-purpose flour
1 teaspoon baking powder
1/8 teaspoon salt
1/2 cup sugar
1/4 cup butter
1 large egg
3 tablespoons milk
1/2 teaspoon vanilla
3 cups sliced peaches, sweetened to taste (about 1/2 cup sugar)

Sift dry ingredients. Cut in butter. Beat egg until thick and ivory colored; beat in milk and vanilla. Add to flour mixture and stir just until smooth.

Arrange peaches in 1 1/2 quart glass dish (8 x 8 Pyrex is fine). Spread batter evenly over peaches. Bake in preheated 350° oven, 35 to 40 minutes.

Goes well with ice cream or whipped cream.

Canned peaches are OK, too, just drain and use less sugar.

Peach Ambrosia Dessert

1 No. 2 can (2 1/2 cups) pineapple tidbits, drained
1 cup Tokay grape halves or seedless white grapes
1 cup orange sections (undrained)
1 cup tiny marshmallows
1 3 1/2-ounce can (1 1/4 cups) flaked coconut
1 cup dairy sour cream
1 No. 2 1/2 can (3 1/2 cups) peach halves

Combine first 5 ingredients, stir in sour cream. Chill several hours or overnight. Serve in chilled, drained peach halves on endive. Makes 6 to 7 servings.

English Trifle

Contributed by
Shirley Hartert

Prepare one recipe of Blanc Mange using 3 eggs. Cover and refrigerate for at least 3 hours.

Continue with the following:
2 packages (3 ounces each) ladyfingers
1/2 cup strawberry preserves
1 package (12 ounces) frozen strawberries, thawed
1 cup chilled whipping cream
2 tablespoons sugar
2 tablespoons toasted slivered almonds

Split ladyfingers lengthwise into halves; spread each half with strawberry preserves. Layer 1/4 of the ladyfingers cut sides up, half the strawberries and half the pudding in 2-quart serving bowl; repeat. Arrange remaining ladyfingers around edge of bowl in upright position with cut sides toward center. (It may be necessary to gently ease ladyfingers down into pudding about 1 inch so they remain upright.) Cover and refrigerate.

Beat whipping cream and 2 tablespoons sugar in chilled bowl until stiff; spread over dessert. Sprinkle with almonds.

Kennedy Square Fountain, 1970.

Apple Dumplings – American

2 cups flour
2 teaspoons baking powder
1/2 teaspoon sugar
1/2 teaspoons salt
4 level tablespoons lard or other shortening
Enough milk to make soft dough
2 cups sweetened (dried) apples

Sift dry ingredients together, spread with sweetened apples. Then roll up like cinnamon rolls and cut about an inch wide. Set rolled slices in pan containing the following ingredients:
3 cups water
3 cups sugar
2 tablespoons butter
1 teaspoon cinnamon
1 teaspoon nutmeg

Bake in moderate oven until brown.

Apple Squares

2 1/2 cups flour
1 teaspoon salt
1 cup shortening
1 egg yolk mixed with 2/3 cup milk
1 cup corn flakes
12 sliced apples
1 cup sugar
1 teaspoons cinnamon
1 egg white

Cut flour, salt and shortening. Add egg mixture. Roll out one-half crust, place on cookie sheet (cover edges). Sprinkle crushed corn flakes on crust. Place apple slices on top of corn flakes. Sprinkle apples with sugar and cinnamon. Top with crust; slit top. Beat egg white until frothy; brush on crust. Bake 375° 50 minutes. Glaze: 1 cup powdered sugar and 3/4 tablespoon milk. Drizzle on top of apples squares while still warm.

Cookies

Scotch Shortbread – 1910

Sift together:
3 cups sifted flour
1/2 cup sugar
Cut in:
1 cup butter thoroughly to form a soft dough.

Divide dough in half. Shape into two balls. Place on ungreased baking sheets and flatten into 7-inch circles, about 1/2 inch thick. Flute edges to form a scalloped edge.

Prick lines on circles with fork, outlining 12 wedges on each.

Bake in moderate oven (375°) 15 to 20 minutes until light golden brown. While warm cut along pricks but do not cut all the way through. Cool; break into wedges. Bake at 375° for 15 to 20 minutes. Makes 2 dozen.

Depression Cookies – 1930

3/4 cup shortening
1/3 cup white sugar
2 cups regular flour
1/2 cup finely cut nuts
Confectioners' sugar

Cream together shortening and sugar. Add nuts and flour. Mix well. Will be crumbly but keep mixing. Make into 1 inch balls. Bake 1 hour at 250°. Cool well. Coat with confectioners' sugar.

Russian Tea Cookies – 1930

1 cup soft butter
1/2 cup sifted confectioners' sugar
1 teaspoon vanilla
2 1/4 cups sifted flour
1/4 teaspoon salt
3/4 cup finely chopped nuts

Mix thoroughly the butter, sugar and vanilla in an electric mixer. Gradually add the sifted flour and salt. Then mix in nuts. Chill dough several hours or overnight. Roll dough into 1 inch balls and place about 2 inches apart on ungreased baking pan. Bake until set, but not too brown, at 400° for 10-12 minutes. While warm, roll cookies in confectioners' sugar; allow cookies to cool. After cooled, roll again in powdered sugar. Makes 5 dozen.

Pumpkin Drop Cookies – 1910

1 1/4 cups sugar
1/2 cup butter
2 eggs, beaten
1 1/2 cups cooked pumpkin
1/2 teaspoon salt
1/4 teaspoon ginger
1/2 teaspoon nutmeg
2 1/2 cups flour
4 teaspoons baking powder
1 teaspoon lemon extract
1 cup raisins
1 cup chopped nuts
1/2 teaspoon cinnamon

Cream butter and sugar. Add eggs, pumpkin, spices and salt. Sift flour and baking powder. Stir into sugar-butter mixture. Add lemon, raisins and nuts. Mix well. Drop by spoonfuls onto greased cookie sheet. Bake at 400° for approximately 15 minutes. Makes 3 dozen cookies.

The "Soft Soap Bath"

An early form of soap was like jelly – soft soap, made from simple home ingredients. A big kettle of water was swung over the fireplace to heat up the water. Then on Saturday afternoon mother would set up the laundry tub with warm water in the middle of the kitchen and send for the oldest boy. She would go down the line to the baby of the family. After they were in bed Mother and Dad were next – in the same water.

Russian Angel Wings – 1930

12 egg yolks
4 teaspoons sour cream
1/2 teaspoon salt
1 tablespoon vinegar
1 tablespoon whiskey
1 teaspoon vanilla
2 cups flour

Beat egg yolks until light; add sour cream, vinegar, vanilla and salt. Knead until smooth, roll out thin; cut into squares; slit center, draw one end of square through slit to make a bow. Fry in hot shortening until light brown. When cool, dust with confectioners' sugar.

Traffic Tower

In 1917, the first "crow's nest"-style square tower appeared on Woodward Avenue to help regulate traffic flow.

Ginger Creams – 1920

1/2 cup shortening
1 cup sugar
1 cup sweet or sour cream
2 eggs
1/2 cup molasses
Pinch salt
3 1/2 cups flour, sifted
2 teaspoons soda
1 teaspoon cinnamon
1 teaspoon ginger

Cream together shortening and sugar. Add cream, eggs, molasses and salt. Add dry ingredients. Add nuts and raisins if desired. Spread on bottom of pan quite thin. Bake in moderate oven (350°) oven 20-25 minutes, or till toothpick tests done. Ice with thin powdered sugar icing.

Chocolate Surprise – No Bake – 1940

Submitted by Gerry Johnson

1 package chocolate chips (dark)
3 ounce can Chinese chow mein noodles
1 cup Spanish peanuts

Slowly melt chips in pan. Add noodles and peanuts. Drop by teaspoon onto wax paper and cool.

Seven Layer Bars – 1940

1/4 cup butter or margarine
1 cup graham cracker crumbs
3 1/2 ounce can flaked coconut
6 ounce package chocolate chips
6 ounce package butterscotch morsels
15 ounce can sweetened condensed milk
1 cup chopped pecans

Melt butter in 9 x 13 baking pan. Add ingredients by layers, in order listed above. Bake at 325° for about 30 minutes. Cool in pan, then cut into squares.

Chocolate Fudge Cookie – No Bake

Submitted by Mary Ellen Busch

Mix:
2 cups sugar
1/3 cup cocoa
1/2 cup milk
1/4 cup butter

Bring to the boil. Remove from heat.
Add:
3 1/2 cups oatmeal
1 teaspoon salt
1/2 cup peanut butter
1/2 cup coconut or 1/2 cup nuts

Drop by teaspoonfuls on waxed paper. Cool.
If using peanuts, use unsalted kind.

This recipe was given to me by Shirley Anderson forty years ago when she was working as a 4H leader. This can be a safe project with children.

Pop Corn Balls

Contributed by Jackie Napolitan

Boil together a cupful each of molasses and brown sugar, and a tablespoon of vinegar. When it has cooked for twenty minutes put in two tablespoons of butter. Then cook until the candy reaches the brittle stage, and stir in enough pop corn, freshly made, to form a mixture as stiff as can be stirred. When it is cool enough to handle, form it into balls with buttered hands and then roll the balls in popped corn until the outside of the balls is coated with all the corn that will adhere to them. Wrap each ball in waxed paper.

Mexican Wedding Cookies – 1940

1 cup butter
1/2 cup confectioners' sugar
1/2 teaspoon salt
1 teaspoon almond extract or 2 teaspoons vanilla
2 cups all-purpose flour
1 1/2 cups ground Brazil nuts, pecans or filberts

Prepare several days ahead: With electric mixer at medium speed, beat butter with 1/2 cup confectionersí sugar until creamy. Mix in salt, extract, flour and nuts until well blended. Refrigerate dough until easy to handle. Heat oven to 350°. Shape dough into 1 inch balls and place on cookie sheet. Flatten dough balls with bottom of glass dipped in flour. Bake 10-15 minutes until lightly golden. Sprinkle with confectioners' sugar. Place on rack to cool. Can be stored well in covered container. Makes 5-6 dozen cookies.

Old Fashion Tea Cakes – African American

1/4 cup butter
3/4 cup sugar
1 egg
3 cups flour (sifted)
2 teaspoone baking powder
Pinch salt
3/4 cup orange juice
1 teaspoon vanilla extract
Grated rind of one orange

Cream butter and sugar, add egg, beat well, add juice and rind, mix thoroughly. Sift dry ingredeints together and add gradually until well mixed. Place on flour board, roll thin and cut in with large biscuit cutter. (Large-mouth glass will work.) Place on greased baking sheets – sprinkle with sugar. Bake in 350° oven until brown. Makes about 5 dozens.

Girls Helping Out

My sister and I used to butter up our fingers and help make the popcorn balls. It had to be done quickly before the candy hardened. They were crunchy to eat, a real treat; usually made at Halloween to take to school for a class treat. – Jackie Napolitan – 1950

Lemon Bars

Crust:
2 cups flour
1 cup butter
1/2 cup sugar
Filling:
4 eggs
1/4 cup lemon juice
Rind of 1 lemon
2 cups sugar
1/4 cup flour
1 teaspoon baking powder

Combine and mix flour, butter and sugar as you would for pie crust. Press into a 9 x 13 inch pan and bake at 350° for 15 minutes. Do not brown. Slightly beat eggs and lemon juice and rind. Sift sugar, flour and baking powder. Combine with egg mixture. Spread over top of pastry mixture. Return to oven and bake for 25 minutes longer. To serve: Cut into squares and sprinkle with powdered sugar.

Cadillac Hotel

The Cadillac began the innovative practice of offering fine orchestral music in the dining room, which soon gained in popularity in the area. Holiday dinners offered by the hotel included special music for the season. It was torn down to make way for the Book Cadillac in 1923.

Turn of the Century Sugar Cookies – 1900

Submitted by Meg Humes

1 cup granulated sugar
1 cup brown sugar, packed
3/4 cup shortening
3/4 cup margarine
1 teaspoon salt
3 whole eggs
1 teaspoon each: baking soda, vanilla, lemon extract, cinnamon and nutmeg
5 cups flour

Mix all ingredients together as per regular cookie recipe. Then put roll of dough between 2 sheets of wax paper. Roll out to 1/2 inch thickness. Cut with floured cookie cutters. Sprinkle with colored sugars before baking. Bake on lightly greased cookie sheets 10-12 minutes at 350°. Store in air tight container.

Refrigerator Fruit Slices – 1940

2 cups butter or margarine
2 cups sifted powdered sugar
2 unbeaten eggs
2 cups chopped nuts (walnuts or pecans)
1 pound candied cherries (red and green)
2 unbeaten eggs
1 teaspoon vanilla
4 1/2 cups sifted flour

In large mixing bowl cream butter and sugar. Add eggs and vanilla. Mix well. Add flour and mix well. Blend in nuts and candied cherries. Chill one hour. Divide dough into fourths. Shape into rolls (12 inches long). Chill overnight. Cut in 1/4 inch slices and place on ungreased cookie sheets. Bake in 325° oven 13-15 minutes until delicately brown on edges.

Pies

Hungarian Cottage Cheese Pie

Contributed by Rose Laus

Pie Crust:

1 cup flour dipped from sack

1 teaspoon salt

1/2 cup lard

4 tablespoons cold water

2 teaspoons butter

Sift flour with salt. Blend lard with flour, add water and mix thoroughly. Divide in two parts. Roll out part for lower crust. Roll the remaining part and dot with butter, fold, and roll again for upper crust.

Pie Filling:

2 cups cottage cheese

2 eggs

1/3 cup raisins

1 teaspoon cinnamon

1/2 cup sugar

1/4 teaspoon salt

Place cheese in dish; break in eggs without beating; add raisins, cinnamon, sugar and salt. Mix all together and put in pastry-lined pie plate. Put on upper crust and bake 30 to 45 minutes in moderate oven.

Hypocrite Pie – 1920

1 package (8 ounces) dried apples or peaches

2 1/2 cups water

3 or 4 tablespoons sugar

1 unbaked 9-inch pie shell

Custard

2 eggs, beaten

3/4 cup milk

3-4 tablespoons sugar

1/2 teaspoon vanilla

Cook dried fruit in water 15 minutes. Mash. During last few minutes stir in sugar, fruit. Preheat oven 425°. Put in fruit. Combine custard and pour over fruit. Bake 10 minutes. Then reduce oven to 350° and bake 40 minutes more.

First Steamboat

The steamboat WALK-IN-THE-WATER, the first to navigate the Great Lakes, was launched May 28, 1818. It was named in honor of the old Wyandotte chief who had been a "good Indian" about Detroit since the war. His Wyandotte name was "Mier" signifying "turtle" which the Indians tried to describe as an animal that walks in the water.

Quiche Lorraine – French

1 9-inch pie crust, unbaked

1 teaspoon butter

1/4 pound lean bacon

1 medium-sized onion, chopped

1/2 cup grated Swiss cheese

4 eggs, slightly beaten

1 cup milk

1 cup heavy cream

Pinch of grated nutmeg

1 teaspoon salt

1/4 teaspoon pepper

Line a 9-inch pie pan with crust. In a small saucepan, cook bacon until crisp. Remove. Add onions to pan and cook until lightly browned. Cool. Cover bottom of pie crust with onions and the crumbled bacon plus half the grated cheese. In mixing bowl, combine remaining cheese with the eggs, milk and cream, nutmeg, salt and pepper. Mix well and pour over bacon. Put in 450° (preheated) oven and bake for 15 minutes. Reduce heat to 350° and continue baking until mixture is set (about 20 minutes). Serve hot – take carefully out of the oven so that the quiche stays high.

Fresh Strawberry Pie

1 baked graham cracker curst

Line crust with fresh strawberries.

Cook until thick and clear:

1 cup sugar

1 cup water

2 tablespoons cornstarch

Then add: 4 tablespoons Strawberry Jell-O powder to hot mixture. Pour over strawberries. Cool and top with whipped cream or Cool Whip.

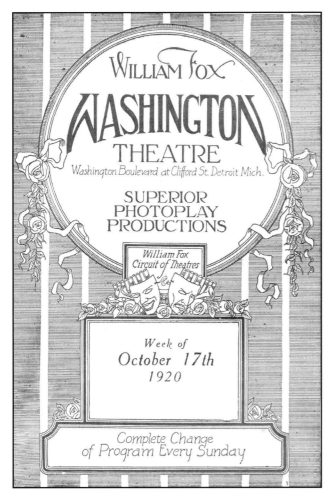

Funeral Pie – 1910

3 cups water
4 cups raisins
1 cup sugar
2 tablespoons cornstarch
1/2 teaspoon grated lemon peel
3 tablespoons lemon juice
1 teaspoon salt
1 tablespoon butter or margarine
Pastry for a 9-inch 2-crust pie

Heat the water to boiling; stir in the raisins. Cook until tender, about 5 minutes. Mix the sugar and cornstarch; stir into the raisins. Heat, stirring constantly, till boiling. Boil and stir for 1 minute. Remove from the heat. Add the remaining ingredients. Pour the filling into the pie shell; cover with the top crust and cut slits into it. Bake at 400° for 35-40 minutes. Cool.

Bertha's Prize-Winning Buttermilk Pie

1 cup sugar
1 stick melted butter
3 tablespoons flour
    Cream together.
    Add 3 eggs one at a time, mixing well after each.
    Add:
1/2 cup buttermilk
1 teaspoon vanilla
    Mix together. Pour into shells. Bake 400° for 10 minutes, 325° for 30 minutes.

Maple Pecan Pie

2 tablespoons butter or margarine
1/2 cup white sugar
2 eggs
2 tablespoons flour
1/4 teaspoon salt
1 teaspoon vanilla
1 1/4 cups maple syrup
1 cup pecans
1/4 teaspoon tarragon or cider vinegar
1 unbaked 8-inch pie shell

Cream the butter and sugar, add unbeaten eggs, and stir. Add flour, salt, vanilla, and syrup. Beat well. Add nut meats. Place in an unbaked crust. Bake about 45 minutes in a 375° oven, or until filling is set when pie is shaken gently.

Glazed Blueberry Pie

1 3-ounce package cream cheese
1 9-inch baked pastry shell
3 cups fresh blueberries
1 cup fresh blueberries
1/2 cup water
3/4 cup sugar
2 tablespoons cornstarch
2 tablespoons lemon juice

Soften cream cheese; spread in bottom of cooled pie shell. Fill with 3 cups berries.

Combine 1 cup blueberries and the water; bring just to boiling, reduce heat, and simmer 2 minutes. Strain, reserving juice (about 1/2 cup). Combine sugar and cornstarch; gradually add reserved juice. Cook, stirring constantly, till thick and clear. Cool slightly; add lemon juice. Pour over berries in pastry shell. Chill.

Serve with whipped cream.

Pumpkin Pie

Submitted by Lenora Stoetzer
From Commercial Milling Co., Detroit
(Henkel's Flour) – 1930
Serves 8
Piecrust:
1 cup sugar, white or brown
1 1/2 cups rich milk
1/2 cups pumpkin
1 teaspoon cinnamon
1/2 teaspoon nutmeg
1/2 teaspoon ginger
1/2 teaspoon salt
2 eggs

Make your own favorite pie crust for 9-inch pan. Line pan with pastry. Trim off edges, flute them if desired. Refrigerate. Pastry should be cold and firm to prevent sogginess.

Heat milk and sugar. Cool. Add pumpkin, in which spices have been mixed; add well-beaten eggs. Pour into unbaked shell. Bake 375°, 1 hour (knife-clean).

Whipped cream may be spread over top of pie just before serving.

Concord Grape Pie – 1950

4 cups Concord grapes

Slip pulp out of skins. Cook pulp to loosen then press through sieve to remove seeds. Combine pulp, skins and add:
3/4 cup sugar
1 1/2 tablespoons lemon juice
1 teaspoon rind (optional)
2 tablespoons tapioca

Let stand 15 minutes. Pour into pastry shell, cover with top crust. Bake 425° 40 minutes.

Bertha's Foolproof Pie Crusts

Submitted by Bertha Madison
4 cups flour
1 teaspoon salt
1 teaspoon baking powder
1 tablespoon sugar
1 3/4 cups shortening

Mix together with pastry cutter. Add together in cup:
1/2 cup ice water
1 tablespoon vinegar
1 egg

Add to above and mix together. Makes 5 pie crusts.

Quick Garden Quiche – 1930

Combine in 10-inch pie plate:
2 cups broccoli or cauliflower, cooked and chopped
1/2 cup onion, chopped
1/2 cup green pepper, chopped
1 cup cheddar cheese, shredded

Beat until smooth:
3 eggs
3/4 cup Bisquick
1/4 teaspoon pepper
1 1/2 cups milk
1 teaspoon salt

Pour over vegetables. Bake until golden brown, 35 minutes. Let stand 5 minutes before cutting.

To Make Hens Lay in Winter

Keep them warm; keep corn constantly by them, but do not feed it to them. Feed them with meat scraps when lard or tallow has been tried, or fresh meat. Some chop green pepper finely, or mix cayenne pepper with corn meal to feed them. Let them have frequent taste of green food, a little gravel and lime, or clam-shells.

Spinach Ricotta Tart – 1920

Prepare and bake 10 minutes: 1 pie shell.

Sautè: 1 small onion, minced

Cook, drain, and squeeze out moisture: 2 packages spinach (10-ounces each).

Combine in large bowl:
3 eggs, slightly beaten
1 carton ricotta (or cottage) cheese (15 ounces)
1 cup light cream or milk
1/2 cup Parmesan cheese
1/2 teaspoon salt
1/4 teaspoon nutmeg
Dash pepper

Add spinach and onion. Pour into baked pastry shell. Bake at 350° for 50 minutes or 'til browned and set. Serve with tossed salad and cornbread.

Old Time Travel

Since 1863, streetcars roamed the streets of the city, but the number of automobiles on the streets made boarding exciting and dangerous and the system came to an end in 1956.

Puddings

Russian Cream

1 cup sour cream
1 cup sweet cream (whipping)
1/2 cup sugar
1/2 cup cold water
1 teaspoon vanilla
1 package plain gelatine

Add sugar to sweet cream and heat until lukewarm. Soften gelatine in cold water. Add to cream and stir. Allow to cool and when it starts to thicken, add sour cream and beat until smooth. Pour into mold. Serve with a sauce of cranberries, raspberries or strawberries. Can also be layered with Jell-O.

Kwanzaa Bread Pudding

Pudding:
2 cups milk
1/2 cup sugar
2 eggs
2 tablespoons butter, melted
1 teaspoon imitation rum extract or 2 tablespoons rum
1 teaspoon vanilla
1/2 teaspoon nutmeg
3 1/2 cups soft bread cubes (about 6 slices)
1 (8 1/2 ounce) can sliced peaches in heavy syrup, cut up and undrained
1/2 cup raisins
Topping:
1 cup whipping cream
2 tablespoons confectionersí sugar
1/2 teaspoon vanilla
1/4 teaspoon nutmeg

Heat oven to 350°. Lightly butter 8- or 9-inch square baking dish. For pudding, whisk or stir vigorously milk, sugar, eggs, butter, rum extract, vanilla and nutmeg in large bowl. Add bread cubes, peaches and raisins, completely soaking the bread cubes. Let stand 5 minutes. Spread evenly in baking dish. Bake 50 to 55 minutes or until top is evenly browned and center is no longer moist.

Beat whipping cream in small bowl, gradually adding confectioners' sugar, then vanilla and nutmeg, until soft peaks form. Serve with warm or chilled pudding. Store pudding and topping tightly covered in refrigerator. Makes 6 servings.

Chocolate Mousse – French

1 teaspoon unflavored gelatin
1 tablespoon cold water
2 tablespoons boiling water
1/2 cup sugar
1/4 cup cocoa
1 cup chilled whipping cream
1 teaspoon vanilla extract

In custard cup sprinkle gelatin over cold water; let stand 1 minute to soften. Add boiling water; stir until gelatin is completely dissolved and mixture is clear. Cool slightly. In small mixer bowl stir together sugar and cocoa; add whipping cream and vanilla. Beat at medium speed, scraping bottom of bowl occasionally, until stiff peaks form; pour in gelatin mixture and beat until well blended. Spoon into serving dishes. Chill about 1/2 hour.

Four 1/2 cup servings.

Sanders

A new establishment. Mr. F. Sanders, late of Philadelphia, will this morning open a confectionery and ice cream establishment in the new store, No. 166 Woodward Avenue. He is a practical confectioner, has a handsome place and will devote his entire attention to customers.
Press release – Detroit Free Press, June 17, 1875.

Sirnaya – 1925
(Russian Cheese Pudding)

4 hardboiled eggs
1 pint cottage cheese3 eggs
1 cup sugar
1/4 cup butter
1/2 teaspoon vanilla
2 heaping tablespoons flour
1/2 cup raisins

Put the yolks of the hardboiled eggs and the cottage cheese through a fine sieve. Beat thoroughly. Cream the egg yolks and the sugar, add the butter, melted and beat well. Fold in the vanilla and the flour and add the raisins.Fold in the egg white, stiffly beaten. Pour into baking dish and bake in a slow oven for 35 to 45 minutes.

Blanc Mange – French

Cornstarch, 4 to 5 tablespoons
Sugar, 1/2 cup
Salt, 1/8 teaspoon
Milk, 3 cups
1 beaten egg, optional
Vanilla, 1 teaspoon

Mix cornstarch, sugar and salt in the top of a double boiler. Slowly stir in milk. Place over boiling water and stir constantly until thick and smooth. Cover and cook for 15 minutes longer, stirring occasionally. Add vanilla and turn into molds or dishes. Chill. Unmold and serve with chocolate sauce, any fruit sauce, or caramel or butterscotch sauce or surround with fresh or canned fruits or berries and top with whipped cream. Makes 4 to 6 servings.

A New Town

The town of Detroit was incorporated in 1802 and government was established under a board of trustees. The charter was granted by the territorial government at Chillicothe, Ohio.

Mocha Bavarian Cream

4 egg yolks
2 cups light cream
1 envelope unflavored gelatin
1/2 cup sugar
1/4 teaspoon salt
2 squares unsweetened chocolate
1 tablespoon instant coffee
1/4 cup brandy
1 cup heavy cream, whipped

Beat egg yolks and light cream until well mixed. Stir gelatin, sugar and salt together in the top of a double boiler. Stir in the yolk and cream mixture. Put the pan over boiling water and stir in the chocolate and coffee. Cook, stirring constantly, until the chocolate is melted and the coffee dissolved. Donít worry about the chocolate flecks. Remove top of double boiler from stove and add the brandy. Beat with a rotary beater until the chocolate is well blended. Chill, stirring occasionally, until the mixture begins to thicken and is about the consistency of cream sauce. (Allow at least an hour for this process.) Fold in the whipped cream. Ladle the mousse into a serving bowl or six individual dessert dishes. Chill for another two hours or until firm.

Creme de Menthe Pudding in a Cloud

Contributed by Shirley Hartert

1 package instant chocolate pudding
1 3/4 cups milk, cold
Large tub Cool Whip
1/4 cup creme de menthe (green)
A chocolate bar to shave curls to garnish

To prepare pudding. Pour 1 3/4 cups milk into a bowl, add pudding mix and creme de menthe. Whip until thickened – it can be done by hand! Chill until serving time. To serve: Line bottoms of champagne glasses with a generous amount of Cool Whip and fill to the top with pudding. Add a dollop of Cool Whip to the center and garnish with chocolate curls.

Serves 4-6

Frangelico Velvet

Contributed by Shirley Hartert

4 eggs, separated
1 tablespoon sugar
6 ounce package chocolate chips
1/4 cup boiling water
1/4 cup Frangelico Liqueur
Chopped hazelnuts or peanuts

Beat egg whites until foamy, gradually adding sugar until stiff, set aside. Whirl chocolate chips in blender until finely grated. Add boiling water and blend until chocolate melts. Add egg yolks and liqueur and blend until smooth. Gently fold chocolate mixture into whites. Spoon into dessert dishes or champagne glasses and chill until set. Garnish with chopped nuts around edges and one whole nut at the center. Note: serving in glasses makes a more stunning presentation!

Serves 6-8.

Jewish Kugel

1 package (8 ounces) wide egg noodles
2 eggs, slightly beaten
1 cup dairy sour cream
1 cup small-curd cottage cheese
1/2 cup golden raisins
1/2 cup sugar
1/2 teaspoon salt
1/4 teaspoon ground cinnamon
1/8 teaspoon ground nutmeg

Cook noodles as directed on package; drain. Mix remaining ingredients; toss with noodles. Pour into greased 2-quart casserole. Bake uncovered in 350˚ oven until golden brown, 40 to 50 minutes. 6-8 servings.

Beverages

Kahlua – 1990

4 cups water
4 cups sugar
4 tablespoons coffee (instant)
A fifth of vodka 100 proof
1 vanilla bean

Bring to a boil water, add sugar and coffee and stir to dissolve. Let cool and add vodka. Put into 3 bottles and break vanilla bean in 3 pieces, one for each bottle. Let sit at least 6 weeks.

Sangria

Bring to a boil 1 cup of water and 1 1/2 cups sugar. Cool for 5 minutes. Slice 1 orange, 1 lemon and 1 lime paper thin. Pour sugar syrup over fruit and chill at least 4 hours. When ready to serve, use 2 cups syrup to 2 bottles of club soda and 1 large bottle of Spanada wine or any sweet red wine you prefer.

If you are using a smaller bottle of wine, only use 1/2 cup syrup.

Behind Closed Doors
There were an estimated 25,000 "blind pigs" and "speak-easies" – illegal drinking establishments that operated in Detroit during the Prohibition years from 1918-1933.

French Punch

Peel of 1 lemon
1 cup sugar
1 cup water
1/2 cup Cointreau (or liquor of your choice)
Juice of 2 lemons
Juice of 2 oranges
2 bottles of Burgundy

Bring to a boil water, sugar and lemon peel. Boil for 3 minutes. Cool.

Add the orange and lemon juices to cooled syrup. Pass through a fine strainer. Refrigerate.

At serving time, pour syrup into the punch bowl, add liquor. Place a large block of ice at the center of the punch. Pour Burgundy over ice.

Makes 14 to 18 cups.

Turkish Coffee – 1910

2 cups water
2 tablespoons sugar
2 tablespoons pulverized coffee

Place the water in a copper pan made especially for the purpose or a small deep saucepan. Add the sugar. Boil 2 or 3 minutes; add the coffee, stir and boil until there is foam on the top. Remove from the fire and repeat the boiling process twice.

Serves 6. Always serve in small after-dinner coffee cups. Pour a small amount of coffee into each cup, then gradually add more until the cups are filled. Do not serve a spoon with Turkish coffee, for there is always a heavy sediment in the bottom of the cup, which must not be stirred.

Frosted Russian Chocolate

2 cups strong boiling black coffee
2 ounces chocolate
1/2 cup sugar
2 cups scalded milk
1 tablespoon cornstarch
Cinnamon
Nutmeg

Dissolve cornstarch in coffee and cook in double boiler with coffee, chocolate, spices and sugar. Then add the milk to this thickened liquid. Stir well and boil for one-quarter hour. Serve chilled with some cracked ice in tall glasses.

Two Christmas Punches – 1940

Contributed by Mary Ellen Busch

One
8 pints of cranberry juice
2 large gingerales or sparkling water
1/2 gallon of orange sherbet
Optional – gin or vodka

Two
1 12-ounce frozen orange juice diluted
1 12-ounce lemonade diluted
1 large can Hawaiian Punch (or 2 frozen – diluted)
1 quart dry gingerale, gin or vodka – or 1 quart of orange sherbet

Spiced Grape Juice

1 pint grape juice
1/2 teaspoon whole cloves
Juice of 1 orange and 1/2 or less of orange rind
2 2-inch piece sticks of cinnamon

Mix all ingredients together. Boil for 10 minutes. Cool and strain. Heat before serving.

Punch – Polish – 1920

4 oranges, peeled and sliced thin
1 lemon, peeled and sliced thin
1 cup sugar
2 quarts white wine
1 quart soda water
1 cup orange juice
Juice of 1 lemon

Sprinkle orange and lemon slices with sugar, cover and refrigerate overnight. When ready to serve, put orange and lemon slices with sugar into punch bowl. Add wine and juices. Add soda water last. You may also add ice cubes.

New Year's Eggnog – American

Eggs, 6
Sugar, 3/4 cup
Cream, chilled, 1 pint
Milk, chilled, 1pint
Whiskey or Cognac brandy, 1 pint
Jamaica rum, about 1/4 cup

Beat egg whites until stiff but not dry; gradually add sugar, beating continuously.

Beat egg yolks until thick and lemon-colored; fold in egg whites.

Gradually add chilled cream, milk, whiskey or Cognac brandy, stirring continuously; add rum to taste; stir until well combined.

Gently turn the thick mixture into a well-chilled punch bowl, or serve directly into small cups, using a ladle; sprinkle each serving with nutmeg. Allow at least 2 servings for each person. Makes about 20 servings.

Irish Coffee

1 jigger Irish whiskey (1 1/2 ounces)
1 to 2 teaspoons sugar
Hot strong coffee
Whipped cream

Pour whiskey into serving glass or mug. Add sugar, stir to dissolve. Fill glass with hot coffee. Top with whipped cream. Makes 1 serving.

Memories Lenora Stoelzer, Born 1909
During Prohibition days liquor was smuggled by night via boats from Windsor. I used to go to "blind pigs" to party – you know young people always know where to find liquor.

Apricot Slush

Boil and cool:
5 cups water
2 cups sugar
Boil and cool:
2 cups water with 3 teabags
Mix above with:
12 ounces frozen orange juice
12 ounces frozen lemonade
1/2 large can of pineapple juice
2 cups apricot brandy

Make ahead of time – store in freezer.

Mulled Cider

2 quarts cider
1/4 cup brown sugar
2 sticks cinnamon
1 teaspoon whole cloves
1/8 teaspoon ground ginger
1 orange, sliced (unpeeled)

Place in crock pot. Cover and heat on low setting for 2 to 5 hours.

Appetizers

"Snacks"
Canapè was an early term for appetizer.

Crab Meat Canapès – 1920's

1 cup crab meat
1 teaspoon Worcestershire sauce
1/4 teaspoon paprika
1/2 teaspoon salt
1 tablespoon lemon juice
1/4 teaspoon mustard
1/2 teaspoon horseradish

Chop crab meat, mix well with seasonings, and spread on thin rounds of untoasted brown bread. Garnish with small cube of lemon.

Savory Oyster Crackers

1/2 bottle popcorn oil
1 package dry ranch dressing
2 teaspoons (rounded) dill seed
Box of oyster crackers

Mix together well and stir gently into box of oyster crackers. Let marinate for 24 hours. Mix a few times before serving.

War & Sanders

Sanders business grew and many new stores opened around Detroit. During the WW II Sanders offered "Ready Cooked Food" for women to take home since many of them found themselves working with not enough time to cook. Advertised in their January 26, 1946, menu you could take home a Veal Croquette with Mushroom Gravy dinner for 15 cents each.

Cantaloupe Cocktail

2 cups cantaloupe
Juice of 1/2 lemon
1/3 cup preserved ginger
2 tablespoons powdered sugar

Cut melon in small cubes, or in balls (using a potato cutter). Add chopped ginger, lemon juice, and sugar, and serve very cold.

Club Canapès – 1920's

Mix devilled ham with a little grated cheese; spread on thin rounds of brown bread, and mark into quarters with finely chopped pickle. Chop fine the white of a hard-cooked egg, and cover two opposite quarters; press the yolk through a sieve, and cover the remaining quarters.

Middle Eastern Hummus

1 can (15 ounces) garbanzo beans (chickpeas), drained (reserve liquid)
1/2 cup sesame seed
1 clove garlic, cut into halves
3 tablespoons lemon juice
1 teaspoon salt
Snipped parsley
Pita bread, crackers or raw vegetable sticks

Place reserved bean liquid, the sesame seed and garlic in blender container. Cover and blend on high speed until mixed. Add beans, lemon juice and salt; cover and blend on high speed, scraping sides of blender if necessary, until of uniform consistency. Garnish with parsley. Serve as spread or dip with wedges of pita bread. Makes 2 cups.

Dried-Beef Dip

1 (8 ounce) cream cheese
1 large jar Armour dried beef, cut into small pieces
1 1/2 cups sour cream
1 medium diced onion
1 large diced green pepper

Mix above ingredients and use Triscuits or salty crackers to dip. Or serve with veggies.

Water Chestnuts

2 cans whole water chestnuts
1 pound bacon, sliced into thirds
Sauce:
3/4 cup ketchup
3/4 cup mayonnaise
1 1/2 cups brown sugar

Wrap bacon around water chestnuts and hold together with toothpicks. Bake 30 minutes at 400°. Drain grease. Pour sauce over chestnuts and bake 30 minutes more.

Nuts and Bolts

1 tablespoon bacon fat
1 pound butter
1/4 cup Worcestershire sauce
2 teaspoons onion powder
2 teaspoons garlic powder
2 teaspoons celery powder
Melt above and pour over:
10 1/2 ounce box Cheerios
12 ounce box Rice or Wheat Chex
5 ounce Pretzel sticks (broken in small pieces)
1 pound mixed nuts

Place all in large roaster and cook 2 1/2 hours at 225°. Stir every 15 minutes. Place in large tin and seal tightly. Warm again before serving.

No Money for Fred

After the store was rented and furnished and the great copper kettles in place in the candy shop, Fred Sanders found that there was not a penny left to buy sugar – the most important ingredient. Mr. Mr. W. H. Edgar, a Detroit merchant, was willing to loan him a barrel of sugar so he could open his store.

Taco Dip – Mexican

2 cans refried beans
1 8 ounce package cream cheese (not fat free)
1 package taco seasoning
2 cloves garlic
1 small bunch green onion
2 cups shredded Mexican cheese
1 medium tomato
1 8 ounce sour cream
1 package corn chips

Spread beans in the bottom of the deep dish baker or square baking dish. Mix cream cheese, garlic and seasonings. Spread over beans. Sprinkle with onions and then cheddar cheese. Bake 20-25 minutes at 350° or microwave 8-10 minutes. Garnish with tomatoes and sour cream.

Hanky-Pankies

1 pound ground beef
1 pound pork sausage
1 pound Velveeta cheese
1 teaspoon ground oregano
1 tablespoon Worcestershire sauce
1 tablespoon catsup
1/2 teaspoon garlic powder
2 loaves party rye bread

Brown ground beef and sausage. Drain off fat. Add Velveeta and seasonings. Stir until well-mixed. Spread on rye bread slices. Freeze. When ready to eat, broil 3 to 4 minutes or bake about 10 minutes.

Puppy Chow

1/2 cup peanut butter
1/4 cup margarine
1 cup chocolate chips
7-8 cups Rice Chex
2 cups powdered sugar

Melt peanut butter, margarine and chocolate chips. Pour over Rice Chex and stir well.

Place in paper bag with powdered sugar and shake well.

Aghavni's Navy Bean Plaki (appetizer) – Armenian

Contributed by Agnes Nigoghosian

2 pounds navy beans cooked, save 4 cups liquid
1 cup olive oil
1 cup vegetable oil
6 cups white onions, chopped
3 cups carrots, chopped
3 cups celery, chopped
3 cloves garlic, chopped
1 cup fresh parsley, chopped
1 tablespoon each chopped: dill, basil
1 tablespoon salt
Pinch black pepper
Pinch cayenne pepper
1 6-ounce can tomato paste
1 12-ounce can tomato sauce

Heat olive and Mazola oils and sautè onions for about 5 minutes. Add garlic, salt, pepper and herbs. Add tomato sauces. Mix in chopped vegetables. Simmer for 15 minutes. Add navy beans and 2 cups of liquid. Cook slow one hour. Add liquid if necessary. Serve warm or cold. Freezes well. Add more liquid to make bean soup.

Soup

Vichyssoise – 1910 – American

4 leeks, sliced (no tops)
1 medium onion, sliced
1/4 cup butter or margarine
5 medium potatoes, peeled and thinly sliced
4 cups chicken broth
2 cups milk
2 cups light cream
1 cup whipping cream
Snipped chives

In saucepan cook leeks and onion in butter till tender but not brown; add potatoes, broth, and 1 tablespoon salt. Cook for 35 to 40 minutes. Rub through fine sieve. Return to heat; add milk and light cream. Season to taste. Bring to boiling. Cool; rub through very fine sieve. Stir in whipping cream. Chill thoroughly before serving. Garnish with chives. Makes 8 servings.

Depression Memories
Known as the decade of hard times, the 1930's was marked by the drama and chaos of the worst economic depression in history. Every family knew what it was to live on bread and cheese gravy.

Lentil Soup – Slovak

1/2 pound lentils
1/2 cup chopped celery
1 large onion, chopped
2 tablespoons flour
2 diced carrots
Finely chopped parsley
Salt and pepper to taste
1/2 cup strained tomatoes
7 cups cold water

Cover lentils with plenty of cold water and let stand overnight. Drain and add 7 cups cold water, cook slowly about 2 hours. Saute onion and celery in hot fat and add the flour. The carrots should be added to the lentils while cooking. The flour mixture is blended into the lentils and then add the seasoning and the parsley. Simmer about 15 minutes and serve hot.

Wedding Soup – Turkish

1 stewing chicken (about 5 pounds), cut up
1 beef soup bone (1 to 2 pounds)
1/2 pound beef marrow bones
1 carrot, cut into 2-inch pieces
1 onion
1 stalk celery, cut into 2-inch pieces
Salt and pepper
3 egg yolks
1/4 cup lemon juice
1 tablespoon butter or margarine, melted
1 teaspoon paprika
1 teaspoon cayenne pepper

Place chicken, soup bone, marrow bones, carrot, onion and celery in Dutch oven. Add water to cover. Heat to boiling. Reduce heat. Simmer uncovered over medium heat, removing film occasionally, until chicken is tender, about 2 1/2 hours. Let chicken cool 30 minutes in broth; discard vegetables. Remove chicken and beef from bones; tear into small pieces. Cover and refrigerate the broth and the meat separately.

Skim fat from top of the broth. Heat broth in Dutch oven over medium heat; season to taste with salt, and pepper. Beat egg yolks and lemon juice until foamy in small bowl; add 1 cup of hot broth gradually to egg mixture. Add egg mixture to remaining broth gradually; stir in chicken and beef. Heat but do not boil. Pour soup into tureen or individual bowls. Mix butter, paprika and cayenne pepper; spoon over soup. 6 servings.

French Onion Soup

Butter, 3 tablespoons
Onion, sliced paper thin, 2 cups
Bouillon, 4 1/2 cups
Salt and pepper
Worcestershire sauce
French bread
Parmesan cheese or other finely grated cheese

Heat butter; add onions; simmer about 10 minutes or until soft and lightly browned.

Add bouillon; bring to a boil, simmer 45 minutes.

Season to taste with salt, pepper and Worcestershire sauce.

Pour the hot soup into earthenware marmites or soup plates.

On top of each serving float a slice of sautèed French bread; sprinkle with grated cheese and pass additional cheese. Makes about 6 servings.

Corn & Wild Rice Soup with Sausage

12 1/2 cups (or more) canned low-salt chicken broth
1 1/4 cups wild rice (about 7 1/2 ounces)
6 1/4 cups frozen corn kernels (about 2 1/2 pounds thawed)
2 tablespoons vegetable oil
10 ounces fully cooked smoked sausage (such as kielbasa), cut into 1/2-inch cubes
3 carrots, peeled, diced
2 medium onions, chopped
1 1/2 cups half and half
    Chopped fresh chives or parsley for garnish

    Bring 5 cups broth to simmer in heavy medium saucepan over medium heat. Add wild rice and simmer until rice is almost tender, stirring occasionally, about 40 minutes.

    Meanwhile, blend 3 3/4 cups corn and 1 1/2 cups chicken broth in processor until thick, almost smooth puree forms. Heat vegetable oil in heavy large Dutch oven over medium-high heat. Add sausage and sautè until beginning to brown, about 5 minutes. Add carrots and onions and stir 3 minutes. Add remaining 6 cups chicken broth and bring soup to simmer. Reduce heat to low and simmer soup 15 minutes.

    Add cooked wild rice, corn puree and remaining 2 1/2 cups corn kernels to soup. Cook until wild rice is very tender and flavors blend, about 15 minutes longer. Mix in half and half. Thin soup with more chicken broth, if desired. Season soup to taste with salt and pepper.

Hearty Soup Mix

14 ounces split peas
12 ounces pearl barley
14 ounces small macaroni
12 ounces lentils
1 1/2 cups brown rice
    Combine and store in glass jar.
    To make soup from mix, combine:
6 cups water
1 1/3 cups soup mix
1 1/2 teaspoons salt
    Simmer 1 1/2 hours. Can then add any variety of vegetables and cooked meat if desired. Simmer 1/2 hour until vegetables are tender.

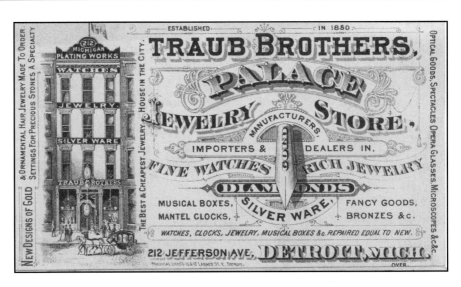

Ham Chowder

Ham shank or picnic shoulder bone, 1
Onion, small, chopped, 1
Celery, 1 stalk
Cold water, 1 quart
Potatoes, sliced or diced, 1 quart
Parsley, chopped, 3 tablespoons
Butter, 3 tablespoons
Flour, 3 tablespoons
Milk, 1 quart
Salt and pepper
Stale bread, 2 slices
Ham drippings, 1/4 cup
    Place ham bone, onion, celery and water in kettle; cover and bring slowly to a boil; simmer gently about 1 hour.

    Remove bone, trim off meat; dice meat and add to stock. Add potatoes and half the parsley; boil gently about 20 minutes or until potatoes are tender.

    Make a white sauce of butter, flour and milk; add to stock and season to taste.

    Cut bread into small cubes and sautè in hot ham drippings until crisp.

    Garnish each serving of hot soup with a few bread cubes and some of the remaining parsley. Makes about 6 servings.

Independence Day 1905

On this day the Russell House offered a complete breakfast, luncheon and dinner menu program to celebrate July 4th. The musical selections were also listed in the program which was printed in the Russell House print shop.

Polish Dill Pickle Soup

This soup tastes best when made from the stock in which fresh Polish sausage (kielbasa) has been cooked. However, it is also very good started with 4 slices of diced fried bacon. Use a 4 quart or larger saucepan with a tight-fitting cover. Makes 6 to 8 servings.

Use 11 cups of cold water, bring to a boil a double link of fresh (unsmoked) kielbasa. Skim foam off and simmer, covered, for 1 hour. Remove sausage for use in other recipes.

While kielbasa is cooking, soak 6 large dried mushrooms in 1 cup cold water, then chop mushrooms finely, reserving mushrooms and liquid for later use in soup. Empty 1 large container (16 ounces) sour cream into medium bowl; leave at room temperature. Add to soup stock the following very finely diced vegetables (about 1/4 inch cubes):

3 medium potatoes
3 carrots
1 medium onion
2 ribs celery with chopped green tops
The mushrooms and liquid
1 large dill pickle, chopped
1 bay leaf
1 teaspoon each Lawry's seasoned salt and garlic salt
1/4 teaspoon seasoned pepper
1 tablespoon dried parsley
1 teaspoon Worcestershire sauce
1/2 cup quick-cooking barley

Bring the whole mixture to a boil. Lower heat, cover tightly and simmer for 1/2 hour. Then remove bay leaf, add 1 cup of dill pickle from jar, cover and simmer about 15 or 20 minutes. To the bowl of sour cream, add 1 serving spoonful at a time of the hot soup liquid until bowl is almost full. Add sour cream mixture to soup pot, stir and heat thoroughly, almost to boiling. Cover and leave on low heat.

This soup tastes better after it stands for awhile, even tastes better reheated.

Canadian Cheese Soup

Cook together in butter for 5 minutes:
1/2 cup diced celery
1/2 cup diced carrots
1 teaspoon minced onion
Blend in 3 tablespoons flour and 1/2 teaspoon salt. Add 2 cups chicken broth and cook slowly until the vegetables are cooked tender. Add 2 cups milk and 1/2 pound diced sharp American cheese. Just before serving, add 1/2 cup beer. Top with salted whipped cream and parsley.

About 4 servings.

Cold Yogurt/Cucumber Soup – Middle East

2 medium cucumbers
1 1/2 cups unflavored yogurt
1/2 teaspoon salt
1/4 teaspoon dried mint flakes
1/8 teaspoon white pepper

Cut 7 thin slices from cucumber; reserve. Cut remaining cucumber into 3/4-inch chunks. Place half the cucumber chunks and 1/4 cup of the yogurt in blender container. Cover and blend on high speed until smooth.

Add remaining cucumber, the salt, mint and white pepper. Cover and blend until smooth. Add remaining yogurt; cover and blend on low speed until smooth. Cover and refrigerate at least 1 hour. Garnish with reserved cucumber slices. 7 servings.

Mushroom and Potato Soup – Russian

1 pound fresh mushrooms, cut up and sauteed in 2 tablespoons oil
1 large onion, diced
2 large potatoes, peeled and diced
3 tablespoons oil or oleo
1 bay leaf
Salt and pepper
1 large bunch scallions

Into 2 quarts water, put salt and onion and bring to a boil. Add potatoes, bay leaf, black pepper and simmer 1/2 hour. Add mushrooms and chopped scallions. Cover and simmer 3/4 hour.

Basque Vegetable Soup

Soak 1 pound white pea beans and 1/2 pound dried peas overnight in water (unless they are the quick-cooking type). Next day, put them in a deep kettle with a meaty ham knuckle, 2 bay leaves, an onion stuck with 2 cloves, 3 quarts water. Cook 1 hour, taste for salt (if ham is salty, it will not be needed). Cook until beans are tender. Drain, reserving liquid. In bean liquid cook 6 potatoes, cut small, 4 slices carrots, 4 diced turnips, 5 cut-up leeks, 6 chopped garlic cloves, 1 teaspoon thyme, 1 bay leaf. When tender, add 1 small shredded cabbage, the beans and peas, meat from ham bone, 12 sausages. Cook until cabbage is just tender and soup very thick. Serve in bowls, sprinkle with grated Swiss cheese, with hot French bread. Serves 6 to 8.

1930's Depression Days
For the girls, they were right at their mother's side observing and learning her ingenuity as a way of life. As a result of the constant need the women became near magicians in their large kitchens, outperforming in putting meals on the table. They improvised warm clothing for the family to sustain them through bitter cold winters where children often walked miles to school.

Egg Drop Soup – Chinese

In a saucepan slowly blend two 13 3/4 ounce cans chicken broth into 1 tablespoon cornstarch. Cook and stir till slightly thickened. Slowly pour in 1 well-beaten egg; stir once gently. Remove from heat. Pour into soup bowls and garnish with 2 tablespoons sliced green onion with tops. Serves 4.

Cream of Broccoli Soup

1 head broccoli, broken in pieces
8 ounces mushrooms
8 ounces butter
1 cup flour
1 quart chicken stock or 4 bouillon cubes in quart of water
1 quart Half and Half
1 teaspoon salt
1/4 teaspoon white pepper

Steam broccoli till tender in 1/2 cup water. Do not drain. Melt butter. Blend in flour. Cook 2 to 4 minutes. Add the rest of the ingredients.

Stain Removal
Don't let spilled wine spoil your prettiest tablecloth. While the stain is still wet, cover it with a mound of ordinary table salt; when dry just brush away. The salt will absorb the wine so completely you won't even have to wash the cloth.

Shaving cream is one of the most useful upholstery cleaners.

To remove water rings and stains from inside small glass or crystal vases, dampen the inside and add any toilet bowl clearer. Let stand 10 minutes. Rinse thoroughly.

Berry Soup

Blueberries, raspberries or other berries, 1 pint
Water, 3 1/2 cups
Apple juice, 2 cups
Sugar to taste
Nutmeg, 1/8 teaspoon
Salt, 1/4 teaspoon
Cornstarch, 2 tablespoons
Lemon juice, 1/4 cup

Combine berries and water in saucepan; bring to boil; cover and cook 20 minutes or until soft; press through sieve.

Add apple juice, salt, nutmeg and sugar to taste; add cornstarch dissolved in 2 tablespoons cold water. Cook until clear, stirring constantly. Chill and add lemon juice.

Top each serving with a puff of whipped cream if desired; sprinkle with chopped mint. Makes about 6 servings.

Berry Cream Coup: After chilling add 1 cup thick sour cream.

Fruit Juice Soup

Water, 1 1/2 cups
Sugar, 1/2 cup
Cinnamon, 1-inch stick
Cranberry juice, 1 1/2 cups
Fruit juices, 3 cups (plum, peach, pineapple, etc.)
Granulated tapioca, 3 tablespoons

Combine water, sugar and cinnamon in saucepan; bring to boil then simmer five minutes.

Add cranberry juice and sweet fruit juices; bring to boil. Gradually add tapioca, stirring constantly; simmer five minutes, stirring occasionally. Chill thoroughly.

Garnish each serving with a thin slice of lemon, if desired. Makes about 6 servings.

Michigan Chowder – 1950

1/4 pound salt pork (cubed)
2 onions, sliced, cooked with pork until yellow
12 ears of corn, cut from the cob
6 medium tomatoes (peeled)

Add a little water, simmer for 2 hours. About 1/2 hour before serving, add:
4 medium potatoes, sliced
1 tablespoon butter
1 1/2 pints milk (depends on the amount of liquid you like)
Salt to taste

Just before serving, add: 12 large soda crackers rolled fine. Serves 6-8.

From (Mrs. Frank B.) Mary Kirk Woodford

Pasta

Linguine with Tomatoes and Basil

Contributed by Rennie Hughes

4 ripe large tomatoes, cut into 1/2-inch cubes
1 pound Brie cheese, rind removed, torn into irregular pieces
1 cup cleaned fresh basil leaves, cut into strips
3 garlic cloves, peeled and finely minced
1 cup plus 1 tablespoon best-quality olive oil
2 1/2 teaspoons salt
1/2 teaspoon freshly ground black pepper
1 1/2 pounds linguine
Freshly grated imported Parmesan cheese (optional)

Combine tomatoes, Brie, basil, garlic, 1 cup olive oil, 1/2 teaspoon salt and the pepper in a large serving bowl. Prepare at least 2 hours before serving and set aside, covered, at room temperature.

Bring 6 quarts water to a boil in a large pot. Add 1 tablespoon olive oil and remaining salt. Add the linguine and boil until tender but still firm, 8 to 10 minutes.

Drain pasta and immediately toss with the tomato sauce. Serve at once, passing the peppermill, and grated Parmesan cheese if you like. 4 to 6 portions.

Lasagna

1 pound ground beef
4 medium tomatoes, cooked
6 ounce can tomato paste
1 envelope spaghetti sauce mix
1/4 teaspoon garlic salt
10 lasagna noodles
6 ounces Mozzarella cheese
1 cup cottage cheese
1/2 cup Parmesan cheese

Preheat oven to 350°. Brown meat and add next 4 ingredients, cover and simmer 40 minutes, stirring occasionally. Cook noodles in boiling salted water until tender (12 minutes) and drain. In ungreased 11 x 8 inch pan put 4 noodles on bottom, cover with 1/3 meat sauce, 1/3 cup of Mozzarella and 1/2 cup cottage cheese, 3 noodles, repeat layers. With sauce on top. Top with Parmesan cheese. Bake at 350° for 25 to 30 minutes. Let stand 15 minutes, then serve.

Creamy Pasta Sauce with Fresh Herbs

1 1/2 cups heavy cream
4 tablespoons sweet butter
1/2 teaspoon salt
1/8 teaspoon grated nutmeg
Pinch of cayenne pepper
1/4 cup grated imported Parmesan cheese
1 cup finely chopped mixed fresh herbs (our favorite combination – basil, mint, watercress, Italian parsley and chives)

Combine cream, butter, salt, nutmeg and cayenne in a heavy saucepan and simmer for 15 minutes, or until sauce is slightly reduced and thickened.

Whisk in Parmesan and fresh herbs and simmer for another 5 minutes. Taste and correct seasoning. Serve immediately.

2 cups sauce, enough for 1 pound of angel's-hair pasta, 6 or more portions as a first course.

Entrance to Woodmere Cemetery, Detroit, Mich.

Fettucine Alfredo – Italian

Contributed by Rennie Hughes
Serves 8
1/2 cup butter, softened
1/4 cup whipped cream, room temperature
1/2 cup grated Parmesan
16 ounces fettuccine (medium)
1 6 ounce can whole mushrooms, drained (about 1 cup)

Cream butter. Beat in whipped cream a little at a time, till well combined. Beat in Parmesan. Set aside at room temperature. Cook fettucine in boiling salted water 10-12 minutes. Stir, drain. Transfer pasta to warm chafing dish. Add cream mix and toss till well coated. Season with a little salt, fresh ground pepper. Stir in mushrooms. Serve pronto.

Baked Macaroni and Cheese – African American

Macaroni, 1 package (8 to 9 ounces)
Thin white sauce, 3 cups
Cheese, grated, 1/4 to 1/2 pound
Onion, grated, 1 tablespoon
Dry mustard, 1/2 teaspoon
Worcestershire sauce, 1 teaspoon (optional)
Buttered crumbs, 1/2 cup

Cook macaroni; drain and rinse.

Combine hot white sauce, grated cheese, onion, mustard and Worcestershire sauce, reserving a little of the grated cheese for topping. Add macaroni. Place in a greased casserole. Top with buttered crumbs, remaining cheese and a dash of paprika.

Bake in a moderate oven (375°) about 25 minutes or until browned. Makes 6 to 8 servings.

Spatzen or Spaetzle – German Egg Noodles

Contributed by Mary Ellen Busch
Beat two eggs in bowl. Combine and add:
1 1/2 cups flour
1/2 cup water
1/2 teaspoon salt
1/4 teaspoon baking powder

Mix very well. Drop dough in tiny pieces into boiling salted water or chicken broth.

I prefer to cut dough in strips off edge of bowl.

Pasta Primavera

1 teaspoon olive oil
1 cup diagonally sliced asparagus
1/2 cup sliced onion (1 small onion)
1 cup sliced fresh mushrooms (about 4 mushrooms)
3/4 cup diced cooked ham
1/2 cup frozen peas, thawed
1/4 cup chicken or vegetable broth
1/4 cup light sour cream
About 2 tablespoons pesto (homemade or store-bought)
1 tablespoon finely chopped fresh parsley (preferably flat leaf)
Salt and black pepper, to taste
6 ounces linguine or other pasta
Grated Parmesan cheese (optional)

Heat oil in a large nonstick skillet over medium-high heat. Add asparagus and onion; cook, stirring, 2 minutes. Add mushrooms; cook, stirring, 1 to 2 minutes. Stir in ham and peas; cook, stirring, 1 minute, or until vegetables are tender-crisp. Add broth, sour cream, pesto, parsley, salt and pepper; mix well. Cook and stir until thoroughly heated.

Meanwhile, cook linguine according to package directions. Drain well.

Put linguine in a warmed serving dish. Spoon sauce over pasta. Sprinkle Parmesan cheese on top, if desired. Serve immediately. 2-3 servings.

Vinegar, King of the Cupboard

Since Biblical times women have known what a touch of vinegar would do for food. Caesar's legions glubbed drinking water laced with it. Uses range from preservatives to deodorants in a room or a fishy fry pan.

Vinegar keeps apples from turning brown, it is a meat tenderizer, and a dash of it in bread and rolls make them delightfully crusty. A tablespoon full used in place of cream of tartar in meringue makes it beautifully high. And yes! Grandmother stirred up a vinegar pie that was equal to any lemon concoction.

Three tablespoons of vinegar to a quart of water takes stains out of carpets. Vinegar with its myriad of uses truly is King of the Cupboard.

A Scenic view of Elmwood Cemetery and Parents Creek
about 1920

Forgotten History

*Few persons who travel along East Jefferson Avenue
corner of Adair Street realize that they are passing the
scene of an important battle of American history – the
Battle of Bloody Run in 1763. This battle, part of the
conspiracy of Pontiac to remove the white man from this
area, is now almost forgotten. Parents Creek still runs
through Elmwood Cemetery.*

Hungarian-Style Noodles

8 ounces medium egg noodles (5 cups)
1 cup low-fat cottage cheese
1/2 cup light sour cream
1/2 cup plain yogurt
1/4 cup finely chopped green onions
1 clove garlic, finely chopped
1 teaspoon paprika
1/2 teaspoon salt
1 or 2 dashes hot pepper sauce

Cook noodles al dente according to package directions.
Drain well.

Meanwhile, combine cottage cheese, sour cream,
yogurt, green onions and garlic in a large serving bowl. Add
noodles; mix gently. Add paprika, salt and hot pepper sauce;
mix again. Serve immediately. Serves 4-5.

Pierogi Ukrainian – 1920

To prepare dough:
2 cups flour
1 egg
1 egg yolk
2 tablespoons sour cream
1 teaspoon butter
1/4 teaspoon salt

Put all ingredients
into a bowl and work
dough into a soft, smooth
ball. Roll out thinly on
lightly floured surface.
Cut into 2 inch rounds.

Place a small spoon-
ful of filling near the center, but to one side; fold
over and pinch edges to
form a triangle. Do not get any filling on the edges because the
two layers of dough will not stick together.

Bring water to a boil, add 1 tablespoon salt and drop 6
dumplings into the boiling water – cook about 5 minutes,
stirring gently at least once while cooking. Drain. Place in
bowl and coat generously with melted butter. After boiling,
these dumplings can be pan fried in butter. pierogi can be
fried in deep fat rather than cooked in boiling water.

Cottage Cheese and Mashed Potato Filling (or Dry
Farmer's Cheese): Mix thoroughly:
1 cup mashed potatoes
1 cup cottage or dry farmer's cheese
A few chives or onion greens, finely cut
Salt and pepper to taste

Cabbage and Mushroom Filling: Cut 1 small head
cabbage into quarters and cook in salted water until tender.
Drain. Cover with cold water, drain. Chop fine and set
aside. Saute in butter:
1 cup chopped mushrooms
1 small, chopped onion
Salt and pepper to taste

Fettucini & Spinach

Contribute by Rennie Hughes

1/2 package (1 pound) medium noodles
1/4 cup salad oil
1 clove garlic crushed
1 package frozen chopped spinach, thawed and drained
1/2 cup canned condensed chicken broth, undiluted
1/2 teaspoon dried basil leaves
1/4 cup chopped parsley
1/4 cup grated Parmesan cheese
1 cup (8 ounces) cottage cheese
Salt and pepper

Cook noodles and drain. In hot oil saute garlic and spinach 5 minutes. Add chicken broth, basil, Parmesan cheese, salt and pepper. Stir over low heat 2 minutes. Toss cheese spinach with noodles. Place in seving dish. Garnish with pimiento strips

Spaghetti Pie

6 ounces spaghetti
2 tablespoons butter
1/2 cup Parmesan cheese
2 well-beaten eggs
1 pound ground beef
18 ounce-can tomatoes, stewed
6-ounce can tomato paste
1 teaspoon sugar
1 cup cottage cheese
1/2 cup chopped onion
1/2 cup chopped green pepper
1/3 cup shredded Mozzarella cheese
1 teaspoon oregano
1 teaspoon garlic salt

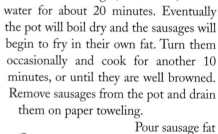

Cook spaghetti and drain. Stir in butter, Parmesan cheese and eggs. Form spaghetti mixture into a crust in a buttered 10-inch pie pan. In skillet, brown ground beef and add onion and green pepper. Drain fat. Add tomato paste, tomatoes, sugar, oregano and garlic salt. Heat through. Spread cottage cheese in pie crust. Cover with meat sauce. Bake at 350° for 30 minutes. Add Mozzarella cheese on top and return to oven until melted.

Pasta with Sausage and Peppers

2 pounds sweet Italian sausage
3 tablespoons best-quality olive oil
1 cup finely chopped yellow onions
3 sweet red peppers, stemmed, ribs and seeds removed, cut into medium-size julienne
1 cup dry red wine
1 can (2 pounds, 3 ounces) Italian plum tomatoes, including the liquid
1 cup water
1 tablespoon dried oregano
1 teaspoon dried thyme
Salt and freshly ground black pepper, to taste
Dried red pepper flakes
1 teaspoon fennel seeds
1/2 cup chopped Italian parsley
6 (or more) garlic cloves, peeled and finely chopped

Prick the sausage links all over with the tines of a fork and put them in a pot with 1/2 inch of water. Set the pot over medium heat and simmer the sausages, uncovered, in the water for about 20 minutes. Eventually the pot will boil dry and the sausages will begin to fry in their own fat. Turn them occasionally and cook for another 10 minutes, or until they are well browned. Remove sausages from the pot and drain them on paper toweling.

Pour sausage fat out of the pot but do not wash pot. Set it over low heat, add the olive oil and onions, and cook them, covered, until tender, about 25 minutes.

Add the peppers, raise the heat, and cook uncovered for another 5 minutes, stirring often.

Add the wine, tomatoes, water, oregano and thyme, and season to taste with salt, black pepper and red pepper flakes. Bring to a boil, reduce heat and simmer, partially covered, for 30 minutes.

Meanwhile, slice the sausages into 1/2-inch-thick rounds. When the sauce has simmered for 30 minutes, add sausages and fennel seeds and simmer, uncovered, for another 20 minutes. Add parsley and chopped garlic and simmer for another 5 minutes. 2 quarts sauce, enough for about 2 pounds pasta.

Salad

Maurice Salad

(Excellent copy of J. L. Hudson's)
Contributed by Mary Ellen Busch
Dressing:
Mix:
1/2 cup salad dressing (Miracle Whip type)
1/4 cup vinegar
1 tablespoon Worcestershire
3 cooked eggs, chopped
1 tablespoon minced onion
1/2 cup pickle relish

Let stand in refrigerator for one hour. Toss with lettuce in bowl. Dress with strips of chicken and ham and wedges of tomatoes.

Tabooleh Salad – Syrian/Lebanese

Submitted by Edward Deeb, President, Michigan Food and Beverage Association
1 cup cracked wheat, fine
1 bunch green onions
2 large bunches parsley
1/2 bunch mint (optional)
4 large tomatoes
Juice of 4 lemons
1/2 cup olive oil
salt and pepper to taste

Soak wheat in water a few minutes. Squeeze dry by pressing between palms. Chop onions, parsley, mint leaves (optional), and tomatoes (very fine). Add wheat, lemon juice, olive oil, salt and pepper. Mix well. Serve with fresh lettuce leaves, grape leaves or Syrian bread used as scoops. Serves 6. Enjoy this healthy creation.

Pepper Salad – Roumania

3 sweet green peppers
1/8 cup wine vinegar
1/4 cup olive oil
Paprika, for seasoning

Sear the peppers over a flame or under the broiler. Remove the thin outside skin; cut the pepper open, remove the seeds and ribs. Cut it into thin slices. Cover with a dressing of the wine vinegar and the olive oil, seasoned with salt, pepper and paprika.

American Potato Salad

Contributed by Lorene Rever
4 cups cubed boiled potatoes
2 tablespoons finely chopped onion
1/2 teaspoon salt
Dash of pepper
3/4 cup mayonnaise + 1 tablespoon vinegar
2 hard-cooked eggs, cut up
1 cup chopped celery
2 tablespoons finely chopped dill pickle and/or 2 tablespoons deli-style mustard (optional)
Chopped green pepper

Place warm potatoes in a bowl and add onion, salt and pepper. Add 1/4 cup mayonnaise and 1 tablespoon vinegar. Chill about 1 hour. Add 1/2 cup mayonnaise (or adjust to your taste) and then blend in rest of ingredients.

High School Days

In 1923 Central High School on Cass Avenue and Warren became College of the City of Detroit and in 1934 it was renamed Wayne University. The original building, still standing, is now called Old Main, part of the large Wayne State University campus.
A new Central High School was built in 1926 at Tuxedo and Linwood.

Colorful Bean Salad

1 can (about 1 pound) each of garbanzo (chick-peas), white kidney beans, red kidney beans, baby lima beans and black-eyed peas
1 pound fresh green beans, or half green and half yellow wax beans
Garlic Dressing
1 cup chopped scallions (green onions)
1/2 cup chopped Italian parsley (garnish)

Drain canned beans, rinse thoroughly with water, and drain again.

Trim, cook and cool beans. Drain, pat dry, and cut into 2-inch lengths.

Toss canned and fresh beans together in a large bowl. Pour in the dressing, sprinkle on the scallions, and toss again. Cover and refrigerate overnight before serving. Garnish with chopped parsley. Serve at room temperature. 10 to 12 portions.

Fort Wayne Gate 1845
Photo courtesy of Robert Watson

Oriental Cabbage Salad
Contributed by Vi Stone
1 pound coleslaw mix
1 bunch diced green onions
2 packages Ramen Chicken Soup Mix
1 cup cashews or slivered almonds (any kind)
1 cup sunflower seeds
1/2 cup sugar
1/3 cup white vinegar
1/4 cup vegetable oil

Mix slaw with uncooked Ramen noodles broken into small pieces and green onions. Mix sugar, oil and vinegar and packets of dry soup mix. Pour over salad and thoroughly mix. Let stand 2 hours. Put in nuts and seeds before serving. Serves 6-8.

Broccoli Salad
Contributed by Pat Wilson
1 bunch broccoli, chopped
1 red onion, chopped
1/2 cup roasted sunflower seeds
1/2 cup raisins
Combine above ingredients.
Mix together at least 1 hour before serving:
2 tablespoons sugar
3 teaspoons vinegar
1 cup mayonnaise

Ambrosia Salad
1 16-ounce package small marshmallows
1/2 cup coconut
1 6-ounce can mandarin oranges (drained)
1 cup crushed pineapple (drained)
1/2 cup maraschino cherries cut-up
8 ounces cream cheese

Prepare marshmallows and fruit. Fold in sour cream with spatula. Chill 2-3 hours before serving.

Szechuan Shrimp Salad
Submitted by Shirley Hartert
1 package fine cooked egg noodles
1/4 cup vegetable oil
2 tablespoons vinegar
2 tablespoons soy sauce
1 tablespoon sesame seeds
1 teaspoon ground ginger
1 teaspoon sugar
1 teaspoon Tabasco or to taste
1 pound small frozen, cooked shrimp
1 package frozen snow peas, cooked 1 minute
1 red bell pepper, cut in match stick strips
1/2 cup scallions, sliced including green ends
3 bananas cut diagonally in 1/2-inch slices

In large Tupperware bowl combine oil, vinegar, soy, seeds, ginger, sugar, red pepper and hot sauce. Add shrimp, snow peas and scallions. Toss to coat. Chill covered until serving time. To serve: place cooked noodles on platter and gently mix sliced bananas into shrimp mix and spoon over noodles. This dish looks stunning and has a spicy oriental flavor. Serve with hot croissants and chilled Soave Bolla wine. 6-8 servings.

Mexican Potato Salad

3 tablespoons vinegar
1/3 cup olive oil or vegetable oil
1 teaspoon salt
1 can (16 ounces) potatoes, drained and sliced
1 can (8 ounces) diced carrots, drained
1 can (8 ounces) diced green beans, drained
1/2 cup sliced pitted ripe olives
3 tablespoons snipped parsley
Lettuce leaves
1 medium cucumber, sliced
1 small tomato, cut into wedges

Mix vinegar, oil and salt; stir in potatoes, carrots, beans and olives. Cover and refrigerate, stirring occasionally, at least 2 hours. Just before serving, toss vegetable mixture with parsley; drain. Pour into lettuce-lined bowl. Top with cucumber and tomato. 6-8 servings.

Winter River Travel - 1800

The desire to cross the river year round resulted in the invention of building a ferry with sloping ends so that the engine would drive it upon the ice breaking it down by the weight of the heavy vessel.

Hot German Potato Salad

Contributed by Lenora Stoetzer

2 quarts cooked sliced potatoes (2 pounds raw)
3/4 cup diced bacon (6 slices)
1/2 cup chopped onion
2 teaspoons salt
1 teaspoon sugar
1 teaspoon flour
1 teaspoon mustard
1/8 teaspoon pepper
1/2 cup vinegar
1/2 cup boiling water
4 tablespoons chopped parsley

Wash potatoes, steam until tender, about 30 minutes. Peel and slice. Fry bacon until slightly browned, then add onion and brown. Blend salt, sugar, flour, mustard and pepper and the onion and bacon. Add the potatoes and then the vinegar and water. Allow to heat through until moisture has been partly absorbed. Add parsley and serve hot.

Mexican Taco Salad

1 can black olives, sliced (optional)
1 head lettuce
1 pound ground beef or ground turkey
1 large tomato
1 onion
1 12-ounce package shredded cheese (Monterey Jack, Mozzarella, Taco)
1 package taco seasoning
1 small bottle Catalina dressing

Brown meat and add taco seasoning. Drain and cool. Chop lettuce, onion and tomato (chop small). Mix lettuce, tomato, onion, shredded cheese, and meat together. Add bottle Catalina dressing. Put mixture into taco shells, or break taco chips into the salad. Additional taco salsa or sour cream added as desired.

Fruit-and-Cabbage Salad – Scandinavian

2 oranges, pared and sectioned
2 apples, chopped
2 cups shredded cabbage (about 1/4 medium head)
1 cup seedless green grapes
1/2 cup whipping cream
1 tablespoon sugar
1 tablespoon lemon juice
1/4 teaspoon salt
1/2 cup mayonnaise or salad dressing

Place oranges, apples, cabbage and grapes in bowl. Beat whipping cream in chilled bowl until stiff. Fold whipped cream, sugar, lemon juice and salt into mayonnaise. Stir into fruit mixture. 6 servings.

Greek Salad

1 head lettuce
1 onion, sliced
1 green pepper, sliced
2 tomatoes, quartered
1 cucumber, sliced
1/2 cup oil
1/4 cup lemon juice
Feta cheese

Cut the head lettuce, wash well and combine with the tomatoes, onion, pepper, cucumber. Mix in a bowl and add salt, pepper to taste, oil and lemon juice. Garnish with Feta cheese, black olives and sprinkle with fresh dill.

Pickles & Preserves

Dill Pickles – Fresh Kosher Style

30 to 36 cucumbers (3 to 4 inches long)
3 cups vinegar
3 cups water
6 tablespoons salt
Fresh or dried dill
Garlic
Mustard Seed

Wash the cucumbers. Make a brine of the vinegar, water and salt. Bring to boil. Place a generous layer of dill, 1/2 to 1 clove of garlic (sliced) and 1/2 tablespoon of mustard seed in bottom of each clean quart jar. Pack the cucumbers into the jars. When the jars are half filled with cucumbers add another layer of dill and complete the packing of the jars. Fill the jars to within 1/2 inch of the top with the boiling brine. Put cap on jars, screwing the band tight. Process 5 minutes in boiling water bath.

Mixed Pickles

2 large heads cauliflower
1 gallon green tomatoes
6 large onions
6 green peppers
6 cucumbers

Separate cauliflower, chop green tomatoes, onions, green peppers and cucumbers. Mix well. Put in a kettle in layers, first a layer of vegetable mixture, then a very thin layer of salt until all ingredients are used, being sure the last layer is salt.

Let stand 24 hours, then squeeze as dry as possible. Make a pickling solution of:
1 quart vinegar
4 cups sugar
2 level teaspoons each of cloves, cinnamon, allspice and mace
If desired little red peppers may be added.

Mix sugar and spices with vinegar, boil 5 minutes and pour over vegetables, stirring well so that vinegar will mix in with them. Allow to stand several hours. Bring pickles to boil and cook 15 minutes, then pack into sterilized jars and seal at once.

Bread and Butter Pickles

25 to 30 medium cucumbers
8 large white onions
2 large sweet peppers
1/2 cup salt
5 cups cider vinegar
5 cups sugar (2 1/2 pounds)
2 tablespoons mustard seed
1 teaspoon turmeric
1/2 teaspoon cloves

Wash cucumbers and slice as thin as possible. Chop onions and peppers; combine with cucumbers and salt; let stand 3 hours and drain. Combine vinegar, sugar, and spices in large preserving kettle, bring to boil. Add drained cucumbers; heat thoroughly but do not boil. Pack while hot into sterilized jars and seal at once. Makes about 7 quarts.

Pickled Beets

Select small, young beets, cook until tender, dip into cold water. Peel off skin. Make the following syrup:

2 cups sugar
2 cups water
2 cups strong vinegar
1 teaspoon cloves
1 teaspoon allspice
1 tablespoon cinnamon

Pour over beets and boil 10 minutes. Pack into sterilized jars and seal.

Peach Preserves

Pare, and add to a pound of peaches one and one-quart pounds best sugar. Cook very fast for a few moments, in a porcelain kettle. Turn out in a bowl, cover with muslin or cambric, set in the sun, stirring every day till they seem quite transparent. They retain their flavor much better this way than when cooked on the fire. Put in jars, cover with paper saturated with brandy, and tip up tightly to exclude the air.

Sweet Tomato Pickle

Slice one gallon green tomatoes, and put a handful salt to each layer of tomatoes. Let them stand twelve hours, then drain off the liquor, and add to them two green peppers, and from two to four onions, sliced; take two quarts vinegar, half a pint molasses, two tablespoonfuls mustard, one teaspoonful allspice, and one of cloves; heat it until it begins to boil, then put in tomatoes, onions, and peppers; let them boil ten minutes; pour into a stone jar, and seal tight. In a fortnight they will be ready for use.

Pineapple Preserves

Parboil the pineapples, then peel and cut in thick slices, carefully taking out the cores, which, if allowed to remain, will cause the preserves to ferment. Put a pound of sugar to a pound of fruit, and let it remain all night to make the syrup. Boil then till done, without adding a drop of water to the syrup.

Social Security
During WWII citizens were urged to take better care of their Social Security Cards so that the government would not have to replace them. They pointed out that 13 bullets could be bought for what it cost to replace one card.

Orange Marmalade

4 oranges
1 lemon
11 cups water
4 pounds sugar

Grind oranges and lemons, mix together, add water and let stand 24 hours, then boil for one hour with cover off. Let stand again 24 hours. Add sugar and boil until it jells, or about one hour. Makes ten glasses.

Grape Conserve

2 quarts stemmed grapes
1 1/2 pounds of raisins
3 oranges
1/2 pound nuts

The grapes should not be over-ripe. Wash grapes and separate pulp from the skins. Cook pulp until soft and pass through a sieve. Remove pulp and juice from oranges and add to the grape skins, pulp and raisins. Measure and add equal amount of sugar. Simmer until ready to jell. Add nuts in broken pieces.

Peach Preserve

Pare, and add to a pound of peaches one and one-quarter pounds best sugar. Cook very fast for a few moments, in a porcelain kettle. Turn out in a bowl, cover with muslin or cambric, set in the sun, stirring every day till they seem quite transparent. They retain their flavor much better this way than when cooked on the fire. Put in jars, cover with paper saturated with brandy, and tip up tightly to exclude the air.

Peach Conserve

15 peaches
1 pint canned pineapple
3 1/2 cups sugar
1 cup almonds

Chop peaches and pineapple; add sugar and let stand one hour. Cook slowly 45 minutes; then add blanched almonds and cook ten minutes longer. Turn into sterilized glasses and when cold cover with melted paraffin.

Spiced Apples

Cut peeled apples into eights or quarters and cook till tender in a syrup of equal parts water, vinegar and sugar, to which has been added a few whole cloves, a few pieces of cinnamon and a little cayenne pepper. Remove the apples with skimmer, boil syrup until thick and pour over the fruit.
A fine relish. Serve cold.

Fox Grape Preserves

Seed the grapes, then pour scalding water on them and let then stand till cold; then draw off the water, put one pound sugar to one pound of gapes, and boil gently about twenty minutes.

Apple Butter – Spiced

16 cups thick apple pulp
1 cup vinegar
8 cups sugar
4 teaspoons cinnamon

Core and slice apples but do not peel. Add only enough water to cook apples until soft. Press through fine sieve and measure. Combine all ingredients. Cook until mixture remains in a smooth mass when a little is cooled (about 1 1/2 hours boiling). During cooking stir frequently to prevent burning. Pour into sterilized jars and seal while hot.

Mint Jelly

2 cups apple juice
1 1/2 cups sugar
1 teaspoon mint extract
Green food coloring

Combine apple juice and sugar and boil rapidly. When mixture is nearing jelly stage, add the mint extract. Boil rapidly to jelly stage. When ready to remove from heat, add green coloring to give desired shade. Pour into sterilized jelly glasses.

Fruit and Combinations of Fruits Making Jelly

Apple: Apple and Mint
Apple and Strawberry
Apricot and Plum
Blackberry
Crab Apple
Crab Apple and Cherry
Crab Apple and Raspberry
Currants, all kinds
Currant and Apple
Currant and Apricot
Currant and Pear
Currant, Peach and Pineapple
Fig and Lemon
Grape
Grape, Muscadine
Grape and Apple
Grape and Apricot
Grape and Orange
Grapefruit
Grapefruit and Cherry
Grapefruit and Roselle
Lemon
Lemon and Cherry
Lemon and Raspberry
Loganberry
Loganberry and Pineapple
Orange
Orange and Apple
Orange and Pineapple
Orange and Plum
Peach and Lemon
Peach and Apple
Peach and Quince
Pineapple and Quince
Plum
Plum and Raspberry
Quince
Quince and Apple
Quince and Apricot
Raspberry
Raspberry and Currant
Roselle

Berry Jam

Wash and pick over berries. Crush and measure berries and juice. Heat through. Add 3/4 cup sugar for each cup berries and juice. Cook, stirring frequently, until of desired consistency. Pour into sterilized jars and seal while hot.

Russell House

Russell House took over the site where the National Hotel had stood. It opened in 1857 and quickly became the foremost Detroit hotel, rising to social prominence. Among its famous guests were the Prince of Wales, who became King Edward VII, and the Grand Duke Alexis of Russia. It soon became the business planning site for the auto industry in its infancy. It was razed in 1905 and replaced by the Pontchartrain in 1907 which was torn down in 1920.

Apricot-Raspberry Jam

2 pounds fresh apricots (6 cups sliced)
1/4 cup water
4 1/2 cups sugar
1 1/2 cups raspberries

Add water to apricots which have been pared and pitted. Add sugar and raspberries and cook until jam is of desired consistency. Pour into sterilized jars and seal while hot.

Plum Jam

4 cups purple plums, pitted
3 1/2 cups sugar
1 teaspoon lemon juice

Chop plums. Mix all ingredients together and let stand 1 hour. Cook until thick, stirring once in a while to prevent sticking. Pour into hot sterile jars and seal. Makes about 6 8-ounce jars.

Grape Jelly

Wash, stem and crush grapes, add small amount of water and boil 15 minutes. Press through jelly bag and strain. Measure juice and bring to a boil. For each cup of juice add 3/4 cup of sugar. Boil rapidly to jelly stage. Pour into sterilized jelly glasses. Crystals often form in grape jelly. To prevent this allow extracted juice to stand overnight in a cool place. Next morning carefully pour juice off sediment in bottom of pan.

Sauces

Hot Fudge Sauce

1 cup sugar
4 tablespoons cocoa
1 tablespoon flour
1/8 teaspoon salt
3/4 cup milk
2 tablespoons butter or margarine
2 tablespoons light corn syrup
1/2 teaspoon vanilla

Combine dry ingredients in cup. Stir in milk. Add butter and syrup. Microwave at high 3-4 minutes until thick, smooth and a rich chocolate color. Stir in vanilla, mixing well. Serve hot or cold. To reheat, microwave at high, covered with plastic wrap, 15-30 seconds for each 1/2 cup of sauce

* COMPLIMENTS OF *

THE DAY MANUFACTURING CO.,

DAY'S SELF HEATER . DETROIT,

MICH.

Butterscotch Sauce

1 cup packed brown sugar
1/4 cup light corn syrup
1 tablespoon flour
2 tablespoons water
3 tablespoons butter or margarine
1/2 cup half and half

Combine all ingredients in measuring cup. Microwave at high 3 minutes. Stir, microwave 4-6 minutes more until slightly thickened. Beat well. Serve warm over ice cream of other desserts.

Caramel Sauce

Melt one cup of sugar in a smooth, clean saucepan, add three-fourths cup of boiling water, and simmer fifteen minutes. Take care that sugar does not burn. Strong coffee may be used instead of water, and, if desired, one-half cup of chopped nut meats may be added.

Cranberry and Apple Sauce

1 cup cranberries
1 cup apple (diced)
1 cup water
3/4 cup sugar (more if sweeter sauce is desired)

Place the apple in the pot, the cranberries over the apples, and the water (the water should not reach to more than half the depth of the fruit). Cover closely and place on moderate flame. After the berries have commenced to pop open, stir sugar into sauce, and then stir mixture occasionally until berries are all mashed and sauce is thick. This is delightful served with meat or vegetables. The apples take away the extreme tartness of the berries and the berries give the apples piquancy. More or less of either fruit may be used.

French Cream Sauce

2/3 cup whipping cream
1/3 cup dairy sour cream
2 to 3 cups assorted fresh fruit
Ground nutmeg or sugar

Gradually stir whipping cream into dairy sour cream. Cover and refrigerate no longer than 48 hours. Serve over fruit. Sprinkle with nutmeg. 4-6 servings.

Suggested fruits are blueberries, raspberries, strawberries, sliced peaches or cubed pineapple.

Fruit Sauce

Heat one cup of sirup of preserved or canned fruit, thicken with one teaspoon of cornstarch moistened with one tablespoon of cold water, and cook ten minutes; add a few grains of salt, a teaspoon of butter, a few drops of red coloring, and serve hot.

Thin White Sauce

Butter, 3 tablespoons
Flour, 2 tablespoons
Salt, 1 teaspoon
Pepper, 1/4 teaspoon
Milk, 2 cups

Melt butter over low heat; add flour, salt and pepper; stir until blended. Remove from heat. Gradually stir in milk and return to heat. Cook, stirring constantly, until thick and smooth. To shorten cooking time milk may be heated separately. Makes 2 cups.

Cheese Sauce: When sauce is thick add 2 cups grated cheese and 1/2 teaspoon Worcestershire sauce. Stir over low heat until cheese is melted. Serve with vegetables, fish loaf, rice, macaroni or hard-cooked eggs.

Lemon Vinaigrette

1 cup best-quality olive oil
2/3 cup lemon juice
1/2 cup snipped fresh chives
2 tablespoons finely minced shallots
2 tablespoons prepared Dijon-style mustard
Salt and freshly ground black pepper, to taste.

Combine all ingredients, with seasoning to taste, in a covered container and shake well until blended. Serve immediately. About 1 3/4 cups.

Hard Sauce

1/2 cup butter or margarine
2 cups sifted confectioners' sugar
1 teaspoon vanilla

Thoroughly cream butter and sugar; add vanilla. Vary flavor with lemon or orange juice and grated peel. Makes 1 2/3 cups.

Garlic Dressing

1 egg yolk
1/3 cup red wine vinegar
1 tablespoon granulated sugar
1 tablespoon chopped garlic
Salt and freshly ground black pepper, to taste
1 cup best-quality olive oil

Combine egg yolk, vinegar, sugar, garlic, and salt and pepper to taste in blender. With the motor running, slowly dribble in the olive oil. Taste, correct seasoning if necessary, and transfer to storage container.

Detroit's Biddle House

The Biddle House hotel at corner of Jefferson and Randolph, was built in 1849. It was successful from the beginning, having famous guests such as General Grant in 1865 and President Andrew Johnson in 1866. Biddle House contained Detroit's largest auditorium. It was used as a concert hall, convention site and theater.

Medium White Sauce

Butter, 4 tablespoons
Flour, 4 tablespoons
Salt, 1 teaspoon
Pepper, 1/4 teaspoon
Milk, 2 cups

Prepare as directed for thin white sauce. Makes 2 cups.

Balsamic Vinaigrette

1 garlic clove, unpeeled
1 tablespoon prepared Dijon-style mustard
3 tablespoons balsamic vinegar
Salt and freshly ground black pepper, to taste
1 cup best-quality olive oil

Cut garlic clove into halves and rub the cut sides over the inner surface of a small bowl. Reserve the garlic. Whisk mustard and vinegar together in the bowl. Season with salt and pepper to taste. Dribble oil into the bowl in a slow steady stream, whisking constantly, until dressing is creamy and thick. Taste and correct seasoning. Add reserved pieces of garlic; cover the bowl and let the dressing stand at room temperature until you need it. Remove garlic and rewhisk the dressing if necessary before using. About 1 3/4 cups.

Fish

Trout with Bacon – Welsh

12 slices bacon
6 drawn whole trout (about 5 ounces each)
2 tablespoons snipped parsley
1 1/2 teaspoons salt
1/4 teaspoon freshly ground pepper
Snipped parsley

Arrange bacon in single layer in broiler pan. Cook uncovered in 400° oven 10 minutes; drain on paper towels. Sprinkle inside of fish with 2 tablespoons parsley, the salt and pepper. Arrange fish in single layer on bacon in pan. Cover and cook until fish flakes easily with fork, about 20 minutes. Split fish down center along backbone; remove as many bones as possible. Serve each dish with 2 bacon slices. Garnish with parsley.

Memories - Lenora Stoetzer - Born 1909
During WWII everyone received ration coupons, young and old, for meat, sugar and canned goods. Times were really hard. We even ate horsemeat. All the really good things were sent overseas to the soldier boys. Nearly every home had a dad, son or brother in the war.

Jambolaya – American

From Mrs. Jean Babcock (James)
Saute 2 slices of diced bacon.
Add and saute lightly:
1 medium onion, diced
1 small green pepper, diced
1/2 cup diced celery
Stir in and brown lightly 1 tablespoon flour. Add:
2 No. 2 cans of stewed tomatoes
1/4 teaspoon paprika
1/4 teaspoon thyme
1 good dash Worcestershire sauce
Bring these ingredients to the boiling point. Stir in:
3 cups cooked rice
1 cup diced cooked ham
1 cup diced cooked chicken
1 pound cooked shrimp
Add salt as needed. Cover and cook over low heat until the meats and rice are thoroughly warm, approximately 30 minutes. An electric skillet is ideal for fixin' this.

Red Snapper Rolls

Contributed by Shirley Hartert
4 tablespoons butter
1/4 cup chopped onion
1 (3 ounce) jar sliced mushrooms (save juice)
1 (7 1/2 ounce) can crab, drained
1/2 cup crushed saltines
2 tablespoons parsley, chopped
1/4 teaspoon pepper
6 red snapper fillets (approximately 2 pounds)
Sauce:
3 tablespoons butter
3 tablespoons flour
1 1/4 cups milk
1/3 cup dry white wine
4 ounces grated Swiss cheese
1/2 teaspoon paprika
Mushroom liquid

Cook onions in butter until tender, add mushrooms, crab, saltines, parsley and pepper. Spread mix on fish fillets and roll up. Secure with picks. Place seam side down in a pretty baker. Sauce: Melt butter, add flour. Add milk and mushroom liquid to make 1 1/2 cups. Add wine to butter-flour mixture, cook and stir until thick. Pour over fillets and bake 25 minutes at 400°. Then sprinkle with cheese and paprika and bake 10 minutes more. To serve, garnish with parsley sprigs between fillets and serve with warm garlic bread, artichokes, semi-dry white wine. 4-6 servings.

Irish Baked Trout

4 green onions, sliced
1 green pepper, chopped
1/4 cup margarine or butter
1 cup soft bread crumbs
1/4 cup snipped parsley
1 teaspoon lemon juice
1 teaspoon salt
1/4 teaspoon dried basil leaves
4 drawn whole trout (about 8 ounces each)
Salt

Cook and stir onions and pepper in margarine until onions are tender; remove from heat. Stir in bread crumbs, parsley, the lemon juice, 1 teaspoon salt and the basil.

Rub cavities of fish with salt; stuff each with about 1/4 cup stuffing. Place fish in greased oblong baking dish, 13 1/2 x 9 x 2 inches. Cook uncovered in 350° oven until fish flakes easily with fork, 30 to 35 minutes. Garnish fish with cherry tomatoes and parsley if desired. 4 servings.

Scampi – Italian

Contributed by Rennie Hughs

48 jumbo shrimp (under 15 count per pound)
6 cloves garlic, crushed
2 teaspoons salt
3/4 cup butter
3/4 cup olive oil
1/4 cup minced parsley
2 tablespoons lemon juice
Freshly ground black pepper
        Garnish:
3 lemons, scalloped cut
1 large green pepper, sliced lengthwise (24 slices)
6 tiny parsley sprigs for center of lemons

Use a knife and devein shrimp and butterfly cut through shell back lengthwise, almost to the tail. Leave feet on and shell intact. Melt butter and add all other ingredients, add shrimp when butter is hot (need 2 frying pans to do this amount of shrimp). Cook shrimp until they ìbutterflyî nicely and are pinkódonít overcook. To serve: place 1/2 cup Lemon Rice in center of plate and flatten in a circle. Place lemon in center and 4 pepper strips outwards from lemon, giving you 4 sections. Stand 2 shrimp per section, cut flesh side down and tails in the air. Spectacular! Serves 6.

Walleye Special – Detroit

Contributed by Frances Deaner

1 1/2-2 pounds walleye, cut in 2-inch strips
10 ounce can of stewed tomatoes
1 medium onion, thinly sliced

Place walleye strips in 9 x 13 baking pan. Cover with stewed tomatoes and onion slices. Bake in 350° oven for 20 minutes.

Salmon Puffs – Jewish

1 (1 pound) can pink salmon
1/2 cup bread crumbs
1/3 cup finely chopped onion
2 eggs
Salt
1 tablespoon lemon juice

Drain juice from can of pink salmon. Put 1/2 cup bread crumbs into juice and let soak. Put salmon into a bowl and break up to fine pieces. Add onion, eggs, salt and lemon juice. Mix into soaked bread and blend well with a fork. Fill buttered muffin cups to the top and dot the top with butter and crumbs or crushed potato chips or crackers. Bake at 375° for 25 minutes. Makes 9 or10 puffs.

Schoolroom 1840, by Frank Hibbler

Stuffed Pike – Austrian

2- to 2 1/2-pound pike, cleaned
1/2 teaspoon salt
1/8 teaspoon pepper
1 small onion, chopped
1/2 cup sliced mushrooms
2 tablespoons margarine or butter
1 cup soft bread crumbs
3 anchovy fillets, mashed
3 tablespoons milk
1 tablespoon snipped parsley
1/4 cup margarine or butter, melted
2 tablespoons lemon juice
1 clove garlic, chopped

Rub cavity of fish with salt and pepper. Cook and stir onion and mushrooms in 2 tablespoons margarine until onion is tender. Mix onion, mushrooms, bread crumbs, anchovies, milk and parsley. Spoon into cavity of fish. Close opening with skewers; lace with string. Place fish in shallow roasting pan. Mix 1/4 cup margarine, the lemon juice and garlic; brush fish with margarine mixture. Cook uncovered in 350° oven, brushing occasionally with margarine mixture, until fish flakes easily with fork, about 1 hour. Garnish with parsley sprigs and thinly sliced lemon if desired. 8 servings.

Salmon, red snapper, lake trout, bass or whitefish can be substituted for the pike.

Fish and Collard Greens – African American

2 medium onions, sliced
1 green pepper, sliced
1/4 cup margarine or butter
1 package (10 ounces) frozen collard greens
2 tablespoons water
1 pound fish fillets
1 1/2 teaspoons salt
1/2 teaspoon paprika
1/4 teaspoon pepper

Cook and stir onions and green pepper in margarine in 3-quart saucepan until onion is tender, about 3 minutes. Add collard greens and water. Heat to boiling; separate greens with fork. Reduce heat. Cover and simmer 5 minutes.

Cut fish into strips, 4 x 3/4 inches each; add to vegetables. Sprinkle with salt, paprika and pepper. Heat to boiling; reduce heat. Cover and simmer until fish flakes easily with fork, about 5 minutes. Garnish with lemon wedges if desired.

Baked Sturgeon – Detroit

Wash the skin well, put in a pan and bake for three-quarters of an hour. Then take it out on a dish; pierce with a knife in several places. Make a stuffing of bread crumbs, onions, parsley, thyme, pepper, and salt, all chopped well together. Stuff the holes with the mixture and put the rest in the gravy; return to the pan and bake until done.

Detroit Memories - Jackie Napolitan
One of my friends reminiscing about his youth in Detroit about 1928-34. Sometimes on a hot night he and his buddies would swim in the Detroit River at the foot of St. Jean. A business there on the river maintained a huge pile of sand at the water's edge making a perfect beach hill for sliding into the water.

Baked Halibut in Tomato Sauce

Boil the halibut and break into small pieces. Make one cup of white sauce, adding one can of tomatoes, strained. Make the white sauce very smooth and stir while adding tomato juice. Place the halibut in a greased baking dish, cover with the sauce, season and cover with cracker crumbs. Dot with pepper and bake for twenty minutes until brown.

African Fish Stew with Vegetables

1 can (15 ounces) tomato sauce
4 cups water
1 cup uncooked regular rice
3 carrots, thinly sliced
1 onion, thinly sliced
1 tablespoon salt
1/2 teaspoon ground red pepper
1 package (10 ounces) frozen okra pods
1 package (10 ounces) frozen green beans
3 cups sliced cabbage
1 1/2 pounds catfish, perch, bass or trout fillets, cut into serving pieces

Heat tomato sauce, water, rice, carrots, onion, salt and red pepper in Dutch oven to boiling; reduce heat. Cover and cook 10 minutes.

Rinse okra and green beans under running cold water to separate; drain. Cut okra lengthwise into halves. Add okra, green beans, cabbage and fish to Dutch oven. Heat to boiling; reduce heat. Cover and cook until fish flakes easily with fork and vegetables are tender. 10 to 12 minutes. 8 servings.

Beef

Veal Piccata – Italian

Contributed by Rennie Hughes

3/4 pound veal round steak, about 1/2 inch thick
1/4 cup all-purpose flour
1/4 cup margarine or butter
2 tablespoons vegetable oil
2 tablespoons lemon juice
Salt and pepper

Cut veal steak into 4 serving pieces; pound until 1/4 inch thick. Coat with flour; shake off excess. Heat 2 tablespoons of the margarine and the oil in 12-inch skillet over medium heat until hot. Cook veal until tender and brown, about 4 minutes on each side.

Remove veal to heated platter. Heat remaining 2 tablespoons margarine in skillet until melted; stir in lemon juice. Pour over veal; sprinkle with salt and pepper. Garnish with parsley and lemon slices if desired. 4 servings.

Big Producer - 1900's

Detroit makes more stoves, more pills, more paint and more freight cars than any other city in the country.

Swedish Meat Balls

1/2 cup fine bread crumbs
1 1/4 cups cream
1 1/2 pounds ground beef
1/2 pound ground pork
1 onion, grated
2 teaspoons salt
1/2 teaspoon pepper
1/4 teaspoon cloves
Allspice
Butter for browning
1 cup water
2 tablespoons flour
1 1/2 cups scalded light cream

Soak bread crumbs in 1 1/4 cups cream, then mix with beef, pork, onion, salt, pepper, cloves and a pinch of allspice. Shape into small balls and brown on all sides in butter. Add 1 cup water to pan, cover and simmer. When done, sprinkle with flour and stir. Gently stir in the light cream and season to taste. Keep hot in chafing dish. Use as appetizers or a main course.

German Dinner in 3 Parts
Contributed by Gertrude Teschke
Translated from original German into English

Rindsrollen – Beef Rouladen

6 to 8 slices of breakfast or chipsteak
6 to 8 slices of bacon chopped in small pieces
1/2 to 1 cup finely chopped pickles (I use sweet relish)
1/2 to 1 cup finely chopped onions
Mustard (about 1/8 cup)
Butter and flour
2 cups water
2 beef bouillon cubes
1/2 to 1 cup sour cream
Cornstarch
Salt and pepper

Pound steaks to flatten and tenderize. Spread with mustard. Place some bacon, pickles and onions in center. Fold sides in and roll up. Secure with string or toothpicks. Roll in flour. Brown in butter, turning frequently. Once all rouladen are browned add 2 cups of water and 2 bouillon cubes. Cook and let simmer 1 and 1 1/2 hours. Add sour cream to gravy and thicken with cornstarch if needed.

Potato Dumplings

2 pounds (6) raw potatoes
4 slices white bread
1 teaspoon salt
1/4 teaspoon pepper
1 onion, grated
1 teaspoon minced parsley
2 eggs, well beaten
1/4 cup flour
1 1/2 quarts boiling salted water

Wash, peel and grate potatoes, soak bread in a little cold water, squeeze out as much water as possible. Mix bread, salt, pepper, onions and parsley. Add potatoes and eggs, mix well. Form into balls, roll lightly in flour, drop into salted boiling water (1 teaspoon salt to each quart water) cover pot tightly, boil 15 minutes.

Use Almost Anything

The people of Detroit used animal skins, stamped playing cards, English pounds, Spanish pieces of eight, York currency, due bills, shin plasters and many other forms of money before a banking system came into being to serve everyone in 1818.

Red Cabbage – Rotkraut

Contributed by Gertrude Teschke

1 head red cabbage (2 pounds)
3 or 4 slices of bacon
1 onion
1 teaspoon of sugar
Salt and pepper
2-3 tablespoons vinegar
1 tablespoon flour
1 apple (or applesauce)
If you like, 1/2 glass wine
Beef broth (or 1 beef bouillon cube, 1 cup water)

Take off the outside bad leafs. Cut in fine strips. Cut bacon in little pieces, put in pot and let it brown a little bit. Add the fine chopped onions, sugar, red-cabbage and the fine cut apple. Let it under diligent shaking steam. Then add salt and pepper, vinegar and beef broth and let it cook. Shortly before itís done add the flour. Before you serve it add the wine. Cooking time 1 1/2-2 hours.

Beef Gumbo – African American

2 pounds beef (stewing or boneless)
1 pound okra
Can tomatoes
1 green pepper
Large onion
Small piece garlic or garlic salt
Black pepper
2 stalks celery
Seasoning salt

Beef should be cut up in small pieces. Wash and put on – let cook – when it has cooked about 45 minutes, add chopped onion, green pepper and celery and seasoning. Let cook for about 30 minutes and add tomatoes. Cut up okra, let cook another 1/2 hour, serve over rice. Shrimp or hot smoked sausage may be added or both together may be added. Add them when you put in tomatoes and okra.

Home Canning

How to feed his army so vexed Napoleon that he offered a prize for a method of preserving food. Nicolas Appert, a Paris confectioner, won the award in 1810 by demonstrating that cooked food packed in glass bottles, heated, and sealed would keep for months – even years. Just why wasn't understood until Louis Pasteur's work more than half a century later.

Once the effect of heat on bacteria was understood, canning techniques improved. John Mason's jar in 1858 helped, too. A rubber gasket fitted the shoulder on his jar and a zinc lid screwed down tight. A later jar had a glass lid, rubber gasket, and a wire bale arrangement. Today's jars use a two-piece metal lid. The flat center portion seals against the glass and a removable screw band holds it.

Water-bath canning of fruits requires only a large, deep kettle with a rack and cover. Filled jars simmer covered with boiling water. Introduction of a kitchen-size pressure canner just before Word War I made possible a safe method for canning low-acid vegetables and meats at home.

During two world wars canning was vital in preserving food from victory gardens. Centers were set up in schools and church basements. Some operated long after the emergency. By the 1950s, however, home freezers and a population shift to cities made canning a lost art for many people. Now, as home gardens sprout again, homemakers once again face the problems of preserving food at home.

Chippewa Bulettes

Take a pot and chop an onion in it, add 4 potatoes peeled and finely cubed, cover with water, cover and simmer while taking one pound of hamburger and make little bitty meat ball shapes, then add this to pot and simmer with salt and pepper to taste. When the hamburger turns grey and is cooked, fill your pot with more water and take one cup milk with a couple tablespoons of flour blended in and add this too. Simmer until thickened.

Pepper Steak – Chinese

From Victor Lims Restaurant

4 tablespoons olive oil
1 clove garlic, crushed
1 teaspoon salt
1 teaspoon chopped green ginger root
1/2 teaspoon pepper

Heat the above in a skillet. Add 1 pound flank steak, cut into thin slices. Brown lightly for a minute or two. Add:

4 tablespoons soy sauce
1/2 teaspoon sugar

Cover the skillet and cook beef for 2 minutes longer. Remove the beef and keep it warm. Add to the pan juices and cook briskly for 3 minutes:

2 cups bean sprouts
2 tomatoes, peeled, seeded and coarsely chopped
2 green peppers, seeded and cut into strips
2 celery strips, chopped coarsely

Add the meat and stir in 1 tablespoon cornstarch blended with 1/4 cup water. Cook until thickened. Sprinkle top when serving with 2 or 3 scallions. Serves 4.

Auto Production

Only four of the 202 different makes of cars being built in 1910 are still in production today: Buick, Ford, Cadillac and Oldsmobile.
(2001 GM announces halt of Olds production.)

Kima – Pakistani

1 pound ground beef
1 cup chopped onion
1 clove garlic, minced
2 tomatoes, peeled and cubed
2 raw potatoes, peeled and cubed
1 (10 ounce) package frozen peas, broken apart
2 teaspoons curry powder
1 1/2 teaspoons salt
Dash of pepper
Flaked coconut
Hot cooked rice

In skillet, cook beef, onion and garlic till meat is browned. Pour off fat. Stir in remaining ingredients except coconut and rice. Cover; simmer for 20 to 25 minutes or until vegetables are tender. Sprinkle with coconut. Serve with hot cooked rice. Makes 6 servings.

Salisbury Steak with Onion Rings – African American

3 pounds hamburger
2 eggs
5 medium size onions—sliced
Seasoning salt
Garlic salt—optional
Celery salt—optional
1 cup bread crumbs
1 cup bacon fat or shortening
1 cup flour
3 or 4 cups water

Combine hamburger, eggs, seasoning, bread crumbs, mix until bread crumbs are completely absorbed into meat. Make oblong steaks, use your own judgment as to size and thickness, flour them on both sides. Pour bacon fat or shortening into large thick skillet and fry steak on both sides. Be sure to cook them only half done. Be careful not to have flame too high. Take them out and place them in small roaster putting a layer of steaks and a layer of onions, use remaining flour to make gravy by browning in remaining fat. Stir until brown, pour in water when blended. Pour over steak and onion and bake in pre-heated oven 350° for about 30 to 40 minutes, add seasoning to gravy before pouring over steaks.

Greek Meatballs

1 pound ground beef or lamb
1/2 cup dry bread crumbs
1/4 cup snipped parsley
1/4 cup milk
1 egg
1 medium onion, finely chopped
1 clove garlic, finely chopped
1 tablespoon snipped fresh mint leaves or 1/2 teaspoon crushed dried mint
1 teaspoon salt
1/2 teaspoon crushed dried oregano leaves
1/4 teaspoon pepper

Mix all ingredients. Shape mixture into 1-inch balls. (For easy shaping, dip hands into cold water from time to time.) Place meatballs in ungreased jelly roll pan or oblong pan. Cook uncovered in 350° oven until light brown, about 25 minutes. 6 servings.

Detroiters, Edward F. Schlee, right and his pilot, William S. Brock took off from Old Orchard, Maine, in 1927 and flew their Stinson monoplane acoss the Atlantic, across Europe, and through Asia, in a world-girdling flight that ended in Tokyo, through monsoon and typhoon. They could not complete the journey due to a lack of a fuel supply from the Navy. A welcome-back dinner to honor them was held at Masonic Temple.

Irish Corned Beef and Cabbage
4-5 pound brisket of beef
3 slices onion
4 cloves
6 whole black peppercorns
1 bay leaf
1/2 teaspoon dried rosemary
1 clove garlic
2 green pepper rings
1 stalk celery
1 carrot
Few sprigs parsley, tied in bunch
1 green cabbage, quartered

Place brisket in large deep kettle and cover with cold water. Add all other ingredients except cabbage. Cover and bring to boil; reduce heat and simmer for 4-5 hours until meat is fork-tender. About 1/2 hour before meat is done, skim off excess fat from water. Arrange cabbage on top of meat and simmer, covered, for 25-30 minutes until cabbage is tender-crisp. To serve, slice meat and place on platter surrounded by cabbage. Makes 8 servings.

Sarma – Armenian
2 pounds ground beef
1 cup raw rice
1 onion, chopped fine
5 fresh tomatoes or 1 No. 2 can tomatoes
20 grape leaves
A few meat bones

Mix the beef, rice, onion, and tomatoes thoroughly and season with salt and pepper. Place a small amount of the mixture on a grape leaf and make into a roll, and continue until the mixture is all used up. In a kettle in which the meat bones have been placed, place the rolls in layers. Cover with water or meat stock, holding the sarma in place with a lid or plate. Boil at least 1 hour.

Memories
In 1937 or 1938 my mother and I took the ferry from Detroit to Windsor to see King George VI and Queen Elizabeth as they rode along on the platform car on the Royal Train. We stood near the railroad tracks and could see them clearly. Years later, my husband and I drove across the Blue Water Bridge between Port Huron and Sarnia to see Queen Elizabeth and Prince Philip. – Margaret Link

Pork

Pork Nicoise

4 tablespoons olive oil
4 tablespoons red wine vinegar
1/4 teaspoon salt
Fresh ground pepper
2 tablespoons each finely chopped chives and parsley
8 small new potatoes, cooked
1 pound green beans, cooked
2 large tomatoes, cut into eighths
2 hard-cooked eggs, peeled and quartered
10 anchovy fillets
1/2 cup pitted ripe olives
1 tablespoon capers
Butter lettuce or chopped romaine
1 1/2 cups cooked pork, cut julienne
Watercress

Shake together oil, vinegar, salt and pepper, chives and parsley. Quarter potatoes, coat lightly with dressing and chill 1-2 hours. Dress beans lightly with dressing, chill. On large platter, arrange potatoes and beans, tomatoes, lettuce. Top with pork, garnish with anchovies, olives, capers, and watercress. Drizzle remaining dressing over all. Serves 4.

Barbecued Pork Chops

Submitted by Rennie Hughes

6 pork chops
1/4 cup flour
1/4 cup vinegar
1/2 teaspoon salt
1/2 teaspoon dry mustard
1 teaspoon celery seed
1 tablespoon Worcestershire sauce
1/2 cup catsup
2 tablespoons brown sugar
1/4 teaspoon Tabasco

Coat chops with flour and brown in skillet. Stir remaining ingredients together in small bowl. Pour over the chops, cover and simmer over low heat until chops are tender and well-cooked. Serves 6

Pork Chops in Orange Sauce

6 pork chops (1/2-inch thick)
1 tablespoon butter
1/4 cup minced onion
1 tablespoon flour
2 bouillon cubes
1 cup boiling water
1/2 teaspoon minced parsley
1 drop of oil of peppermint
1 teaspoon dry mustard
Juice of 1 lemon
Juice of 1 orange
1 teaspoon salt
1/8 teaspoon pepper

Brown chops on both sides. Melt butter; add minced onion; cook until soft. Stir in flour; dissolve bouillon cubes in boiling water; add gradually to butter, onion, flour mixture, stirring constantly. Simmer 8 minutes. Add parsley, peppermint oil, mustard, fruit juices, salt and pepper; add chops. Cover and simmer for 3 hours.

Vernors Mock Sangria

Mix equal parts of Vernors and grape juice. Serve cold over ice for a refreshing summer drink. Serve hot in mugs with a thin lemon slice for warming winter drink.

Potatoes Stuffed with Ham – Romanian

1 large baking potato for each person
1/2 tablespoon butter
1/4 pound boiled or baked ham
1 tablespoon grated Swiss cheese
Parsley, fennel, chives
Pepper and salt

Wash potatoes, bake in oven. When done, let them cool, then slice off the tops and scoop out the insides, leaving a not too thin shell. In a mixing bowl, add potatoes, 1 1/2 tablespoons butter, 1/4 pound ham (diced), 1 tablespoon grated cheese, finely chopped parsley, fennel, chives, pepper and salt to taste. Mix well. Stuff the potatoes not quite to the top. Place potatoes on a baking dish. Add a pat of butter to top of stuffing, sprinkle on a little parsley. Replace the slice off potato tops. Place in a hot oven uncovered and bake until heat has penetrated the stuffed potatoes. Serve hot.

Independence Day
1905
The Russell House
Detroit
Chittenden Co. Ltd
Proprietors

Pig Feet – Slovak

3 pounds pig feet, cut in half lengthwise
Water
1 tablespoon salt
Pepper
1/4 red paprika (optional)
Clove of garlic

Singe pig feet by holding over flame. Wash – and cover with water. Bring to boiling point and skim. Simmer slowly and add garlic, onion, salt and pepper and paprika. Cook until bones fall apart (about 4 or 5 hours). Pour into deep dishes and let stand overnight in a cold place. The liquid will jell.

Vernors New Yorker

Submitted by Carol White, Woodhaven, Michigan

In blender or shaker mix six ounces Vernors, two tablespoons chocolate syrup, two tablespoons cream or evaporated milk and crushed ice. Serves one.

Jewelled Crown Roast of Pork with Champagne Dressing

Submitted by Shirley Hartert

7 pounds crown roast of pork
3 tablespoons lime juice
1 teaspoon ground ginger
1 tablespoon flour
1 teaspoon celery salt
1/2 teaspoon ground pepper
Parsley (garnish)
Green grapes in clusters
Small red crab apples
Kumquats, drained
Stuffing (recipe follows)

Pour lime juice over roast. Mix together ginger, flour, salt and pepper and sprinkle over meat. Roast at 350° watching carefully not to overcook. After one hour drain fat and fill with dressing. Return to oven and cover lightly with foil until done. To serve: place pork on platter and surround with a wreath of parsley sprigs. Place bunches of green grapes on top of parsley. Small red crab apples are a pretty contrast between clusters.

"Spear" kumquats on toothpicks on tops of ribs like jewels atop a crown. If kumquats are unavailable, substitute paper frills made from typing paper.

Champagne Dressing

Submitted by Shirley Hartert

1 cup chopped onion
1/2 cup crushed pineapple, drained
4 strips bacon, fried and crumbled
1/3 cup ripe olives, chopped
2 tablespoons parsley, chopped
1 cup celery, chopped, sauteed 5 minutes in butter
2 cups wild rice cooked in champagne or dry white wine, not water
1 teaspoon marjoram
1/2 teaspoon thyme
2 eggs, beaten
1 cup raw mushrooms, chopped

Combine all ingredients and stuff center of pork roast. Prepare after roast has been started and add after first hour of roasting.

Pork Cordon Bleu – French

4 boneless pork chops, each about 3-4 ounces
2 ounces proscuitto or wafer-thin ham
2 ounces Swiss cheese, cut into 2-inch by 1/4-inch rectangles
1 teaspoon dried thyme leaves
1/2 cup flour
1 egg, beaten with 1 teaspoon water
1/2 cup fine dry bread crumbs

Slice each chop lengthwise almost in half to butterfly. Between two pieces of plastic film, pound each butterflied chop to 1/8-inch thickness. On half of each chop, place 1 ounce proscuitto and 1 piece of cheese. Sprinkle with 1/4 teaspoon thyme. Roll chops to enclose filling. Coat with flour, dip into egg wash, and roll in bread crumbs.

In 12-inch frying pan, melt 3 table-spoons butter. Add pork and cook 10-12 minutes, turning frequently to brown all sides. Garnish with lemon wedges and parsley. 4 servings.

Where Are The Roads?

For more than a century, no roads led to or from Detroit. On Woodward, from six-mile to Royal Oak lay a swamp so fearsome that no contractor would undertake to bridge it. Until 1850 Detroit continued to wallow in mire. Then, as a result of the Plank Road Act (1848), plank roads were finally under construction.

Polynesian Pork

4 cups bite-size pork cubes
3 tablespoons soy sauce
1 clove garlic, minced
1/4 teaspoon ginger
1/3 cup vinegar
1/3 cup brown sugar
3/4 cup pineapple tidbits and juice
3 cans tomato sauce (8 ounces each)

Lightly brown pork cubes in a small amount of fat in skillet. Blend soy sauce with garlic, ginger, vinegar, brown sugar, pineapple and tomato sauce; pour over meat, cover and simmer about 40 minutes; serve with hot rice. Serves 6.

Ham Hocks and Turnip Greens – African American

3 large ham hocks
2 pounds turnip greens
1 small onion

If greens have bottoms to them, cut these off and save. Wash greens, easiest is to cover up, drain and wash them right in the sink. This gets off all the soil and dirt. Wash ham hocks and put them in a boiler and let them come to a boil and pour off this water and add water not quite enough to cover them (the water from your greens will supply the rest). Let cook about 1 hour slow before adding greens. Place greens in pot with ham hocks. Let cook until the ham hocks feel tender. Peel turnip bottoms, quarter them and lay them on the top of greens and let cook slowly until done.

Baked Spare Ribs – African American

Spare ribs
1/2 cup flour
Seasoning salt
Black pepper
3 cups water

Wash spare ribs and cut into serving size. Season with salt and black pepper. Dredge with flour, place ribs in roaster and put water in, add extra flour. Put in oven 350° and cook about one hour and keep basting.

Almondigas – Philipines

1 cup ground pork or ground beef (or both mixed in equal portion)
1 egg
Misua (Chinese thin noodles)
1/2 cup green onion
1 onion, sliced or chopped
Salt to taste
Pepper to taste
1 cup ground shrimp (optional)
1/2 tablespoon Accent (optional)
Shrimp extract if available
Garlic

Mix the meat (pork or beef) with shrimp, chopped onion and desired seasoning (salt, pepper and Accent). Shape into small balls about the size of a cherry tomato.

Saute the garlic and chopped onion and about 3 cups of water (and shrimp extract if any). Bring the mixture to a boil, then drop meat balls individually. Add the Misua and remove from fire. Add salt to taste if needed. Sprinkle with green onion. Serve hot.

Cajun Chops

4 boneless pork chops, cut 1/2 inch thick
1 tablespoon paprika
1 teaspoon seasoned salt
1 teaspoon rubbed sage
1/2 teaspoon cayenne pepper
1/2 teaspoon black pepper
1/2 teaspoon garlic powder
2 tablespoons butter

Combine seasonings; coat chops with seasoning mixture on both sides. Heat butter over high heat just until it starts to brown. Put chops in pan, reduce heat to medium. Fry on both sides until dark brown, about 8-10 minutes. Serves 4.

Pigs Feet and Beans – African American

Pigs feet, split in half (amount according to family)
Large onion, chopped
Salt
Black pepper
Cup beans – 1 pound larger family

Clean and wash feet, pick and wash beans thoroughly and put on together with onion and let cook about 1 1/2 hours. Serve with cole slaw.

Pig snouts prepared same way, same cooking time.

Pig tails prepared same way, same cooking item. With pinto beans cook 2 to 2 1/2 hours.

With black eyes cook black eyes alone for 20 minutes. In separate pot pour off water and add to already cooking tails, feet or snouts.

Roast Glazed Loin of Pork

1 4 1/2 to 5 pound loin of pork (10 chops)
2 teaspoons alt
Freshly ground pepper
1 cup orange juice
1/2 cup light brown sugar
1 tablespoon ginger
1/4 teaspoon powdered cloves

Preheat the oven to 325°. Place pork, fat side up, in a roasting pan. Insert thermometer; do not let it touch bone. Rub in the salt and pepper. Roast for 35 minutes to the pound, or until it reaches 170°. Meanwhile, in a small saucepan, mix the orange juice, sugar, ginger and clove together. Simmer for 30 minutes. Brush this glaze generously over the roast, at least twice, during the last hour of roasting time. Serves 6.

First Envelopes

Up to 1839 all letters written in Detroit were so folded as to form their own envelope and sealed with hot wax, but during that year manufactured envelopes came into use.

Leftover Ham in Sour Cream

1 cup cooked ham in julienne strips
1/4 cup chopped onion
2 tablespoons butter or margarine
1 tablespoon flour
1 cup dairy sour cream
1 small can sliced mushrooms, drained
Hot cooked rice

Cook ham and onion in butter until tender but not brown. Sprinkle with flour; gradually stir in sour cream. Add mushrooms. Cook over low heat, stirring constantly, just until mixture thickens, 2 to 3 minutes. Garnish with parsley or add chopped parsley to the mixture for color. Serve over cooked rice. Makes 3 or 4 servings.

This is a good recipe for buffet-type serving.

Vernor's Passion-Party Punch

In punch bowl mix two quarts chilled orange juice, one bottle light rum and two quarts chilled Vernors. Garnish with fresh or canned fruit cocktail.

Teriyaki Pork – Japanese

1 pound pork tenderloin, cut into 6x1/2 x 1/8-inch slices
2 tablespoons sliced green onion
1 tablespoon brown sugar
1/2 teaspoon ginger
1 clove garlic, minced
1/2 cup soy sauce
1/4 cup dry sherry

Combine all ingredients except pork strips, mix well. Add pork to marinade, cover and marinate in refrigerator at least one hour. Thread meat onto skewers. Broil or grill, turning frequently, 4-5 minutes. Serve with rice, if desired. 4 servings.

Lamb

Lamb Curry – India

1 cup butter
2 medium onions, chopped
2 pounds lamb, cubed
2 teaspoons salt
1/2 teaspoon cayenne pepper
1 tablespoon coriander
1 tablespoon sugar
1 pound small turnips, peeled and halved
1 cup plain yogurt
1 1/2 teaspoon curry powder

Melt butter in large pan, add onions and brown. Add the rest of the ingredients and cook about 25 minutes or until meat browns. Reduce heat; cover and simmer for 45 minutes or until meat is tender. Serve with hot fluffy rice and offer bowls of condiments such as raisins, peanuts, chutney, and coconut. Serves 6.

Crown Roast of Lamb

Have the butcher prepare the ribs for "crown roast." The center may be filled with bread stuffing, cooked vegetables, boiled chestnuts or mashed potatoes.

Cover the ends of the ribs with greased brown paper to prevent charring. Roast one and one-quarter hours or until tender in a hot oven.

Serve with fancy paper chop holders. Serves 4-6.

Lamb Shanks

4 lamb shanks
2 tablespoons flour
1 tablespoon fat (salad oil, etc.)
1 cup water
2 tablespoons horseradish
2 tablespoons Worcestershire sauce
2 tablespoons vinegar
1/2 teaspoon salt
Pepper

Mix flour, salad oil or fat; add water.

Cook 2 to 3 hours until mixture thickens into a delicious gravy and meat falls away from bone. Serves 4.

Roast Leg of Lamb

Bone the lamb, dredge with flour, sprinkle on salt and pepper. Roast in a roasting pan in a hot oven. When brown, baste every quarter hour and add water if necessary. Cook for two hours.

Serve with mint sauce or pour one glass currant or gooseberry jelly over the meat just before serving. Serves 8-10.

Memories - Lenora Stoetzer - Born 1909
When I was a girl it seems like everything came by our neighborhood via horse-drawn vendors. There was the milk man, the vegetable man (usually Italian), egg man, junkman, fresh fish and even Awreys & Mills Bakeries. We also used to take our little red wagon to the ice house twice a week to get ice for mother's icebox.

Arabic Shish Kabob

1 pound lamb boneless shoulder, cut into 1-inch cubes
1/4 cup lemon juice
2 tablespoons olive or vegetable oil
2 teaspoons salt
1/2 teaspoon dried oregano leaves
1/4 teaspoon pepper
1 green pepper, cut into 1-inch pieces
1 medium onion, cut into eighths
1 cup cubed eggplant

Place lamb in glass or plastic bowl. Mix lemon juice, oil, salt, oregano and pepper; pour over lamb. Cover and refrigerate, stirring occasionally, at least 6 hours.

Remove lamb; reserve marinade. Thread lamb on four 11-inch metal skewers, leaving space between each. Set oven control to broil and /or 550°. Broil lamb with tops about 3 inches from heat 5 minutes. Turn; brush with reserved marinade. Broil 5 minutes.

Alternate green pepper, onion and eggplant on four 11-inch metal skewers, leaving space between. Place vegetables on rack in broiler pan with lamb. Turn lamb; brush lamb and vegetables with reserved marinade. Broil kabobs; turning and brushing twice with marinade, until brown, 4 to 5 minutes. 4 servings.

Detroit Opera House and Fountain, 1910.

Meat and Potato Balls

1 pound ground lamb
2 onions, chopped fine, browned in fat
1 cup mashed potatoes
1 egg
Salt and pepper, for seasoning

Mix the ingredients together and make into balls. Place in a pan with a small piece of butter on each ball and put under broiler. When the tops are brown turn the balls and brown the other side.

Meat Balls for a Pasha – Syrian

2 pounds ground lamb
1 large onion, diced
1/2 cup uncooked, washed rice
2-ounce can tomatoes, drained
2 tablespoons salt
4 tablespoons dried dill weed
1/4 cup chopped parsley
4 tablespoons cornstarch stirred into 1/2 cup water
2 eggs
Juice of 1 lemon
Pepper to taste

Put 3 3/4 inches water plus 2 1/2 tablespoons salt in a saucepan about 11 inches in diameter. Cover and bring to a boil. Knead meat with onion, rice, drained and mashed tomatoes, salt, pepper, dill and parsley. Roll into 2-inch balls and drop one by one into boiling water. Simmer for 1 1/2 hours, then thicken juice with cornstarch mixture.

In a separate bowl, beat eggs and lemon juice together. When mixture has cooled to below boiling temperature but still is hot, gradually beat in some of the liquid, tablespoon by tablespoon, taking care the egg does not solidify. Then stir egg-lemon broth into rest of mixture. Warm slightly. Serve in a tureen or large bowl. Can be used as a soup or main dish with plain rice pilaf. Serves 10-12.

Memories - Lenora Stoetzer - Born 1909
Growing up I remember wreaths on the door that signified a quarantine or death in the home. The color of the wreath told what the problem was. Measles and Chicken Pox – yellow wreath; Diphtheria – blue wreath; Scarlet Fever – red wreath; Death of baby – white wreath; Death of young child – pink or gray wreath; Death of older person – dark color wreath.

Irish Stew

6 large potatoes, peeled and cut into 1 1/2 inch cubes
2 teaspoons salt
1/2 teaspoon pepper
6 large onions, sliced
3 carrots, sliced
2 ribs celery, sliced
2 medium tomatoes, cubed
3 pounds boneless lamb, cut into 1 inch cubes
1 1/2 cups water

In a heavy saucepan place a layer of potatoes and sprinkle with a little salt and pepper. Add layers of the remaining vegetables with seasoning. Place a layer of lamb on top and season. Repeat until all ingredients are used up; the top layer should consist of potatoes. Pour water over it and cover. Bring to a boil and cook over low heat for 1 1/2 hours, or until lamb is tender. Serves 8-10.

Bourekia – Greek
(Pastries Stuffed with Lamb)

1 pound ground lamb
1 medium onion, finely chopped
Oil
2 tablespoons chopped fresh parsley
1 teaspoon basil or to taste
Salt to taste
Freshly ground pepper
1/2 cup pine nuts or slivered almonds
3/4 pound phyllo dough
1/2 pound butter, melted

Preheat oven to 325°. Saute lamb, onion and green pepper in oil until lamb takes on color and vegetables are soft. Add parsley, basil and salt. Season with lots of pepper. Add nuts and set aside to cool

Remove one sheet of phyllo and brush it with melted butter. With a sharp knife, cut phyllo lengthwise into four 2-inch wide strips. Place a heaping teaspoonful of filling on one end of the pastry strip and fold over one corner to form a triangle. Continue folding the pastry from side to side in the shape of a triangle (as you would fold a flag) until all the dough is folded over the filling. Repeat this process strip by strip until all the filling has been used.

Place bourekia on buttered baking sheet and bake 20 minutes or until golden brown. Serve hot. Makes about 4 dozen pastries.

Lamb Chops with Vegetables and Fruits

6 boned loin lamb chops, cut 1 1/2 inches thick, about 6 ounces each, trimmed weight
Salt and freshly ground black pepper, to taste
3 kiwis, peeled and scooped into balls
2 cups seedless red or green grapes
24 asparagus spears, trimmed, blanched and sliced diagonally
2 thin cucumbers, peeled and scooped into balls
1/3 cup minced fresh mint and parsley, more or less half and half, or to taste

Preheat oven to 350°.

Tie chops into neat rounds with kitchen twine. Arrange each on a piece of foil and season to taste with salt and pepper. Scatter fruits and vegetables around chops, dividing equally. Sprinkle chopped mint and parsley over all. Seal the foil packets, and set on a baking sheet. Bake about 20 minutes for medium rare. Transfer packets to serving plates and allow guests to open them at table. 6 portions.

Grilled Lamb Kabobs

1 cup chopped onions
3 cloves garlic, minced
2/3 cup cider vinegar
1/4 cup vegetable oil
1/4 cup olive oil
3 tablespoons honey
1 tablespoon dried rosemary
2 teaspoons chopped fresh mint
1/2 teaspoon salt
1/2 teaspoon seasoned pepper
2 pounds boneless lamb, cut into 24 cubes
1 large onion, cut into 12 wedges and halved
12 plum tomatoes, halved
24 small fresh mushrooms

Combine first ten ingredients. Mix well.

Add lamb cubes; stir to coat evenly. Refrigerate, covered, 6 to 8 hours; stir occasionally.

When ready to grill, drain meat, reserving marinade. Put marinade in a medium saucepan and heat to boiling. Reduce heat and let marinade simmer until needed. On each of 6 metal skewers, thread 1 piece onion, 1 meat cube, 1 tomato half and 1 mushroom; repeat 3 times. Place kabobs on a grill over medium-high heat 4 to 6 inches from medium-hot coals. Cook 12 to 15 minutes, basting several times with heated marinade. Discard remaining marinade. Makes 6 servings.

Hollywood Theatre Flyer

Poultry

Duckling a L'Orange

Submitted by Shirley Hartert

1 ready-to-cook duckling (4 to 5 pounds)
2 teaspoons grated orange peel
1/2 cup orange juice
1/4 cup currant jelly
1 tablespoon lemon juice
1/8 teaspoon dry mustard
1/8 teaspoon salt
1 tablespoon cold water
1 1/2 teaspoons cornstarch
1 orange, peeled and sectioned
1 tablespoon orange-flavored liqueur (optional)

Fasten neck skin of duckling to back with skewers. Lift wings up and over back for natural brace. Place duckling breast side up on rack in shallow roasting pan. Prick skin with fork. Roast uncovered in 325° oven until done, about 2 1/2 hours, removing excess fat from pan occasionally. (If duckling becomes too brown, place piece of aluminum foil lightly over breast.) Duckling is done when drumstick meat feels very soft. Let stand 10 minutes for easier carving.

Heat orange peel, orange juice, jelly, lemon juice, mustard and salt to boiling. Mix water and cornstarch; stir into sauce. Cook over medium heat, stirring constantly, until mixture thickens and boils. Boil and stir 1minute. Stir in orange sections and liqueur. Brush duckling with some of the orange sauce; serve with remaining sauce.

Street Lights of Detroit
Detroit installed whale oil lamps in 1830 on the city streets, but they proved to be cumbersome as well as a fire menace and were soon discarded. By 1851 the first gaslights came into being and lamp posts were erected at the corners of principal streets.

Coke Chicken

1 package whole chicken parts
Ketchup
Coke
1 medium onion, sliced

Mix equal parts of coke and ketchup; enough to completely cover. In large frying pan place chicken pieces. Cover with ketchup and coke mixture. Place sliced onions on top. Cook on top of stove for 2 hours on low, covered.

Spanish Chicken and Vegetables

6-8 servings
3 to 4 pound broiler-fryer chicken
1/4 cup margarine or butter, melted
3 tomatoes, cut into wedges
2 green peppers, cut into rings
2 medium onions, sliced
1 clove garlic, chopped
1/4 pound fully cooked smoked ham, cut up (1 cup)
8 pitted ripe olives, cut into halves
1 teaspoon salt
1/4 teaspoon pepper

Fasten neck skin of chicken to back with skewer. Fold wings across back with tips touching. Tie or skewer drumsticks to tail. Brush with margarine. Place chicken breast side up in Dutch oven. Cook uncovered in 375° oven, brushing with margarine every 30 minutes, until thickest pieces of chicken are done, about 1 1/2 hours. Add tomatoes, green peppers, onions, garlic, ham and olives. Sprinkle chicken and vegetables with salt and pepper. Cover and cook until green pepper is tender, about 20 minutes. Place chicken on serving platter; arrange vegetables and ham around chicken. Serve with hot cooked rice.

Chicken Oregano – Greek

2 1/2- to 3- pound broiler-fryer chicken, cup up
1/2 cup olive oil or vegetable oil
1/4 cup lemon juice
2 teaspoons dried oregano leaves
1 teaspoon salt
1/2 teaspoon pepper
1 clove garlic, chopped
Lemon slices

Place chicken in ungreased oblong pan, 13 x 9 x 2 inches. Mix remaining ingredients except lemon slices; pour over chicken. Cook uncovered in 375° oven, spooning oil mixture over chicken occasionally, 30 minutes. Turn chicken; cook until thickest pieces are done, about 30 minutes. Garnish with lemon slices. 6-8 servings.

Downtown Detroit Lights
Detroit citizens gathered at Grand Circus Park, along with Thomas Edison, Henry Ford and Harvey Firestone in 1928 to celebrate the Anniversary of the Electric Light. All the lights went off for one minute and then were turned on by Edison.

Christmas Goose

1 ready-to-cook goose (8 to 10 pounds)
2 cups water
1 small onion, sliced
1 1/4 teaspoons salt
6 cups soft bread crumbs
3 tart apples, chopped
2 stalks celery (with leaves), chopped
1 medium onion, chopped
1/4 cup margarine or butter, melted
2 teaspoons salt
1 teaspoon ground sage
1/2 teaspoon ground thyme
1/4 teaspoon pepper
1 teaspoon salt
1/4 cup all-purpose flour

Trim excess fat from goose. Heat giblets, water, sliced onion and 1 1/4 teaspoons salt to boiling; reduce heat. Cover and simmer until giblets are done, about 1 hour. Strain broth; cover and refrigerate. Chop giblets; toss with remaining ingredients except 1 teaspoon salt and the flour. Rub cavity of goose with 1 teaspoon salt. Fold wings across back with tips touching. Fill neck and body cavities of goose lightly with stuffing. Fasten neck skin of goose to back with skewers. Fasten opening with skewers; lace with string. Tie drumsticks to tail. Prick skin all over with fork. Place goose breast side up on rack in shallow roasting pan.

Roast uncovered in 350° oven until done, 3 to 3 1/2 hours, removing excess fat from pan occasionally. Place a tent of aluminum foil loosely over goose during last hour to prevent excessive browning. Goose is done when drumstick meat feels very soft. Place goose on heated platter. Let stand 15 minutes for easier carving.

Pour drippings from pan into bowl. Return 1/4 cup drippings to pan. Stir in flour. Cook over low heat, stirring constantly, until smooth and bubbly. Remove from heat. Add enough water to reserved broth if necessary to measure 2 cups. Stir into flour mixture. Heat to boiling, stirring constantly. Boil and stir 1 minute. Serve goose with apple stuffing and gravy. 6-8 servings.

Detroit Remembrances from Dorothea Hibbler

Riding to downtown Detroit on the Dexter Double Decker Bus. We would sit on top and the conductor would come around to collect one dime from each of us that he would insert in a handheld machine.

Chicken a la Maria

3/4 cup Italian bread crumbs
1/4 cup grated Parmesan cheese
6 large chicken breasts, skinned, boned, split lengthwise
1/2 cup sliced green onion
2 tablespoons butter
2 tablespoons flour
1 cup milk
1 10-ounce package spinach or broccoli
1 4-ounce package boiled ham slices – diced

Combine bread crumbs and cheese; dip chicken breast halves in crumb mixture; coat lightly. Arrange in 9x13-inch pan. Set remaining crumb mix aside. In saucepan cook onion in butter till tender. Blend in flour; stir in milk. Cook and stir till thickened. Cook and stir 1 minute. Stir in spinach and ham. Spoon spinach/broccoli mix over chicken; sprinkle with the rest of crumb mixture. Bake, uncovered, in 350° oven 40-45 minutes or until done. Makes 12 servings.

If you use fresh broccoli, chop and parboil first.

Tributes to Cadillac

Cadillac is remembered often by the citizens of France. For the Detroit Bi-Centennial in 1901 they presented to Detroit a painting of Cadillac being commissioned in Versailles to travel to the New World to establish a new colony for trading purposes. In 1951 a cast bronze bust of Cadillac was a gift and is on display at the Detroit Historical Museum. To help celebrate its 300th birthday, France is giving Detroit a 7 1/2 foot bronze likeness of Cadillac which will stand at Hart Plaza not far from the spot where he beached his canoe in 1701.

Chicken Fajitas

2 to 3 pounds boneless chicken breasts
1 teaspoon seasoned salt
1 1/2 tablespoons minced onions
1/8 teaspoon garlic powder
1 teaspoon salt
2 tablespoons lemon juice
1/2 cup soy sauce
2 tablespoons honey
1 to 2 packages soft, flour tortillas
Chopped tomatoes
Shredded lettuce
Shredded cheese
Sour cream
Guacamole dip
Picante sauce

Mix seasoned salt, onions, garlic powder, salt, lemon juice, soy sauce and honey. Pour over chicken and marinate about 24 hours. Charcoal broil on medium hot fire approximately 5 minutes on each side – or until done. Slice diagonally in strips. Fill tortillas with remaining ingredients as desired.

Glazed Blueberry Chicken

1 chicken, 2 1/2 to 3 pounds, cut into quarters
1/2 cup blueberry vinegar*
1 teaspoon dried thyme
Salt and freshly ground black pepper, to taste
1/3 cup Blueberry Chutney*
Chopped Italian parsley (garnish)
Grated orange zest (optional garnish)

Combine chicken quarters, blueberry vinegar and thyme in a bowl and marinate for 2 hours, turning occasionally.

Preheat oven to 300°.

Arrange chicken pieces, skin side up, in a baking dish, reserving the marinade. Season chicken lightly with salt and pepper to taste and coat it with the chutney. Set the pan on the center rack of the oven and bake, uncovered, for about 40 minutes, or until done. You may need to bake the dark meat sections for another 5 to 10 minutes. Transfer chicken to a serving platter, cover, and keep warm.

Skim fat from cooking juices and set the baking dish over medium heat. Add the marinade and bring to a boil, stirring and scraping up any browned bits in the pan. Reduce by one-third, or until sauce is lightly thickened. Pour sauce over chicken and garnish with parsley and orange zest. Serve immediately. 2 to 4 portions.

*available in specialty food stores

French Country-Style Chicken

3- to 4-pound broiler-fryer chicken
2 tablespoons margarine or butter
1 can (10 3/4 ounces) condensed chicken broth
1 teaspoon salt
1/4 teaspoon pepper
1/4 teaspoon dried thyme leaves
8 medium carrots, cut into fourths
8 small whole white onions
4 medium turnips, cut into fourths
1/2 cup dry white wine
2 tablespoons cold water
1 tablespoon cornstarch

Fold chicken wings across back with tips touching; tie drumsticks to tail. Heat margarine in Dutch oven until melted. Cook chicken in margarine over medium heat until brown on all sides, 20 to 30 minutes. Pour broth over chicken; sprinkle with salt, pepper and thyme. Cover and cook in 375° oven 45 minutes. Arrange carrots, onions and turnips around chicken. Cover and cook until thickest pieces of chicken are done, 1 to 1 1/2 hours.

Remove chicken and vegetables to warm platter; remove string. Keep chicken warm. Stir wine into chicken broth. Heat to boiling. Mix water and cornstarch; stir into wine broth. Heat to boiling; stirring constantly. Boil and stir 1 minute; skim fat. Serve sauce with chicken. 8 servings.

The Letter Writer

One of the most industrious letter writers in all Detroit's history was its founder, Antoine de la Mothe Cadillac. He wrote numerous letters to advisors and business partners in France, although Detroit did not have a post office until 1803.

Chicken Enchiladas

10 (8 inch) flour tortillas (room temperature)
1 small onion, chopped
8 to 12 ounces cream cheese, softened
3 cups cooked seasoned chicken
1 cup whipping cream, unwhipped
2 cups shredded Monterey Jack cheese

Cook chicken and shred. Saute onion in 2 tablespoons oleo. Add the chicken and cream cheese. Mix well. Divide chicken mixture over the 10 tortillas. Roll up and place seam side down in greased 9 x 13 inch pan. Top with cheese (Monterey Jack). Drizzle with whipping cream. Bake uncovered at 375° for 20 to 25 minutes or until bubbly.

Detroit Memories - Margaret Link (80 years old) - 2001

When I was a little girl my father took me to one of the first J. L. Hudson parades. We took the streetcar downtown, leaving my mother behind to prepare the Thanksgiving dinner. It was a cold day and I don't remember much about the parade itself, except Santa Claus, but on the way home I asked my father why there were so many cross Daddys in the crowd.

My dad also took me to some of the big Memorial Day parades which marched along Woodward Avenue. I can remember him pointing out to me the Civil War Veterans who were too infirm to march, so they rode in automobiles.

Chilean Chicken Stew

1 medium clove garlic, split
2 tablespoons butter or margarine
1 broiler-fryer (2 1/2 pounds), cut up
1 cup chopped onion (1 large)
3 green onions with tops, chopped
1 medium carrot, diced
1 cup diced celery (about 3 ribs)
2 cups shredded cabbage
1/2 teaspoon salt
1/2 teaspoon crushed red pepper
1/4 teaspoon pepper
1 1/2 cups chicken bouillon

    In large skillet saute garlic in butter until lightly browned; discard garlic. In garlic butter lightly brown chicken; remove and set aside. Saute onion until brown. Add green onions, carrot, celery, cabbage, salt and peppers. Cook about 10 minutes, stirring occasionally. Add chicken and bouillon. Cover and cook 30 minutes or until chicken is fork-tender. Serves 4.

Detroit Historical Museum Paving

Cobblestones were commonly used to pave sidewalks and streets in the 1840's in Detroit. By the 1870's, the new paving was 5-inch thick sections of small cedar trees set close together on a 4 inch bed of gravel and covered in tar. The Streets of Detroit in the Detroit Historical Museum has a permanent exhibit where examples of both these types of paving can be seen.

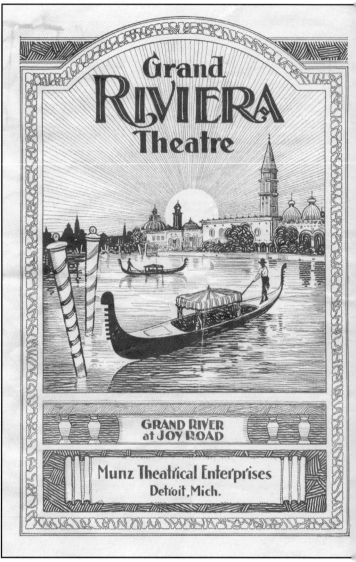

Turkey Crunch

Contributed by Pat Wilson

4 cups cubed turkey
2 cups diced celery
2 cans cream of chicken soup
1 cup shredded cheddar cheese
2 cans or 1 large can Chinese noodles
1 1/2 cups mayonnaise
1 green pepper, chopped
4 tablespoons onions, chopped
4 tablespoons lemon juice
1/4 teaspoon salt

    Mix all together. Put in 13 x 9 inch pan. Bake at 350° for 40 minutes.

Vegetables

Mixed Vegetable Casserole – Scandinavian

3 medium carrots, sliced
2 cups green beans, cut into 1-inch pieces
1/2 small head cauliflower (about 2 cups)
1 small onion, sliced
2 tablespoons butter
2 tablespoons flour
1/2 teaspoon salt
1/8 teaspoon pepper
1/2 cup whipping cream
1/4 cup grated Parmesan cheese

Cook carrots, beans, cauliflower and onion until tender. Drain and place in baking dish. (Save liquid.)

Heat margarine over low heat until melted. Blend in flour, salt and pepper. Cook over low heat, stirring constantly, until mixture is smooth and bubbly; remove from heat.

Stir in 1 cup of the reserved liquid and the whipping cream. Heat to boiling, stirring constantly. Boil and stir minute; remove from heat. Pour sauce over vegetables; sprinkle with cheese.

Broil until top is light brown and bubbly, 3 to 5 minutes.

Horse Boat Ferry

In 1825 John Burtis produced a ferry powered by horses on a treadmill that turned the propeller by means of a huge cogwheel arrangement. It was built on a catamaran plan.

Sweet Potato Pone – African American

2 pounds of grated raw sweet potato
1 1/2 pounds of sugar
6 eggs (well beaten)
1 quart of milk
Juice and grated rind of 1 lemon
1/2 cup of melted butter or margarine
1/2 teaspoon of nutmeg
1/2 teaspoon of cinnamon
1/2 teaspoon mace
1 teaspoon of salt

Mix all the ingredients. Grease the baking dish. Bake in an oven at about 250° for about 2 hours.

Rice Pilaf – Armenian

4 tablespoons butter
2 cups rice or cracked wheat (bulgur)
1 cup tomato juice
4 cups water or clean meat broth

Brown the rice or bulgur slowly in melted fat for about 20 minutes, stirring constantly. Add the tomato juice to the water or meat broth; season with salt and boil. Pour over the partially cooked rice or bulgur. Boil until it absorbs water or broth. Remove pan from fire; cover top of pan with clean dry cloth. Cover with close fitting lid and let stand for about 10 to 15 minutes. This helps to remove extra moisture. Serve with matzoon.

Baked Pumpkin – Native American

1 small sugar pie pumpkin, whole and unopened
1/4 cup apple cider/juice
1/8 cup honey
1/8 cup real maple syrup
1/4 cup raisins or currants
1/4 cup dried apples
"Dollop" of butter or margarine, softened to room temperature.

Wash the pumpkin well, place on a pie pan, and bake in a moderate oven (350°) for 1 and 1/2 hours.

As soon as the pumpkin is in the oven, mix together the apple cider/juice, honey, and maple syrup. Pour the liquid over the dried fruits and set aside.

Remove the pumpkin from the oven (after 1 and 1/2 hours) and cut a hole in the top of the pumpkin about 3-inches to 4-inches in diameter. Scoop out pulp and seeds. Using a metal spoon, gently scrape the "flesh" loose from the walls of the pumpkin. Add in the dried fruit and liquid mixture, and the dollop of butter and stir, being careful not to puncture the "shell."

Replace the top, return to moderate oven and continue to bake for another 35 to 40 minutes longer. Serve whole, scooping out the individual portions at the table, or cut into wedges as you would a melon. Ladle a little of the juice over each serving.

Sweet Potato Casserole – American

3 cups mashed sweet potatoes
1 stick butter or margarine (1/2 cup)
1 teaspoon vanilla
1 cup sugar
2 eggs, beaten

Mix the ingredients together with an electric mixer on low speed until well blended. Pour into a greased rectangular baking pan.

Topping:
1/3 cup flour
1/3 cup butter or margarine
1 cup brown sugar
1/3 cup milk
1 cup chopped nuts (pecans)

Mix the topping ingredients together with an electric mixer on low speed until well blended. Spread evenly on top of the potato mixture. Bake at 325∫ for 30-40 minutes or until set in the center.

Man of Enterprise

David C. McKinstry was in the business of amusement enterprises. In 1834 he was operating a theater, a circus, a museum and a public amusement garden. The public garden was the most profitable. On a block bounded by Randolph and Brush, Lafayette and Monroe, there was a fruit tree orchard where he laid out walkways for strollers around the gardens and trees.

Vegetable Bacon Stew – African American

1 1/2 pounds green beans
1/2 pound sliced bacon
2 large onions
1/2 stick butter or margarine
Salt
Black pepper

Wash green beans, cut off ends and break in 3 pieces, put them on to boil. While beans are cooking, peel and cut up onions and potatoes, small. Cut up bacon in small pieces. Put in skillet and fry on low flame. Add onions. Onions should be cut very small, let cook with bacon, pour beans, add potatoes and butter, cover and let cook slow about 40 minutes.

Sub Gum Chow Mein – Chinese

3 cups finely shredded, cooked chicken
1/2 cup oil
1 1/2 cups diced, canned water chestnuts
1 1/2 cups diced, canned bamboo shoots
3 cups diced celery
2 cups sliced Chinese cabbage
3/4 cup diced mushrooms
1 large green pepper, diced
3/4 cup toasted almonds
3/4 cup thinly sliced green beans
9 scallions, chopped
2 garlic cloves, chopped
3 cups chicken bouillon
1 tablespoon sugar
3 tablespoons cornstarch
1 tablespoon salt
Freshly ground black pepper
Chow mein noodles

Fry vegetables, sugar, salt and pepper in oil for 1 minute, stirring briskly. Add bouillon. Bring to a boil, then reduce heat, cover and simmer for 10 minutes. Combine soy sauce, cornstarch and 4 tablespoons water. Add to vegetable mixture and cook until thickened, stirring constantly. Add chicken and cook for 5 minutes. Serve with noodles, garnish with almonds. Serves 6.

Welcome Back Potato Skins

Preheat oven to 425°. Rub 4 large baking potatoes with butter and bake 1 hour. Remove potatoes from oven. Slice in half horizontally and scoop out pulp with a spoon. Use pulp in another recipe. Brush the inside of the skins with about 2 tablespoons melted butter, salt to taste. Sprinkle with paprika to taste. Return skins to oven and bake 20 minutes or until crisp. Serve with sour cream or plain yogurt, if desired. Makes 4 skins.

Can add shredded cheese and bacon, crumbled in potato skins and heat in oven until melted.

McKinstry's Public Garden - 1834

The garden had a small pavilion for the band that played on Saturday evenings. There was a restaurant and near the restaurant was a bathhouse consisting of plain stalls containing a wooden tub for private bathing. Since homes had no bathtubs at the time, his place was busiest on Saturday nights where one could bathe in privacy.

Sweet Potatoes and Apples – Mexican

6 servings
6 medium sweet potatoes or yams (about 2 pounds)
2 tart apples, cored and cut into 1/4-inch rings
1/2 cup orange juice
1/4 cup packed brown sugar
1/4 teaspoon ground ginger
1/4 teaspoon ground cinnamon
2 tablespoons margarine or butter

Heat enough water to cover potatoes to boiling. Add potatoes. Heat to boiling; reduce heat. Cover and simmer until tender, 30 to 35 minutes. Cool slightly; slip off skins. Cut potatoes into 1/4-inch slices.

Layer potatoes and apples in greased oblong baking dish, 10 x 6 x 1 1/2 inches. Pour orange juice over potatoes and apples. Mix brown sugar, ginger and cinnamon; sprinkle over apples. Dot with margarine. Cook uncovered in 350° until apples are crisp-tender, about 30 minutes.

New Men's Store

In 1881 when J. L. Hudson opened his store for men in Detroit, the City had grown to a population of 116,000.

Sauerkraut with Meats – French

2 tablespoons oil
2 medium onions, sliced
1 clove garlic, minced
1 tart apple, pared and diced
1 carrot, sliced thin or grated
1 cup dry white wine or beer
1 bay leaf
8 juniper berries
10 peppercorns
2 cloves
Parsley sprigs
2 (16 ounce) cans sauerkraut
1 pound Canadian bacon or ham, sliced 1/4 inch
4 knockwursts or other sausage

To prepare: In a heavy pot, cook the oil, onions, garlic, apple and carrot, covered, until onions brown slightly. Add wine and herbs. Let simmer while you briefly rinse sauerkraut (skip rinse for more "sauer" flavor) and press dry. Stir into pot, then add meats and cook till well heated 20-25 minutes. Serves 2 (twice), 4 or double for 8.

Hasselback Potatoes – Swedish

Contributed by Shirley Hartert
6 medium baking potatoes
1/4 cup margarine or butter, melted
Salt
Pepper
1/4 cup grated Parmesan cheese
2 tablespoons dry bread crumbs
Paprika

Cut potatoes crosswise into 1/8-inch slices, cutting along 3/4 through. Place cut side up in greased oblong baking dish, 11 x 7 x 1 1/2 inches. Brush with margarine; sprinkle with salt and pepper.

Bake in 375° oven, brushing with margarine once or twice, 45 minutes. Mix cheese and bread crumbs; sprinkle on potatoes. Sprinkle with paprika. Bake until tender, 20 to 30 minutes. 6 servings.

Potatoes can be baked with a roast at 325° 1 hour. Brush with meat drippings; sprinkle with cheese mixture. Bake until tender, about 30 minutes.

Potato Latkes – Jewish

6 large potatoes
1 large onion, grated
2 tablespoons flour
2 eggs
1 teaspoon salt
1/2 teaspoon pepper
1/2 teaspoon baking powder
1 to 1 1/2 cups vegetable oil, enough to fill the skillet 1/4-inch deep
2 cups sour cream (optional)
1 cup applesauce (optional)
Granulated sugar to taste (optional)

   Peel potatoes and grate into a large bowl. Drain off a little of the liquid by pushing with a spoon. Add onion, flour, eggs, salt, pepper and baking powder; mix well. Heat oil in a large skillet over medium heat. Drop batter into oil, using a 1/4-cup measure. Brown well on both sides until crispy, about 30 seconds on each side. Drain on paper towels. Serve immediately with sour cream, applesauce or sugar on the side. Makes 35 to 40 three-inch pancakes. (You may keep latkes warm in 200° oven as you finish frying the batch, but they will lose a little crispness.)

Cauliflower – African American

1 head cauliflower
1/2 lemon
2 eggs
3 tablespoons butter

   Soak cauliflower, head downward, 1/2 hour or longer in cold salted water. Cook in boiling salted water 15 to 20 minutes. Drain and put on serving platter. It is cut in sections. Boil eggs and mix chopped egg yolk with butter and pour over cauliflower. Use lemon juice if desired.

Cabbage and Tomatoes – Croatian

1 tablespoon lard
1 large onion, sliced
1 quart tomatoes
1 medium head of cabbage, chopped fine
1 tablespoon paprika

   Slightly brown the onion and the cabbage in the lard. Season with salt and pepper and the paprika. Add the tomatoes and cook for 15 minutes.

Mushroom Stuffed Tomatoes

Contributed by Shirley Hartert

6 whole medium tomatoes
1/2 cup sliced fresh mushrooms
3 tablespoons butter
2 tablespoons tomato paste or ketchup
2 tablespoons water
1/2 teaspoon salt
1/8 teaspoon pepper
1 egg yolk, beaten
1/4 cup Parmesan cheese
Butter for topping
1/4 cup bread crumbs

   Cut stem ends off tomatoes and scoop out seeds, leaving a firm wall. Filling: Saute mushrooms 3 minutes. In another pan combine tomato paste, water, salt and pepper and cook until well blended and let cool approximately 4 minutes. Add egg yolk gradually a spoonful at a time. Add tomato-egg mixture to mushrooms and stuff tomatoes. Sprinkle tops with crumbs and cheese, top with a dot of butter. Bake at 425° for 10 minutes – do not overcook as tomatoes become mushy. An attractive vegetable garnish with roasts. 6 servings.

Lindbergh Family

Charles Lindbergh was the only child of Minnesota Congressman Charles A. Lindbergh and his wife, the former Evangeline Land. His mother was determined that her child be born in Detroit because Detroit was her hometown. He was born at his grandmother's house at 258 West Forest Avenue on February 4, 1902.

Gumbo Beans

1 can green beans, drained
1 can wax beans, drained
1 can navy beans, drained
1 can Lima beans, drained
1 can pork and beans, use juice
1 can kidney beans, use juice
1 can tomato paste
1 can tomato soup
1 pound pork sausage fried with onions
1 tablespoon BBQ sauce
1 tablespoon chili powder

   Mix together. Bake 350° 1 hour or use crockpot. Very nice for picnics.

Supper

at the

London

CHOP HOUSE

whereat you will find GOOD FOOD, *temptingly prepared under the supervision of* EDWARD DOBLER, *the Perch King of America;* DANCING *in the American and South American manner to two orchestras* --- FRANK GAGEN AND HIS MUSIC *and* SAMMY DIBERT'S *orchestra with* ETHEL HOWE *also Featuring Lovely* MARTHE ERROLLE — *and you may have your* CARICATURE *drawn by* HY VOGEL, *as has many a famous person.*

Potato Paprikash

2 pounds potatoes, sliced lengthwise (approximate amount)
1 large onion, diced
1 tablespoon paprika
2 tablespoons oil, chicken fat, or lard
1 pound smoked sausage, cut in circles (smoked ham or hot dogs may also be used)
Salt and pepper to taste

Dice the onions and saute in the fat until light brown. Add the paprika, salt, and pepper. (If desired, slices of tomato and green pepper may also be added.)

Add the potatoes, sausage, and enough water to barely cover the potatoes. Cover the skillet and cook until the potatoes are done.

Microwave Garden Vegetable Casserole

2 small yellow summer squash, sliced
1 medium zucchini, sliced
1 small white onion, sliced
1 tomato, sliced
2 tablespoons grated Parmesan cheese
1/2 teaspoon seasoned salt
1/2 teaspoon basil
1/2 teaspoon thyme

Place all sliced vegetables in versatility pan and mix all other ingredients. Toss lightly. Cover and microwave on full power for 8-10 minutes. For conventional oven: Place in oven for 20-25 minutes at 350˚.

Pet Treats

Pets have become an important presence in Detroit. Across the United States people own about 70 million cats and 68 million dogs. The pet and wild bird industry is growing phenomenally. I thought it appropriate to include some recipes for our furry and feathered friends.
– The Editor

DOGS

Bacon Biscuits

Dog Biscuits – Bacon Flavored
Makes 40 servings
5 cups whole wheat flour
1 cup milk
2 eggs
10 tablespoons vegetable oil or bacon fat
1 teaspoon onion or garlic powder
1/2 cup cold water

1 tablespoon vegetable oil or bacon fat (original recipe didn't say why this was listed but I suspect this last tablespoon is to grease cookie sheet with)

Mix all ingredients well. Pinch off pieces of the dough and roll them into two-inch balls. Put them on a greased cookie sheet. Bake them at 350° for 35 to 40 minutes. Let them cool, then store in an airtight container.

Baby Food Doggie Cookies

3 jars baby food – beef or carrots
1/4 cup Cream of Wheat
Chicken
1/4 cup dry milk powder

Combine ingredients in bowl and mix well. Roll into small balls and place on well-greased cookie sheet. Flatten slightly with a fork. Bake in preheated 350° oven for 15 minutes until brown. Cool on wire racks and store in refrigerator. Also freezes well. Can substitute wheat germ for Cream of Wheat and then use a tablespoon to make cookie sized drops on plate. Microwave for 4 minutes on medium high. Suggest keeping an eye on them in microwave and perhaps start out for only 3 1/2 minutes. They do come out soft. Also suggest using Beef/Vegetable Dinner baby dinner

Wheaty Dog Treats

2 1/2 cups whole wheat flour
1/2 cup powdered milk
1/2 teaspoon salt
1/2 teaspoon garlic powder
1 teaspoon brown sugar
6 tablespoons butter
1 egg, beaten
1/2 cup ice water

Butter, margarine, shortening or meat juices may be used. Combine the flour, milk, salt, garlic powder and sugar. Cut in butter until mixture resembles cornmeal. Mix in egg then add enough ice water to make a ball. Pay dough to 1/2 inch thick on a lightly oiled cookie sheet. Cut out shapes with a cookie cutter or biscuit cutter and bake on cookie sheet for 25 minutes at 350°. Remove from oven and cool on a wire rack. To vary the flavor and texture, at the time the egg is added, add any of the following: 1 cup pureed cooked green vegetables or carrots; 6 tablespoons whole wheat or rye kernels; 3 tablespoons liver powder. (Last two items available in health food stores)

Leave unknown dogs alone.
Children should be taught never to approach a dog they don't know. This is especially true of dogs who are tied up, as they tend to be very territorial. Instruct children always to ask permission from a dog's owner before petting a dog.

Peanut Butter Treats

1/4 cup peanut butter
8 ounces yogurt

Mix together and freeze in ice cube trays. Dogs love them.

Puppies

Pups you want to live in the house should at first be started in their own outside penned area and brought inside only after obedience training.

Crunchy Dog Biscuits

3/4 cup hot water or meat juice
1/3 cup margarine
1/2 cup powdered milk
1/2 teaspoon salt
1 egg, beaten
3 cups whole wheat flour

Mix well – roll in to small logs in your hands and bake at 325° for about 50 minutes. Makes 12 treats.

Respect the Family Pet

Teach your children to never disturb a dog when it is eating, sleeping, playing with a toy or caring for puppies.

Oatmeal Wheat Germ Dog Biscuits

3 cups whole wheat or rye flour
3 cups uncooked oatmeal
1/2 cup plain wheat germ
6 tablespoons margarine
1/4 cup molasses
1 cup evaporated milk
1 cup water

Mix together the first 3 ingredients. Then thoroughly mix in the last 4 ingredients. Dough will be stiff. Chill for a half hour. Roll rounded teaspoonfuls into balls. Flatten, place on greased cookie sheet, and bake for 1 hour at 300°

Safer Pets

Before traveling with your pet, make a special ID tag for his collar. Instead of using your home number, use the number of someone you know will be reachable in case your pet gets loose.

CATS

Kitten Delight

1/3 slice of white bread
1/8 cup milk or 1/8 cup chicken broth (whatever preferred)

Pour milk into a measuring cup then pour into the bowl. Repeat with chicken broth. Break bread into tiny bits, then dump into the mixing bowl. Heat in the microwave for approximately 1 minute. When finished, let cool then serve to kitten.

Kitty Salad

1 small carrot, peeled and grated
1/4 cup peeled and grated zucchini
1/2 cup chopped alfalfa sprouts
1 teaspoon chopped fresh parsley
1/8 cup chicken stock
1/4 teaspoon dried or fresh catnip
(optional)

　　Combine vegetables in a medium bowl. Add chicken stock and toss. Sprinkle with catnip and serve at room temperature. Store leftovers in the refrigerator for up to 3 days (do not freeze). Makes 1 to 2 cups.

Lots of Cats

The American cat population reached nearly 68 million in 1996. American Demographics magazine estimates that's about 200 million kitty yawns per hour and a whopping 425 million catnaps each day! Talking Cats Cats have about 100 different vocalization sounds. In comparison, dogs have about 10!

Tuna Treats

　　Makes approximately 60 treats
1/2 cup whole wheat flour
1/2 cup nonfat dry, powdered milk
1/2 can tuna, in oil or 1/2 cup cooked chicken, chopped into small pieces
1 tablespoon vegetable oil or cod liver oil
1 egg, beaten
1/4 cup water
Catnip (optional)

　　Heat oven to 350°.

　　In bowl cut tuna or chicken into smaller pieces. Then add flour and milk. Mix well. Add water and oil. Mix well again. Beat egg until foamy and add. The dough will be sticky. Use fingers to shape small, marble size balls. Place on greased cookie sheet and flatten. Bake 10 minutes. Remove from oven and turn over. Bake another 10 minutes until brown. Cool completely. Store in airtight container.

I Hate Hairballs

Mixing 1 teaspoon of mineral oil with your cat's food once or twice a week will help prevent hairballs and constipation!

DETROIT SOAP CO.'S
QUEEN ANNE SOAP
The Best Family Soap in the World

Meat Loaf for Cats

2 eggs
1 cup milk
1 tablespoon vegetable oil
1 teaspoon bonemeal
1 tablespoon finely chopped cooked vegetables (corn, green beans, or broccoli)
1 pound raw lean hamburger meat or ground chicken
4 slices whole-wheat bread, crumbled

　　Mix eggs, milk, oil, bonemeal, and chopped vegetable. Add meat and bread pieces; stir. Do not overmix. Press into a greased 9x5-inch loaf pan and bake at 350° for 50 minutes. Pour off excess juices. Let loaf set for 20 minutes before serving. Store leftovers in the refrigerator for up to 5 days, or wrap in foil in serving portions and freeze.

Well Styled

25% of cat owners blow dry their cats' hair after a bath.

Tuna Treats

Makes approximately 60 treats
1/2 cup whole wheat flour
1/2 cup nonfat dry, powdered milk
1/2 can tuna, in oil or 1/2 cup cooked chicken, chopped into small pieces
1 tablespoon vegetable oil or cod liver oil
1 egg, beaten
1/4 cup water
Catnip (optional)

Heat oven to 350°.

In bowl cut tuna or chicken into smaller pieces. Then add flour and milk. Mix well. Add water and oil. Mix well again. Beat egg until foamy and add. The dough will be sticky. Use fingers to shape small, marble size balls. Place on greased cookie sheet and flatten. Bake 10 minutes. Remove from oven and turn over. Bake another 10 minutes until brown. Cool completely. Store in airtight container.

The Hunters
Cats aren't hunters by nature;
their mothers teach them to hunt!

Fake Mouse Treats

1/2 cup whole-wheat flour
1/2 cup nonfat dry milk
1/4 cup wheat germ
1/4 cup bonemeal
1/2 teaspoon brewer's yeast
Pinch of catnip (optional)
1/2 beaten egg
1 teaspoon vegetable oil or cod liver oil
1/2 cup chicken stock
5 ounces boneless mackerel or canned tuna, packed in oil; or chopped cooked chicken

Mix dry ingredients and catnip, if using, in a large bowl and add egg, oil, and chicken stock. Mash fish or meat with a fork and add to mixture in bowl. Blend well. Shape into dime-size balls. Place onto a lightly greased baking sheet and press to flatten. Bake at 350° for about 8 minutes, until golden, turning once. Let treats cool before serving. Store in an airtight container in the refrigerator for up to a week, or wrap in foil in packets of 10 and store in the freezer. Makes about 60 treats.

Too Small?
Whiskers tell a cat whether the space they are entering is
big enough for it

Avoiding Cat Bites
Cats almost never bite with warning. Luckily, it's not too difficult to avoid being hurt by a cat, since felines would rather run than fight. Never sneak up on a cat. Say hello in a medium tone and avoid sudden movements. Put down a wriggling cat and watch out for subtle signs the animal is agitated, like the stiffening or twitching of its tail. Never pet him

Kitty Tuna-Pops

Drain liquid from tuna packed in spring water. Freeze liquid in small ice cube trays or little square pill boxes available at most drug stores. Give no more than 2 cubes at one time as a treat. Reuse your can of drained tuna placing in it an airtight container and covering with filtered water overnight for a second tuna-pop water.

Proud
The domestic cat is the only cat species able to hold its tail vertically while walking. All wild cats hold their tails horizontally or tucked between their legs while walking.

WILD BIRDS

Bird Cakes

1 cup crunchy peanut butter
1 cup lard
2 cups quick cook oats
2 cups cornmeal
1 cup flour
1/3 cup sugar

Melt the peanut butter and lard and add remaining ingredients and cool.

Sure-Fire Suet Mix

1 part peanut butter (I use crunchy)
1 part shortening
1 part flour
3 parts cornmeal
1 part cracked corn
I also add black oil sunflower seeds and/or mixed seed

Watering Birds

In a dry spell, provide birds with an outdoor pond. Use a child's 4 foot hard plastic pool with sand on the bottom and a few flat rocks; add a few water ferns for a natural look.

Soft Peanut Butter Mix

1 cup fresh ground suet
1 cup peanut butter
3 cups yellow corn meal
1/2 cup white or whole-wheat flour

Melt suet in a saucepan over low heat. Add peanut butter, stirring until melted and well blended. Mix the rest of the ingredients together in a large bowl. Allow the suet-peanut-butter blend to cool until slightly thickened, then stir it into the mixture in the bowl. Mix thoroughly.

Hard Suet Tidbit Cakes

1/2 pound fresh ground suet
1/3 cup sunflower seed
2/3 cup wild bird seed (mix)
1/8 cup chopped peanuts
1/4 cup raisins

Melt the suet in a saucepan over low heat. Allow it to cool thoroughly, then reheat it.

Mix the rest of the ingredients together in a large bowl. Allow the suet to cool until slightly thickened, then stir into the mixture in the bowl. Mix thoroughly. Pour onto pie pan or form, or pack into suet feeders.

Optional or substitute ingredients: millet (or other bird-seed), cornmeal, cooked noodles, chopped berries, dried fruit.

Sunflower Seed Heads

Place sunflower seed heads in a dark, dry place to dry. Attach to a porch pillar so birds can eat seeds during the winter.

Hard Peanut Butter Mix

2 cups fresh ground suet
1 cup peanut butter
2 cups yellow corn meal
2 cups fine cracked corn

Melt suet in a saucepan over low heat. Allow it to cool thoroughly, then reheat it. Add peanut butter, stirring until melted and well blended. Add dry ingredients to the suet-peanut-butter blend, and mix well. Pour into forms or suet-feeders, and cool until hardened.

Homemade Nectar for Hummingbirds

4 cups water
1 cup sugar

Boil and cool. Freeze for future use.

Wild Bird Safety

Hang bird feeder from an arbor to prevent swooping attacks. Place tomato cage upside down in the birdbath. Encircle feeder with a three foot high wire fence about two feet away from feeder to protect ground feeding birds.

Soft Suet Medley

4 1/2 cups ground fresh suet
3/4 cup dried and fine ground bakery goods (whole-wheat or cracked-wheat bread or crackers are best)
1/2 cup shelled sunflower seeds
1/4 cup millet
1/4 cup dried and chopped fruit (currants, raisins, or berries)
3/4 cup dried and fine ground meat (optional)

Melt suet in saucepan over low heat. Mix the rest of the ingredients together in large bowl. Allow the suet to cool until slightly thickened, then stir it into the mixture in the bowl. Mix thoroughly. Pour or pack into forms or feeders; smear onto tree trunks or overhanging limbs and branches; or pack into pine cones.

Hot Weather Bird Treats

2 cups quick-cooking oats
2 cups cornmeal
1 cup flour
1/2 cup sugar
1 cup lard
1 cup crunchy peanut butter

Combine the oats, cornmeal, flour and sugar in a large bowl. Melt the lard and peanut butter in microwave oven and add to the dry ingredients. Mix well. Pour the mixture into a square pan about 2 inches deep, or spread it directly onto the tree limbs.

Bully Birds?

Place an overturned plastic storage crate on top of the feeder and secure with wire. Cover top with anything flat and hold down with a brick. Allows smaller birds to eat and keeps out bullies.

Detroit Historical Society Guild

Guild Officers 2001-2002

Shirley Hartert – President
Marguerite Humes-Schwedler – Vice President
Recording Secretary – Nancy Schmidt
Corresponding Secretary – Lorene Rever
Treasurer – Mary Ellen Busch
Directors
Nancy Schimmel
Lenore Stoetzer
Rennie Hughes

Recognition of Guild Founders 1951

In 1951 when the present Detroit Historical Museum was built, Margot Pearsall, Curator who became Assistant Director of the Detroit Historical Museum, and Barbara Paulson Nolan, secretary to the Detroit Historical Society, founded the Detroit Historical Society Guild by contacting some of their friends, who in turn gathered a few of their friends who were interested in preserving the history of the City of Detroit.

The purpose of the Guild was then, as it is today, "To further the aims of the Detroit Historical Society and the Detroit Historical Museums by any service which shall be approved by the Board of Directors of the Detroit Historical Society, the Detroit Historical Commission and/or the Board of Directors of the Detroit Historical Society Guild." It has been our privilege for the past fifty years to serve these goals.

A Letter From the Guild President

We invite you to join us at Detroit's frontier campfires to warm yourself and sample our home cooking as we explore how our early grandmothers made a homelife for their families. This is the fourth cookbook the Guild has published, but none to date were of this magnitude and inclusive of Detroit's history and culture. The project was first suggested in 1999 by Dorothea Hibbler, to be a commemorative cookbook for the Guild's Golden Anniversary. A small committee of three saw this cookbook take shape with the contributions of Guild members and friends and become one that will celebrate Detroit's cooking heritage.

Our cookbook chairperson and editor, Marguerite Humes, skillfully piloted the book through all phases, and we express our gratitude and honor her long hours of work and dedication to the project.

The Guild is a group of people unified in purpose across cultural barriers with a common love of history and the goal of preserving Detroit history and supporting its Museums. Our major commitments are the Old Detroit Gift shop, Cadillac Café and two Flea Markets at Historic Fort Wayne annually, in April and October.

Shirley (Stoetzer) Hartert, *President*
Detroit Historical Society Guild

Members of the Detroit Historical Society Guild 2001

Belen Bajos
Mitzie Bean
Joan Belanger
Barbara Belcher
Jamie Kendrick Bloomberg
Pat Bramley
Alice Brandon
Ruth Bruce
Mary Ellen Busch
Marjorie Chalk
Bette J. Clary
Grace Colter
Mary Cooper
Carol Cramer
Veradee Dunaskis
Sallianne Edwards
Kelly Fortune
Mittie Grosscup
Shirley Hartert

Joan Herrington
Dorothea Hibbler
Barbara Howe
Elizabeth Huffman
Rennie Hughes
Alexandra Jackman
Natalie Jacobson
Beatrice Jobagy
Gerry Johnson
Margaret Link
Jackie Napolitan
Evelyn Osgood
Sandra Osgood
Elizabeth Padgett
Mary Ann Perrin
Patricia Phenix
Lisa Pollack
Lorene Rever
Valerie Revitzer

Mary Ross
Alexandra Sauber
Nancy Schimmel
Nancy Schmidt
Marguerite Humes Schwedler
Marguerite Scott
Ginny Smith
Mary Smith
Viola Stone
Lenore Stoetzer
Fern Sturgis
Mary Sucnenek
Margaret Weber
Pat Weeks
Senja Willmarth
Patricia Wilson
Cynthia Boyes Young
Lawrence Zaranski

Recipe Contributors

Linda Humes
Jean Babcock
Agnes Nigoghosian
Viola Stone
Jackie Napolitan
Lorene D. Rever
Dorothea Hibbler
Margaret Link
Mary Ellen Busch
Shirley Anderson
Mae Jarecki
Monica Sloan
Helen Ciernick
Amy Laus
Carol Hinz
Rennie Hugnes
Shirley Hartert
Edward Deeb

Lenore Stoetzer
Rose Laus
Christopher Humes
Gertrude Teschke
Liz Jackson
Bertha Madison
Evie Douglas
Elizabeth Ball Doerr
Alice Wendling Snider
Meg Humes
Alice Busch
Pat Wilson
Rita Bennett
Theresa Flachs Coville
Gertrude Grubb Coatsworth
Catherine Kowalski
Georgia Shurn
Margueite Schwedler

Gifts from the Detroit Historical Society Guild to the Detroit Historical Society and Museums From 1951 to 2001

Several Projectors and Cameras
Oil Painting of Lewis Cass
Support for Educational Television Foundation
Artifacts – Furniture Exhibits Decorative pieces
Map Collection
Support for School Bus Tours
Published Lewis Cass Lectures
Support for films for Museum Education Programs
Purchased Chandler Indian Collection—The Indian
Museum opened June 1969
Thirty Oil Paintings of Great Lakes Vessels for Dossin
Museum
Reference Books for Museum Library
Signs for Freedom Train Visit
Support for Presidential China Exhibit
Uniforms for Guides at Fort Wayne
Support for Restoration at Fort
Support of exhibits at Main Museum
Support for Furnishings of restored Commandant's House
Support for Kresge/Van Dusen Endowment Fund
Radios for Security Department
Awning for Cass Entrance – Main
Awning for Kirby Entrance – Main
Doors for Visitor Center – Fort
Support for Costume Collection—Special storage boxes
Flags for Main and Fort
Photo Murals for Exhibit
Support for Gothic Room restoration

Hudson Team 500 Fund
Support for Pilot House at Dossin
Curator Supplies and Publications
Cadillac Café Equipment and Staff
Annual Hanging of Greens
Assist with Old Detroit Shop
Places and Events Supported
Detroit Historical Museum
Dossin Maritime Museum
Historic Fort Wayne
Moross House
Old Detroit Shop at Museum
Cadillac Café – Provide staff
Indian Museum at Fort Wayne
Show Houses – Gift Shop
Hanging of the Greens
Frontier Pioneer Days
Annual Patriotic Awards
Lantern Tours at Fort Wayne
Civil War Days at Fort Wayne
Lewis Cass Lectures
Noel Night / Detroit
Society Holiday Party
Flea Markets – Two each year
Birthday Celebration for Detroit
Festival of the Arts
Speaker's Bureau / History Programs
Gift Shop at Fort Wayne

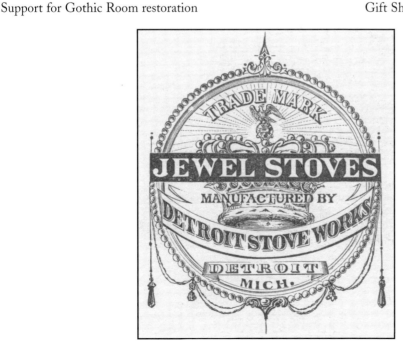

The People Who Built Detroit

The Settling of Detroit's Larger Immigrant Populations

Who They Were and When They Came		Where They Settled First Approximate area	Where They Settled Next Approximate area
	American Indian-3 tribes; Chippewa, Ottawa, Potawatomi	They lived for hundreds of years in the Great Lakes Area.	Detroit Metropolitan Area
1701	French	Ribbon farms along the Detroit River on both side seventually including Grosse Pointe	Detroit to Monroe
1763	British/Scots	Fort Pontchartrain / Detroit	Mixed in Detroit / Windsor
1820 1920	German	Jefferson to Gratiot Trappers Alley	Sterling Heights / Warren
1830	African Americans	Blackbottom / East Side Vernor / Lafayette Park	Bush, Hastings, Gratiot and
1840 1890	Irish	Corktown / Michigan / Bagley	Metro Detroit Area
1849	Scandinavian	Metro Detroit Areas	Oakland / Wayne County
1850	Jews	Hastings Street / Jefferson	Oakland County
1855	Italian	East Side of Detroit	St. Clair Shores / Eastpointe
1860	Polish	Hamtramck area	Warren, Sterling Heights
1880	Greek	Greektown – Monroe Street	Ecorse / St. Clair Shores
1885 1940	Ukraine	Hamtramck and Warren	Greater Detroit areas
1890	Hungarian	Delray Southwest Detroit	Springwells & Suburbs
1900	S.E. Asian	Detroit / North Oakland County	Troy, Madison Heights
1900 1920	Mexican/Latino	Corktown / Michigan Ave.	Bagley / Michigan Ave.
1915	Armenian	Dearborn, Highland Park	Oakland County
1920	Caribbean	Canfield / St. Aubin	Greater Detroit Area
1930	E. European: Czechs, Lithuanian, Russian, Serbian, Yugoslavian, Romanian, Croatian, Macedonian, Albanian and Bulgarian	Detroit area	Five County Area
1940	Arab	Highland Park	Dearborn / Hamtramck
1940	Japan	Detroit	Tri-County Area
1940	Asian	Detroit	Troy, Madison Heights, North Oakland County
1940	Japan	Tri-County Area	Detroit
1940	Chinese	Chinatown/Cass/Peterboro	Ann Arbor, Detroit, Canton
1950	Korean	Detroit	Oakland County
1960	Indian (India)	Garden City, Troy, Sterling Heights	Farmington, North East Suburbs
1965	Philippines	Metro Detroit Area	Metro Detroit Area
1975	Indo-Chinese	9 Mile and Hoover Area	Metro Detroit, Warren

Measurements and Weights

Dash = 1/8 teaspoon (or less)
3 teaspoons = 1 tablespoon
16 tablespoons = 1 cup
4 saltspoons = 1 teaspoon
2 teaspoons = 1 dessert spoon
4 tablespoons = 1 wineglass = 1/4 cup
4 tablespoons = 1/2 gill = 1/4 cup
1 tablespoon = 1 ounce
1 gill = 4 ounces = 1/2 cup
2 gills = 1 cup = 1/2 pint
2 wineglasses = 1 gill = 1/2 cup
1 common sized tumbler = 1/2 pint
4 gills = 1 pint
1/4 cup = 4 tablespoons
1/3 cup = 5 tablespoons plus 1 teaspoon
1/2 cup = 8 tablespoons
2 cups = 1 pint
4 cups = 1 quart = 32 ounces
2 pints = 1 quart
1 cup = 8 ounces
4 quarts = 1 gallon
8 quarts = 1 peck
4 pecks = 1 bushel
16 ounces = 1 pound
Butter size of an egg = 2 ounces
Butter size of a walnut = 1 ounce
1 jigger = 3 tablespoons
1 medium lemon = 3 tablespoons of juice
1 medium lemon = 1 tablespoon grated peel
1 medium orange = 1/3 cup of juice
1 medium orange = 2 tablespoons grated peel
1 medium lime = 2 tablespoons of juice
1 large onion = 3/4-1 cup chopped onion
1 cup regular rice = 3 cups cooked rice
8 ounces sour cream = 1 cup
8 ounces cottage cheese = 1 cup
1 cup whipping cream = 2 cups whipped cream
1/4 pound cheese = 1 cup shredded cheese
1 slice of bread = 1/2 cup bread crumbs
1 pint of berries = 3/4 cup

1 cup macaroni = 2 cups cooked
1 envelope unflavored gelatin = 1 tablespoon
1 (6 ounce) package chocolate chips = 1 cup
10 whole eggs = 1 pound
5 whole eggs = 1 cup
12-14 egg yolks = 1 cup
8-10 egg whites = 1 cup
15 marshmallow = 1/4 pound
4 teaspoons vinegar or 1 1/2 tablespoons lemon juice added
1 cup of sweet milk = 1 cup of sour milk
1 stick of margarine = 1/2 cup
Butter, when soft, 1 pound = 1 pint
1 cup = 1/2 pint
2 pints = 1 quart
Butter, 2 tablespoons solidly packed = 1 ounce
Butter, 2 cups solidly packed = 1 pound
Chocolate, 1 square = 1 ounce
Coffee, 4 1/3 cups = 1 pound
English walnuts, chopped, 5 cups = 1 pound
Wheat Flour 1 pound = 1 quart
Indian meal 1 lb. 2 ounce = 1 quart
Flour, 4 tablespoons = 1 ounce
Flour, Pastry, 4 cups = 1 pound
Flour, Bread, 4 cups = 1 pound
Flour, Entire Wheat, 3 7/8 cups = 1 pound
Flour, Graham, 4 1/2 cups = 1 pound
Meat, 2 cups finely chopped = 1 pound
Oatmeal, 2 2/3 cups = 1 pound
Oats, Rolled, 5 cups = 1 pound
Rice, 1 7/8 cups = 1 pound
Rye Meal, 4 1/3 cups = 1 pound
Sugar, Brown, 2 2/3 cups = 1 pound
Sugar, Confectioners, 3 1/2 cups = 1 pound
Sugar, Granulated, 2 cups = 1 pound
Sugar, Powdered, 2 2/3 cups = 1 pound
Sugar, or Salt, 2 tablespoons = 1 ounce
Loaf sugar, broken, 1 pound = 1 quart
White sugar, powdered, 1 pound 1 ounce = 1 quart
Best brown sugar, 1 pound 2 ounces = 1 quart

Weights and Measures for the 1851 Kitchen

We recommend to all families that they should keep in the house a pair of scales, (one of the scales deep enough to hold flour, sugar, etc. conveniently,) and a set of tin measures; as accuracy in proportioning the ingredients is indispensable to success in cookery. It is best to have the scales permanently fixed to a small beam projecting (for instance) from one of the shelves of the store-room. This will preclude the frequent inconvenience of their getting twisted, unlinked, and otherwise out of order; a common consequence of putting them in and out of their box, and carrying them from place to place. The weights (of which there should be a set from two pounds to a quarter of an ounce) ought carefully to be kept in the box, that none of them may be lost or mislaid.

A set of tin measures (with small spouts or lips) from a gallon down to half a gill, will be found very convenient in every kitchen; though common pitchers, bowls, glasses, etc. may be substituted. It is also well to have a set of wooden measures from a bushel to a quarter of a peck.

Teacup Measure
12 tablespoons dry material is 1 teacup.
1 teacup liquid is 2 gills or 1/2 pint.
1 teacup butter is 1/2 pound.
1 heaping teacup flour is 1/4 pound.
2 teacups granulated sugar is 1 pound.
2 heaping teacups pulverized sugar is 1 pound.
1 teacup suet is 1/2 cup butter.

Dry Measure
Half a gallon is a quarter of a peck.
One gallon – half a peck.
Two gallons – one peck.
Four gallons – half a bushel.
Eight gallons – one bushel.

Oven Temperatures and Terms
Slow Oven   250º
Medium Oven   300º
Hot Oven   350º
Quick Oven   400º
Very Hot Oven   450º
Broil   500º
Roast   600º

Kitchen Substitutions

Ingredients: If you need . . .	Substitute . . .
1 cup sugar	1/3 cup firmly packed brown sugar
Baking powder, 1 teaspoon	1/4 teaspoon soda plus 1/2 teaspoon cream of tartar
Butter, 1 cup	7/8 cup vegetable shortening
Catsup or chili sauce, in cooking	1 cup tomato sauce plus 1/2 cup sugar plus 2 tablespoons vinegar
Chocolate, unsweetened, 1 square (1 ounce)	3 tablespoons regular cocoa plus 1 tablespoon butter or margarine
Cornstarch, 1 tablespoon	2 tablespoons flour
Egg, 1 whole	2 egg yolks (in custard) or 2 egg yolks plus 1 tablespoon water (in cookies)
Flour (for thickening), 2 tablespoons	1 tablespoon cornstarch or 1 tablespoon arrowroot
Flour, cake, 1 cup sifted	7/8 cup sifted all-purpose flour
Garlic, 1 clove fresh	1/8 teaspoon garlic powder
Herb, fresh, 1 tablespoon	1 teaspoon dried herb
Honey, 1 cup	1 1/4 cup sugar plus 1/4 cup liquid
Milk, whole, 1 cup	1 cup reconstituted nonfat dry milk plus 2 tablespoons butter
Milk, sour, 1 cup	1 tablespoon vinegar plus sweet milk to make 1 cup (let stand 5 minutes)
Mustard, dry, 1 teaspoon	1 tablespoon prepared mustard
Sour cream, 1 cup	7/8 cup buttermilk plus 2 tablespoons melted shortening, whipped
Yeast, compressed, 1 cake	1 package or 2 teaspoons active dry yeast

When something goes wrong

Pale gravy

Color with a few drops of Kitchen Bouquet (available at grocery stores)

To avoid the problem in the first place, brown the flour well before adding liquid. This also helps prevent lumpy gravy.

A different way of browning flour is to put some flour into a custard cup and place beside meat in the oven. Once the meat is done the flour will be nice and brown, ready to make a rich, brown gravy.

Gravy – smooth as silk

Keep a jar with a mixture of equal parts of flour and cornstarch. Put 3 or 4 tablespoons of this mixture in another jar and add some water. Shake, and in a few minutes you will have a smooth paste for gravy.

Microwave to the Max

For fastest results, place food in shallow container; this exposes more surface area to the microwaves.

Avoid any casseroles or dishes with sloping sides; food along edges will overcook.

Arrange uneven foods with the thinner areas toward center.

Cover with lid or plastic wrap to hold in moisture. If using plastic, vent so steam can escape.

Thin gravy

Mix water and flour or cornstarch into a smooth paste. Add gradually, stirring constantly, and bring to a boil.

Try instant potato flakes instead of flour.

Greasy gravy

Add a small amount of baking soda if it is quite greasy.

Too salty

For soup and stew, add cut raw potatoes and discard once they have cooked and absorbed the salt. Another remedy for salty soup and stew is to add a teaspoon each of cider vinegar and sugar.

Or simply add sugar.

Too sweet

Add salt.

If it's a main dish or vegetable, add a teaspoon of cider vinegar.

Stir food or rotate dish midway through to ensure even cooking.

Allow standing time to finish cooking.

Baking Basics

Take butter and eggs out of refrigerator 1 hour in advance. No time? To soften butter quickly, pound wrapped stick several times with a rolling pin. Place eggs in warm tap water bath for a few minutes; those right from the fridge yield less volume when beaten.

Standard recipes assume you will use large eggs.

Heat oven to desired temperature 10 to 15 minutes before beginning.

For dry ingredients, use nested cups in 1/4-, 1/3-, 1/2- and 1-cup sizes. Spoon flour and sugar into the appropriate cup and level top by sweeping excess away with the straight side of a knife. For brown sugar and shortening, pack cup firmly before leveling off. For liquids, use measures, usually made of glass, with increments on the side and a pouring spout.

Buy and install an oven thermometer to double-check your unit's built-in thermostat.

Glossary

Alum: A double sulfate of aluminum and potassium, used as a styptic and astringent.

Amber Gum: Probably ambergris, the wax-like secretion of the sperm whale, now used in perfumery, formerly in cookery.

Benzoion Gum: A resin from various East Indian plants used in medicine and as perfume.

Bladder and Leather: Pieces of each substance to be tied over the mouths of jars and bottles to secure the contents against air.

Blanch: To boil briefly in water or to pour boiling water over food for a few moments. This loosens skins or peels, sets colors, seals in juices, or prepares food for freezing or canning.

Borox: A white crystalline borate of sodium having various uses, as in soap and glass manufacture.

Bouquet Garni: Soup seasoning generally added to the soup in a cheesecloth bag which is later discarded.

Braise: To brown in a small amount of fat and then cook slowly on top of the stove or in the oven in a small amount of liquid.

Brine: A strong saline solution: water saturated or strongly impregnated with common salt.

Broil: To cook over, under, or in front of direct heat in an oven or live coals.

Bruise: To partially crush therefore releasing flavor.

Bunged: To plug with a stopper in the bunghole (which is used for emptying or filling a cask).

Calipash: That part of the turtle adjoining the upper shell.

Calipee: That part of the turtle adjoining the lower shell.

Carmelize: To melt sugar slowly over low heat to turn it brown and give it a special flavor.

Caul: An enveloping membrane.

Chine: A "joint" made up of part of the backbone and adjoining flesh.

Clarify: To clear a liquid by separating and removing the solids.

Cob: Corn cob.

Coddle: To poach gently in simmering water.

Crape: To make curly.

Crimp: To seal the edges of a pie crust by pinching.

Cure: To preserve meat, fish, or vegetables by drying, salting, smoking, or some other method.

Currants: A small round acid berry used for making jelly.

Deglaze: To heat stock or wine together with the sediment left in a roasting pan or pan to form gravy (after first draining off any excess fat).

Dredge: To sprinkle or dust with flour before cooking.

Elderberry: The drupe of a shrub of the honeysuckle family.

Emptins: Semiliquid prepared yeast.

Fair (of water): Clean; pure.

Fricasse: To cook gently in liquid; generally applies to poultry.

Frost Grape: A native American species, also called "chicken grape."

Frowy, Froughy: Stale; sour; musty.

Frumenty: Hulled wheat cooked in milk and seasoned with spice, sugar, etc.

Gallipot: A small earthen pot.

Garnish: To decorate with colorful or flavorful foods.

Gem Pans: Baking pans with scalloped edges.

Gilt: Plural is Gilding: Gold or something that resembles gold laid on the surface of an object.

Glaze: To coat with a syrup or thick liquid to add a sheen to a food's surface.

Groats: The hulled kernal of oats, barley, or buckwheat.

Gruel: A liquid food made by boiling a porridge.

Haslet, Harslet (Heartslet): Edible entrails: liver, heart, etc.

Hops: The ripened and dried pistillate cones of the hop plant used chiefly to empart a bitter flavor to malt liquors.

Islinglass: Gelatin made from air bladders of fish.

Jagging Iron or Doughspur: An instrument used for ornamenting pastry, in the form of a toothed wheel, set in a handle, frequently a product of the carving (scrimshaw) done on whaling vessels.

Julienne: To cut food in thin strips.

Jump in the Pan: A characteristic action of eels while in the process of cooking.

Knead: To work dough by pressing with the hands and turning.

Lade: To transfer as with a ladle or scoop.

Mango: A pickled green melon stuffed with various condiments.

Neat's foot: The foot of an ox.

Oil of Bergamont: A greenish or brownish yellow fragrant essential oil expressed from the rind of the fruit of a citrus tree. The fruit is pear shaped.

Orange Flavor Water: A liquid distilled from orange blossoms.

Orange Water: A liquid distilled from oranges.

Orris Root: The dried rootstock of a species of iris having a scented root.

Pannikin: A small metal vessel.

Parboil: To boil until partially cooked.

Patty Pans: Individual pot pie pans.

Pearlash: A salt obtained from the ashes of plants.

Pippin: A variety of apple.

Pomatum: A perfumed dressing used for the hair which is made from fragrenced plants.

Proof: To test yeast for strength or effectiveness.

Puree: To mash until smooth.

Race: A root.

Ragout: A thick, well seasoned stew.

Reduce: To boil a liquid so that volume will be reduced by evaporation.

Render: To melt or clarify.

Roast: To cook by dry heat in an oven.

Roux: Mixture of melted fat and flour, generally for thickening sauces, soups, or liquids.

Run Out or Depreciate: To decline in quality with each planting (particularly true of potatoes grown from seed rather than from cuttings of the tuber itself).

Rusk: Plain or sweet bread that is sliced after baking and then toasted or baked a second time until it is brown and crisp: Also a light, soft, sweet biscuit (rosca), twisted loaf of bread.

Sago: The powdered pith of any of several varieties of East Indian Palm used as a thickening agent.

Saleratus: Either of two salts used as leavening agents; a) potassium bicarbonate; b) sodium bicarbonate.

Salmander: A long handled flat iron utensil heated and placed over foods to brown them.

Salsify: A plant with purple composite flowers and white, edible root of oysterlike flavor.

Sal Soda: Sodium carbonate.

Salt Pork: Side of a hog which has been cured; fattier than bacon and with no smoked flavor. Used for flavoring and adding fat to dishes such as baked beans, stew, etc.

Saute: To cook in a small amount of fat, turning frequently (to pan fry).

Scald: To heat a liquid to just below the boiling point.

Scallop: To bake in a sauce or other liquid.

Scant: Not coming quite up to the stated measure.

Score: To make shallow cuts through the outer covering of food to tenderize and help maintain the shape.

Scrage: The lean part of neck of mutton or veal.

Scum: To skim.

Sear: To brown quickly over very high temperature to improve color and seal in juices.

Secure from Wet: To place or cover so that water does not boil over into food.

Send it up: To send to the table.

Sift: To use a strainer or sifter to remove any lumps or to lighten dry ingredients.

Simmer: To cook slowly in a liquid that is kept below the boiling point (about 185° F).

Slack (of heat): Not strong; moderate.

Snipe: Any of several game birds that reside in marshy areas; and resemble but are more slender than the related woodcocks. They have very long slender bills.

Spermaceti: A white crystalline waxy solid that separates from sperm oil especially from the head cavities and from the oils of related cetaceans, and is used chiefly in ointments, cosmetics, creams, and candles.

Spider: A long handled iron frying pan often having legs.

Steam: To cook or heat over boiling water without touching the water.

Stew: To cook slowly in a small amount of liquid over a long period of time.

Stir: To mix ingredients in a circular motion to blend or prevent from sticking.

Stive: To pack tightly.

Suet: The hard fat about the kidneys and loins melted and freed from the membranes forms tallow.

Syllabub, Sillabub: A mixture of milk or cream with wine, cider, or other acid, usually whipped to a froth.

Tin Kitchen: A roasting pan.

Toast: To brown until crisp over direct heat.

Toss: To mix ingredients lightly.

Tripe: The lining of the ruminate stomach wall of an animal in the cow, sheep or deer family.

Truss: To tie poultry meat with skewers so that it will hold its shape during cooking.

Volatile Salts: Ammonium Carbonate.

Wallop: A bubbling motion made by rapidly boiling water, hence the duration of one such motion used as a measure of time in cooking.

Whip: To beat rapidly in order to increase volume and lighten the mixture.

Whip Dasher: A kitchen utensil made of braided coiled wire or perforated metal with a handle and used in whipping eggs.

Eastern market Flower Day, May 2001. Annual event which draws thousands of people to Detroit. The photo on page 125 shows the same building in 1905.

Bibliography

Cookbook Bibliography

Beecher, Catherine E. Miss Beecher's Domestic Receipt-Book (1858). New York: Dover Publications, Inc., 2001.

Berolzheimer, Ruth. Culinary Arts Institute Encyclopedic Cookbook. New York: Grosset & Dunlap, 1952.

Child, Lydia Maria. The American Frugal Housewife (1844). New York: Dover Publications, Inc., 1999.

Christian, Eugene and Mollie Griswold. 250 Meatless Menus and Recipes. New York: Eugene Griswold and Mollie Griswold Christian, 1910.

Cuisine International. Members of the International Institute. Detroit: International Institute, 1979.

Dessert Cook Book, Better Homes & Gardens (1960). New York: Meredith Corporation, 1970.

A Cook Book, Detroit Historical Society Guild, 1962. Festival Fare, Detroit Historical Society Guild, 1975.

E. Hutchinson. Ladies Indispensable Assistant (1852). New York: 1852.

Gillette, Mrs. F.L. Whitehouse Cook Book (1879). Chicago: R.S. Peale Company, 1879.

Graves, Eleanor. Great Dinners from LIFE (1969). Alexandria: Time–Life Books, 1979.

Hale, Sarah Josepha. Early American Cookery 1841. New York: Dover Publications, 1996.

Hoffman, Matthew, ed. Home Remedies for Dogs and Cat. Pennsylvania: Rodale Press, Inc., 1996.

Better Homes and Gardens Heritage Cook Book. United States: Meredith Corporation, 1975.

Betty Crocker International Cookbook, General Mills. New York: Random House, 1980.

Twentieth Century Cookbook, Mrs. Harding's. The Geographical Publishing Co. Chicago: John Thomas, 1921.

Kirk, Dorothy, ed. Woman's Home Companion Cook Book (1951). New York: P.F. Collier & Son Corporation, 1955.

Leslie, Eliza. Miss Leslie's Directions for Cookery (1851). New York: Dover Publications, 1999.

Massie, Larry B., and Priscilla. Walnut Pickles and Watermelon Cake. Detroit: Wayne State University Press, 1990.

Meal-in-One Microwave Cooking, Litton. Minneapolis: Litton Microwave Cooking Products, 1979.

Nichols, Nell B., ed. Homemade Bread. New York: Farm Journal, Inc., 1969.

Old Frenchtown Cookery 1700's, Frenchtown Families. Monroe: Monroe County Historical Society, 1979.

Old World Foods For New World Families, Merrill-Palmer Motherhood & Home Training School, Detroit (1931). Detroit: Wayne State University Press, 1947.

Paske, Janet Van Amber. Stories and Recipes of the Great Depression of the 1930's. Wisconsin: Van Amber Publishers, 1986.

Practical Recipes for the Housewife, Detroit Times. Detroit: Detroit Times, 1933.

Roberson, John and Marie. The Meat Cookbook. New York: Holt, Rinehart & Winston, Inc., 1953.

Simmons, Amelia. A Facsimile of "American Cookery", 1796. New York: Dover Publications, 1984.

Swell, Barbara. Children at the Hearth. Asheville: Native Ground Music, Inc., 1999.

The French Cookbook, Culinary Arts Institute Staff. Chicago: Culinary Arts Institute.

Tyree, Marion Cabell, ed. Housekeeping in Old Virginia 1879. Louisville: John P. Morton & Company, 1965.

Waddles, Charlesetta, Rev. Mother, Soul Food Cookbook 2nd edition. Detroit: Perpetual Mission, 1970.

Historical Bibliography

Billard, Jules B., ed. The World of the American Indian. Washington D.C.: National Geographic Society, 1974.

Boyle, Kevin & Victoria Getis. Muddy Boots and Ragged Aprons. Detroit: Wayne State University Press, 1997.

Catlin, George B. The Story of Detroit. Detroit: The Detroit News, 1926.

Deur, Lynne. A Story of Indians in Michigan. Spring Lake, MI: River Road Publications, Inc. 1981.

Gabrilovich, Peter & Bill McGraw. The Detroit Almanac. Detroit: Detroit Free Press, 2000.

Danner, Marcia & Patricia Banker Peart, ed. Global Journeys in Metro Detroit. Detroit: New Detroit, 1999.

J.L. Hudson Company Sixtieth Jubilee Year ~ 1881 – 1941. Detroit: Detroit Free Press, 1941.

Lodge, John C. I Remember Detroit. Detroit: Wayne State University Press, 1949.

Peckham, Howard H. Pontiac and the Indian Uprising (1947). Detroit: Wayne State University Press, 1994.

Woodford, Frank B. and Arthur M. All Our Yesterdays. Detroit: Wayne State University Press, 1969.

Web Sites

French-Canadian Culture (frenchcaculture.tqn.com)
Native American Technology and Art
(nativetech.org/food)
Native Way (wisdomkeepers.org)

Index

Appetizers

Aghavni's Navy Bean Plaki, 170
Club Canapes, 169
Crab Meat Canapes, 169
Dried Beef Dip, 169
Hanky-Pankies, 170
Mexican Taco Dip, 170
Middle Eastern Hummus, 169
Nuts and Bolts, 170
Puppy Chow, 170
Savory Oyster Crackers, 169
Water Chestnuts, 169

Beef

Beef and Kidney Pie, 42
Beef Gumbo – African-American, 191
Beef Liver with Onions, 110
Beef Ribs – English, 43
Beef Stew, 107
Beef Stroganoff – Russian, 108
Chippewa Bulettes, 191
Cornish Pastries, 110
French Boiled Dinner, 109
Fricasseed Beef, 107
Greek Meatballs, 192
Irish Corned Beef and Cabbage, 193
Kima – Pakistani, 192
Meat Pie – English, 43
Meat Pies, 110
Oxtail Stew – English, 45
Pepper Steak – Chinese, 192
Rindsrollen – Beef Rouladen, 190
Roast Beef Pie, 109
Salisbury Steak with Onion Rings – African American, 192
Sarma – Armenian, 193
Small Hot Patties – French, 42
Steak and Kidney Pie – English, 109
Swedish Meat Balls, 190
To Cure Beef Ham, 107
Tourtierre – French, 45

Veal Birds – Italian, 108
Veal Picatta – Italian, 190
Veal Stew – Hungarian, 108

Beverages

Apple Beer, 37
Apricot Slush, 168
Birch Beer, 90
Cider Syllabub, 35
Corn Soup Liquor, 18
Dandelion Wine, 90
Eau Sucre, 34
English Eggnog, 89
English Syllabub, 37
Field Mint Tea, 18
Fine Milk Punch, 86
For a Summer Draught, 89
French Punch, 167
Frosted Russian Chocolate, 167
Grape Wine, 90
Honey Drink, 18
Kahlua, 167
Lemon Cordial, 89
Lichen Tea, 18
Mint Flavored Punch, 89
Mulled Cider, 168
New Year's Eggnog – American, 168
Old Time Home Brew, 90
Polish Punch, 168
Possum Grape Drink, 18
Russian Tea, 90
Sage Tea – Ojibwa, 17
Sangria, 167
Simple Root Beer, 90
Spiced Grape Juice, 168
Switchel, 89
Turkish Coffee, 167
Two Christmas Punches, 167
Wassail, 90
White Tea, 34
Wild Grape Wine, 37
Wild Peppermint Tea, 28

Bread and Corn

Acorn Bread – Traditional, 26
Ash Cake – Chippewa, 16
Baked Green Corn, 31
Baking Powder, Recipe, 69
Bannock – Chippewa, 26
Biscuit, Egg, 68
Biscuits, Buttermilk, 145
Boston Corn Bread, 68
Bread Twist, 69
Bread, Light, 68
Breakfast Bread, Excellent for, 64
Buttermilk Muffins, African American Corn Meal, 146
Campfire Corn Bread – French, 36
Chestnut Bread, Indian – Traditional, 16
Cinnamon Rolls, 143
Corn and Beans - Chippewa, 17
Corn Balls – Ottawa, 17
Corn Bread Baked on Bark, 17
Corn Cake, Spider, 67
Corn Pone, 67
Corn, Boiled Parched, 17
Corn, Parched – Ottawa, 17
Cornbread, Old Fashioned Northern, 146
Cornmeal Gravy, 26
Cranberry Bread – Early American, 144
Crusty Oatcakes – Scottish, 146
Dried Pumpkin Seeds, 33
Dumplings, 32
Dumplings – Huron, 21
English Crumpets, 36
English Pancakes, 35
French Bread, 32
French Crepes, 33
French Toast, 33
Fried Bread – French, 33
Hazelnut Cakes – Chippewa, 26
Hot Cross Buns – English, 35
Irish Soda Bread, 143

Jalapeno Bread, 142
Johnnie Cake, 68
Kuchen, Evieís Apple, 142
Molasses Bread, Old Fashioned
    African-American, 145
Molasses Gingerbread, 35
Nothings, 69
Nuts, Roasted, 17
Pastry for Meat Pies, 32
Potato Dumplings, 190
Puffs, Fried Bread India, 144
Puffs,Nunís, 69
Pumpkin Fritters – French, 34
Quick Bread Sticks, 144
Rolls, French, 67
Rolls, Parker House Unfermented, 68
Rolls, Standard Yeast, 144
Rolls, Velvet, 67
Rolls,Pocketbook, 68
Sally-Lunn, 68
Scones, English, 69
Soft Bread – Ojibwa, 26
Sour Cream Coffee Bread, 145
Sour Dough Biscuits, 34
Sourdough Starter, 35
Stuffing for Baked Fish, 105
Yeast, to Make, 66
Yorkshire Pudding, English, 146

Breakfast Dishes

Applesauce Puffs, 148
Black Fruit Salad, 148
Breakfast Casserole, 72
Cakes, Buttermilk, 71
Cakes, Sour Milk, 71
Coconut French Toast, Phillipines,
    149
Egg and Ham Pudding, 70
Egg Pie, 72
Eggs and Bacon, Mixed, 71
Eggs for Breakfast, 70
Eggs Scalloped, 70
Eggs, Cheese, Sausage Bake, 147
Eggs, Scotch, 73
Familia, 148
Flannel Cakes, 72
Gravy for Biscuits, 72
Griddle Cakes, Corn-Meal, 71
Griddle Cakes, Wheat, 71

Ham Pie, 73
Oatmeal with Stewed Apples, 72
Omelet Apple, 71
Omelet of Herbs, 71
Omelet, Asparagus, 71
Orange Pancake Puff, 72
Pancake, Banana Nut, 147
Pancake, Daisyís Baked, 147
Pancakes 1920, Janets Buttermilk,
    149
Pancakes, Pina Colada, 149
Pancakes, Sour Cream Blueberry, 147
Savory Herb Omelet, 32
Scrambled Eggs, Peppers and
    Tomatoes, Shirley's, 148
Syrup, Brown Sugar, 149
Topping, Buttery Peach, 83
Topping, Creamy Fruit, 72
Waffles, Sunday Supper, 147

Cakes

Apple Sauce Cake, 151
Bride's Cake, Old Fashioned, 74
Cake Without Eggs, 75
Canada War Cake, 151
Chunky Apple Walnut Cake –
    American, 152
Civil War Gingerbread, 77
Coffee Cake, 77
Cream Cake, 75
Danish Raisin Cake, 150
English Pound Cake, 76
French Chocolate Cake, 75
Fruit Cake, White, 75
German Pound Cake, 151
Greek Baklava, 150
Greek Honey Syrup, 150
Groom's Cake, Old Fashioned, 77
Italian Cream Cake, Rennie's, 153
Jelly Cakes – Marguerites, 75
Jewish Coffee Cake, 150
Making Fruit Cakes, 75
Mexican Fruitcake, 152
Millenium Cake – 2000, 153
Molasses Gingerbread, 35
Old Tyme 1-2-3-4 Cake, 77
Orange Cake, 76
Orange Glaze, 151

Orange Glazed Poundcake – French,
    151
Poppy Seed Cake – Polish, 150
Pound Cake, 33
Pound Cake – German, 76
Rich Devil's Food Cake – 1950, 152
Scripture Cake, 152
Southern Delight Loaf Cake – 1920,
    153
Sweet Strawberry Cake, 74

Cookies

Chocolate Cookies, 80
Chocolate Fudge Cookie, 160
Chocolate Surprise, 160
Cookies, 80
Depression Cookies, 159
Fruit Cookies, 81
Ginger Creams, 160
Hard Tack, 82
Honey Cakes, 81
Lemon Bars, 161
Maple Butternut Sugar Cookies, 81
Mexican Wedding Cookies, 160
Nutmeg Cookies, 80
Old Fashioned Tea Cakes, 161
Pop Corn Balls, 160
Pumpkin Drop Cookies, 159
Raisin Drop Cookies, 82
Refrigerator Fruit Slices, 161
Russian Angel Wings, 159
Russian Tea Cookies, 159
Scotch Shortbread, 159
Seven Layer Bars, 160
Shortbread, 82
Sour Cream Cookies, 81
Sugar Cakes, 81
Surprise Sugar Cookies, 81
Turn of the Century Sugar Cookies –
    1900, 161
White Cookies, 81

Fish

Baked Fish –1858, 105
Baked Halibut, 189
Baked Sturgeon, 189
Boiled Whitefish, 46

Codfish Cakes – English, 45
Crayfish, 46
Crayfish – Traditional, 20
Dried Fish with Maple Sugar, 46
Egg Soup, 21
English Pickled Fish, 46
Fish & Collard Greens – African-
  American, 189
Fish and Mush – Algonquin, 19
Fish Baked in Clay – Ojibwa, 21
Fish Baked on a Campfire – 1830,
  105
Fish Balls, 46
Fish Chowder, 106
Fish Chowder – Bouillabaisse, 46
Fish Hash – French, 45
Fish Soup, 20
Fish Soup, 106
Fish Soup – Traditional, 20
Fish Stew with Vegetables – African,
  189
Fish with Peas – French, 46
German Fish Stew – 1852, 104
Jambalaya, 187
Pan Fish, 104
Parsley Butter, 105
Planked Fish, 105
Red Snapper Rolls, 187
Salmon Puffs, 188
Scampi, 188
Stuffed Pike – Austria, 189
Stuffing for Baked Fish, 105
Terrapin Stew, 106
To Cook Turtle, 105
To Fry Perch, 104
Trout Baked Irish Style, 187
Trout with Bacon – Welsh, 187
Turtle Soup, 106
Walleye Special Detroit, 188

Frostings and Fillings

"Sanders" Butter Cream Frosting, 154
Apple Filling, 79
Boiled Frosting, 79
Broiled Coconut Frosting, 155
Coconut Pecan Frosting, 155
Butter Cream Frosting – 1940, 154
Butter Frosting, 154

Caramel Butter Frosting, 155
Chocolate Cream Cheese Fluff, 155
Chocolate Frosting, 79
Chocolate Glaze, 155
Chocolate Icing, 78
Cream Eggs, 78
Cream Filling, 78
Cream Filling, 156
Cream Icing, 78
Crystallized Flowers, 155
Easy Chocolate Frosting, 154
French Custard Filling, 156
Frosting Without Eggs, 78
Gelatine Frosting, 79
Icing for Cakes, 79
Lemon Filling, 156
Lemonade Filling, 156
Orange Filling, 78
Orange Filling, 156
Orange Icing, 79
Pineapple Filling, 156
Plain Chocolate Icing, 78
Quick Strawberry Preserve Frosting,
  154
Tutti Fruiti Icing, 79
Whipped Cream Frosting, 154

Fruit Desserts

Apple Dumplings – American, 158
Apple Squares, 158
Apple Tart – French, 37
Baked Apples, 19
Berries and Wild Rice, 18
Corn Cob Syrup, 37
English Trifle, 158
French Peach Cobbler, 157
Fresh Fruit Flan, 157
Hot Fruit Compote, 157
Maple Sugar and Fruit, 19
Maple Syrup Pie – French, 36
Peach Ambrosia Dessert, 157
Stewed French Pears, 37

Game

Baked Beaver – Ojibwa, 25
Baked Raccoon – Ottawa, 28
Baked Raccoon – Potawatomi, 24

Barbecued Pig – French, 40
Barbequed Squirrel, 100
Beaver Tail Soup, 29
Beaver Tail Stew – Huron, 24
Bird – Traditional, 24
Blackbird Pie, 39
Broiled Bear Chops, 102
Broiled Partridges, 103
Brunswick Stew, 100
Chippewa Dill Jellied Eel, 29
Cooking Game, 100
Creamed Fried Partridges, 39
Dried Beans – Leather Britches, 25
Dried Bear, 25
Dried Fish, 25
Fish and Dandelion, 30
Fried Muskrat, 39
Fried Quails, 39
Game Soup, 91
Groundhog Stew – Ojibwa, 24
Haunch of Venison, 101
Hunter's Partridge, 41
Indian Jerky, 29
Opossum, 25
Pemmican – Traditional, 25
Pheasant, 24
Quail – Traditional, 24
Rabbit Pie – English, 102
Roast Hare or Rabbit, 101
Roast Muskrat – French, 39
Roast Opossum, 103
Roast Raccoon, 100
Roast Wild Duck, 39
Roast Wild Shoat (Young Pig) –
  French, 102
Squirrel, 100
Squirrel – Algonquin, 24
Stewed Duck, 103
Stewed Pigeons, 40
Stewed Venison, 101
Stuffed Duck, 103
Tourtierre, 45
Turtle Soup, 41
Venison and Wild Rice Casserole, 29
Venison and Wild Rice Stew, 28
Venison Pie or Pastry – French, 101
Venison Steaks, 41
Waboos – Rabbit, 24
Wild Turkey, 103
Woodcock, 40

Lamb

Bourekia – Greek Pastries, 200
Crown Roast of Lamb, 198
Grilled Lamb Kebobs, 200
Irish Stew, 199
Lamb Chops with Vegetables & Fruit, 200
Lamb Curry – India, 198
Lamb Shanks, 198
Meat and Potato Balls, 199
Meatballs for a Pasha – Syrian, 199
Roast Leg of Lamb, 198
Shish Kabob – Arabic, 198

Pasta

Baked Macaroni, 93
Baked Macaroni and Cheese – African American, 176
Cornmeal Dumplings, 93
Creamy Pasta Sauce with Fresh Herbs, 175
Dumplings – French, 32
Dumplings – Huron, 21
Egg Dumplings for Soup, 93
Egg Noodles for Soup, 93
Fettucine Alfredo, 176
Fettucini and Spinach, 178
French Glacies – Drop Noodles, 36
Ham Dumplings, 93
Hungarian-Style Noodles, 177
Lasagna, 175
Linguine with Tomatoes and Basil, 175
Macaroni, 93
Pasta Primavera – Italian, 176
Pasta With Sausage and Peppers, 178
Pierogi – Ukranian 1920, 177
Spaetzle – German, 176
Spaghetti Pie, 178

Pet Treats

For Dogs
Bacon Biscuits, 210
Baby Food Doggie Cookies, 210
Wheaty Dog Treats, 210

Oatmeal Wheat Germ Dog Biscuits, 211
Peanut Butter Treats, 211
Crunchy Dog Biscuits, 211

For Cats
Kitty Salad, 212
Kitten Delight, 211
Kitty Tuna-Pops, 213
Meat Loaf for Cats, 212
Fake Mouse Treats, 213
Tuna Treats, 212

For Wild Birds
Bird Cakes, 213
Hard Suet Tidbit Cakes, 214
Sunflower Seed Heads, 214
Homemade Nectar for Hummingbirds, 214
Sure-Fire Suet Mix, 213
Soft Peanut Butter Mix, 214
Soft Suet Medley, 214
Hot Weather Bird Treats, 214
Hard Peanut Butter Mix, 214

Pickles and Preserves

Apple Jelly, 97
Cold Eggs for A Picnic, 97
Cranberry Jelly, 97
Piccalili, 96
Pickles and Catsups, 96
Pink Pickles, 97
Preserved Apples for Winter Use, 97
Raspberry Jam, 97
Sweet Cucumber Pickles, 96
Tomato Marmalade, 97
Walnut Pickles, 96

Pies

Apple Cream Pie, 84
Apple Pandowdy, 83
Apple Tart, 37
Beef and Kidney Pie, 42
Bertha's Foolproof Pie crusts, 164
Bertha's Prize Winning Buttermilk Pie, 163
Concord Grape Pie, 164

Cranberry Pie, 85
Cream Tarts, 85
Custard Pie, 85
English Meat Pie, 42
French Apple Tarts, 33
Fresh Strawberry Pie, 162
Funeral Pie, 163
Glazed Blueberry Pie, 163
Hungarian Cottage Cheese Pie, 162
Hypocrite Pie, 162
Lemon Pie, 83
Lemon Tarts, 85
Maple Pecan Pie, 163
Maple Syrup Pie – French, 36
Mince Meat, 84
Mock Cream Pie, 83
Molasses Pie, 84
Onion Quiche – French, 38
Pastry (Paste), 83
Pastry for Meat Pies, 32
Peach Meringue Pie, 83
Peach Pie, 84
Pineapple Pie, 85
Pumpkin Pie, 164
Quiche Lorraine, 162
Quick Garden Quiche, 164
Rhubarb Pie, 84
Spinach Ricotta Tart, 164
Strawberry Short Cake, 83
Sugar Pie, 36
Tourtierre – French, 38
Whipped Cream Pie, 84

Pork

Almondigas – Phillipines, 196
Baked Spare Ribs – African American, 196
Barbecued Pork Chops, 194
Cajun Chops, 197
Champagne Dressing, 195
Cornmeal Mush and Pork, 44
Cretons – French, 44
English Meat Pie, 43
Filling Sausage, 113
Fried Ham, 111
Ham Hocks and Turnip Greens – African – American, 196
Jewelled Crown Roast of Pork, 195

Leftover Ham in Sour Cream, 197
Leg of Pork Stuffed, 111
Pig Feet – Slovak, 195
Pigs Feet and Northern Beans –
    African/American, 197
Polynesian Pork, 196
Pork Chops in Orange Sauce, 194
Pork Cordon Bleu – French, 196
Pork Nicoise – French, 194
Pork Pot Roast – French, 45
Potatoes Stuffed With Ham –
    Romanian, 194
Roast Glazed Loin of Pork, 197
Roast Loin of Pork, 111
Sauerkraut with Pork – Alsatian, 48
Sausage, 44
Sausage Cakes Baked with Apple, 112
Sausage Casings, 113
Scrappel, 111
Small Hot Patties – French, 42
Spare-Ribs, 111
Teriyaki Pork – Japanese, 197
To Cure Bacon, 112
Toad in the Hole – English, 112
Tourtiere – French-Canadian, 112

Poultry

Chicken a la Maria, 202
Chicken and Macaroni, 115
Chicken Enchiladas – Mexican, 203
Chicken Frajitas, 203
Chicken Fricassee – French, 117
Chicken Oregano – Greek, 201
Chicken Paprikas – Hungarian, 116
Chicken Pudding, 115
Chicken Stew – French, 44
Chicken with Raisin/Almond
    Dressing – Polish, 116
Chicken, Fried, 114
Chilean Chicken Stew, 204
Christmas Goose – English, 202
Coke Chicken, 201
Duckling a' L'Orange, 201
French Country Style Chicken, 203
Glazed Blueberry Chicken, 203
Pollo Alla Cacciatora – Italian, 115
Roast Chicken, 117
Roast Goose, 114
Roast Turkey, 114

Spanish Chicken and Vegetables, 201
Turkey Crunch, 204
Ukranian Chicken Kiev, 114

Puddings

Baked Custard, 86
Baked Indian Pudding, 86
Bavarian Cream, 87
Blanc Mange, 166
Blueberry Pudding, 88
Bread Pudding, 88
Canadian Pudding, 88
Charlotte Russe, 86
Cinnamon Custard, 33
Cottage Cheese – English, 33
Crème de Menthe Pudding in a
    Cloud, 166
English Custard, 33
Frangelico Velvet, 166
French Chocolate Mousse, 165
French Pudding, 87
Fruit Pudding, 87
Hard Sauce, 87
Jewish Kugel, 166
Kwanzaa Bread Pudding, 165
Maple Pralines, 33
Mocha Bavarian cream, 166
Molasses Pudding, 86
Mrs. Spence's Pudding, 87
Pudding Without Milk or Eggs, 86
Pumpkin Pudding, 35
Rice Pudding, 86
Russian Cream, 87
Russian Cream, 165
Sirnaya – Russian Cheese Pudding,
    165
Spanish Cream, 86
Tapioca Cream, 86
Teacup Pudding, 87
Whip Cream Substitute, 88
Whipped Cream, 88
Ye Olde Van Antwerpen Plum
    Pudding, 88

Salads and Dressings

Ambrosia Salad, 180
American Potato Salad, 179

Bottle Salad Dressing 1850, 95
Broccoli Salad, 180
Bubble and Squeak – English, 95
Colorful Bean Salad, 179
Dressing for Cabbage, 94
French Potato Salad, 95
Fruit and Cabbage Salad, 181
Greek Salad, 181
Hot German Potato Salad, 181
Hyden Salad – 1875, 94
Irish Potato Salad, 95
Maurice Salad, 179
Mexican Potato Salad, 181
Mexican Taco Salad, 181
Oriental Cabbage Salad, 180
Pepper Salad – Roumania, 179
Szechuan Shrimp Salad, 180
Tabooleh Salad, 179
Tarragon Dressing, 95

Sauces

Applesauce, 98
Balsamic Vinaigrette, 186
Bechamel Sauce, 98
Butterscotch Sauce, 185
Caramel Sauce, 185
Chili Sauce, 99
Cornmeal Gravy, 26
Cranberry and Apple Sauce, 185
Cranberry Sauce, 99
Drawn Butter, 98
Egg Sauce, 99
French Cream Sauce, 185
Fruit Sauce, 186
Garlic Dressing, 186
Hard Sauce, 186
Hollandaise Sauce, 98
Hot Fudge Sauce, 185
Lemon Vinaigrette, 186
Medium White Sauce, 186
Thin White Sauce, 186
White Sauce, 98

Soup

"Habitant" Pea Soup, 42
Basque Vegetable, 173
Berry Soup, 174

Canadian Cheese Soup, 173
Chinese Egg Drop Soup, 174
Cock-a-Leekie, 92
Cold Yogurt/Cucumber Soup, 173
Corn & Wild Rice Soup, 172
Corn Casserole, 27
Corn Soup – Ottawa, 27
Cream of Broccoli Soup, 174
Dumplings – Huron, 21
Egg Soup, 21
Fish and Mush, 19
Fish Soup, Ojibwa, 20
French Onion Soup, 171
Fruit Juice Soup, 173
Game Soup, 91
Ham Chowder, 172
Hearty Soup Mix, 172
Irish Potato Soup, 91
La Garbure – French Cabbage Soup, 42
Lichen Soup, 27
Michigan Chowder, 174
Mushroom and Potato Soup, 173
Pea Soup, 91
Peasant Fish Soup, 42
Polish Dill Pickle Soup, 173
Polish Fruit Soup, 92
Pumpkin Soup, 42
Pumpkin Soup, 92
Pumpkin Soup – Woodland Indians, 27
Scotch Broth, 92
Slovak Lentil Soup, 171
Soupe a la Baillarge – Traditional French, 41
Split Pea Soup, 42
Squash Soup, 42
Squirrel Soup, 91
Sunflower Seed Soup – Ottawa, 27
Tomato Soup, 92
Traditional Fish Soup, 20
Turkish Wedding Soup, 171
Vichyssoise, 171

Vegetables

Apples and Potatoes – German, 122
Baked Corn, 31

Baked Pumpkin – Native American, 201
Baked Pumpkin with Wild Rice and Meat, 23
Beans with seeds, Nuts, Wild Rice and Meat, 23
Boston Baked Beans, 120
Bubble and Squeak, 95
Cabbage and Tomatoes – Croatian 1920, 208
Cauliflower – African American, 208
Colcannon – Irish, 122
Cold Slaw, 120
Dried Beans / Leather Britches, 25
Fiddle Head Fern and Cattail Salad, 21
Fried Cauliflower – Polish, 118
Fried Corn – American Indian, 121
Gastony Style Eggs – French, 38
Green Beans – French Style, 39
Green Peas – French Style, 38
Greens, 23
Gumbo Beans, 201
Hasselback Potatoes – Swedish, 207
Iron Skillet Vegetables and Bacon – French, 38
Large Mushrooms, 27
Maple Sugar Candy, 24
Mashed Potatoes with Turnips, 39
Microwave Garden Vegetable Casserole, 209
Milkweed Buds, 23
Mixed Vegetable Casserole – Scandinavian, 205
Mushroom Stuffed Tomatoes, 208
Mushrooms, 38
Onion Quiche – French, 38
Onions Baked, 119
Parched Corn, 38
Parsley Butter, 105
Pine Needles for Stomach Cramps, 23
Pommes De Terre Potatoes – French, 121
Potato and Egg Casserole – Hungarian, 122
Potato Dumplings, 190
Potato Latkes – Jewish, 208
Potato Paprikash – Hungarian, 208

Potato Pie – English, 120
Potato Puff, 122
Red Cabbage, 191
Rice and Vegetables – Italian, 118
Rice Pilaf – Armenian 1920, 205
Sauerkraut with Meats – French, 207
Sauerkraut with Pork – Alsatian, 38
Scalloped Potatoes – Kentucky Style, 120
Scalloped Tomatoes, 119
Sour-Crout, 119
Steamed Cattails, 22
Stuffed Eggplant – Italian, 121
Stuffed Pumpkin – American Indian, 119
Sub Gum Chow Mein – Chinese, 206
Sweet Corn Mixture, 28
Sweet Potato Casserole – American, 206
Sweet Potato Pone – African American, 205
Sweet potato Pudding – American, 205
Sweet Potatoes and Apples – Mexican, 207
To Fry Cymlings (Squash), 121
To Stew, Fry or Broil Mushrooms, 118
Tomatoes, To Peel, 119
Vegtable Bacon Stew – African American, 206
Watercress, 28
Welcome Back Potato Skins – American, 207
Wild Cabbage, 28
Wild Green Salad – Algonquin, 22
Wild Peppermint Tea, 28
Wild Rice, 23
Wild Rice, 38
Wild Rice – American Indian, 121
Yellow Dock, 28
Young Milkweed Pods, 21
Young Milkweed Spears – Ojibwa, 22